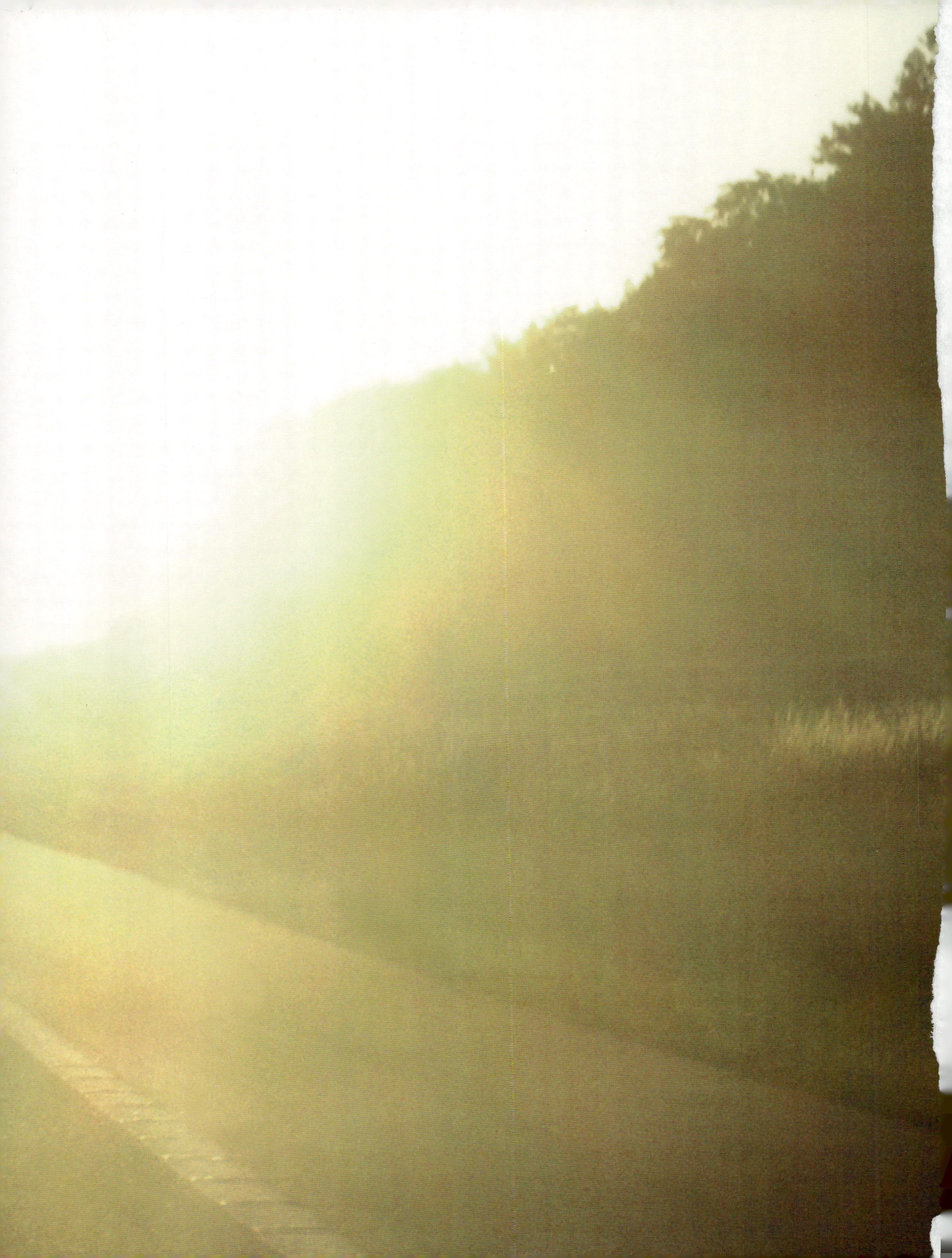

Louis Vuitton
The Art of the Automobile

Serge Bellu

**Abrams,
New York**

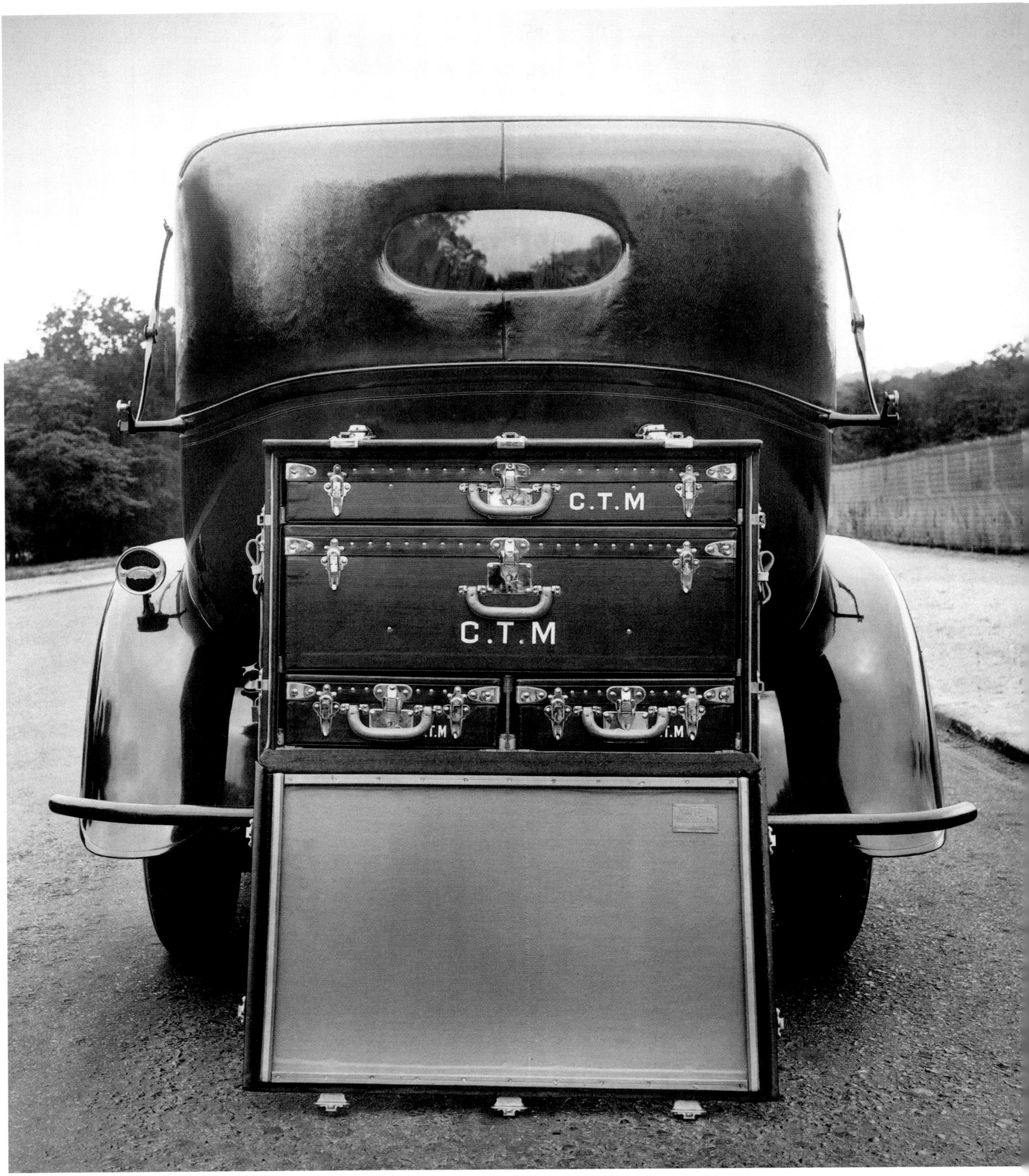
C.T.M
C.T.M

Encounters

Preface

The paths of the Louis Vuitton company and the automobile world have often crossed. These encounters did not take place by chance. Since the beginning of the twentieth century the car has been associated with changes in our life-styles, the acceleration of communications, and the joy of mobility: altogether, the art of travel.

Working in partnership with coachbuilders, the Louis Vuitton company developed complementary accessories and quickly became immersed in the art of bodywork, a specialized field that brings together technology and aesthetics.

When car designers, engineers, and craftspeople combine their know-how, the automobile becomes a masterpiece of the applied arts. It was this extraordinary expression of elegance that Louis Vuitton, at the instigation of company president Yves Carcelle, sought to highlight by organizing its magnificent concours and car rallies.

This book explores Louis Vuitton's remarkable contributions to the automotive world, with accounts of those special events and detailed studies of the most outstanding examples of style and design. In addition to sponsoring the great concours d'elegance, run by Christine Bélanger, Louis Vuitton has always valued and rewarded contemporary creativity.

Thanks to the passion of collectors and the support of automakers, this book provides a wide audience the opportunity to encounter some of the most exceptional cars of the century.

Let's go!

Louis Vuitton
The Art of the Automobile

7 Encounters
Preface

1 Founding

12 **The rise of Louis Vuitton and the birth of the automobile**

2 Travel

32 **Introduction**

34 **From Singapore to Kuala Lumpur**
Louis Vuitton Vintage Equator Run
1993

40 **Around Lake Geneva**
Tour du Léman, Louis Vuitton Trophy
1995–97

46 **The Italian Renaissance**
Louis Vuitton Italia Classica
1995–97

56 **The Charms of Asia**
Louis Vuitton Classic China Run
1998

64 **From Budapest to Prague via Vienna**
Louis Vuitton Classic Bohemia Run
2006

3 Elegance

- 72 Introduction
- 74 **Parisian Classics**
  From Bagatelle to Saint-Cloud
  1989–2003
- 112 **Concours in and around London**
  Stowe, Hurlingham, Waddesdon Manor
  1990–2004
- 130 **Classics in the Heart of Manhattan**
  1996–2000
- 138 **Louis Vuitton Rewards Creativity**

4 Applied Arts

- 146 Introduction
- 148 **Bugatti 50-T** 1932
- 152 **Talbot Lago SS** 1937
- 158 **Voisin Aérosport** 1937
- 164 **Alfa Romeo 8C 2900 Spider** 1937
- 168 **Delage D8-120 Cabriolet** 1938
- 174 **Delahaye 135 MS** 1948
- 180 **Bentley Mark VI** 1951
- 186 **Maserati Sport 2000** 1954
- 192 **Alfa Romeo 2000 Sportiva** 1954
- 198 **Ferrari 375 MM** 1956

5 Innovations

- 206 Introduction
- 208 **Nivola** 1990
- 212 **Chrysler 300** 1991
- 216 **Bugatti EB 112** 1993
- 220 **BMW Z13** 1993
- 224 **Lagonda Vignale** 1993
- 228 **Cadillac Cien** 2002
- 232 **Peugeot RC** 2002
- 236 **Renault Fluence** 2004
- 240 **Birdcage 75th** 2005
- 244 **Citroën C-Métisse** 2006
- 248 **A Discerning Eye**
- 254 **The Best of the Best**
  Best of Show Winners,
  1989–2004
- 256 Photograph Credits and Acknowledgments

1

Founding

12 The dawn of the twentieth century saw both the rise of the Louis Vuitton company and the birth of the automobile industry.

When Louis Vuitton created his first trunk for cars, in 1897, the automobile industry was in its infancy. Only six years earlier two pioneering French firms, Peugeot and Panhard-Levassor, had introduced their first automobiles. They both began manufacturing in 1891, Peugeot at Valentigney, in the Jura region of eastern France, and Panhard at Porte d'Ivry, in Paris. But at the time of these isolated, early initiatives, only a few people foresaw the future that lay ahead for the automobile. One of those visionaries was Louis Vuitton.

He had left his native Jura at the age of thirteen to discover the exciting world he imagined beyond the beautiful, austere mountains he knew so well. After a long and circuitous journey he arrived in Paris, where he marveled at everything, gained experience, improved his mind, engaged in a swirl of diversions, and then finally resolved to learn a trade. In the fall of 1837 he was taken on as an apprentice by a *layetier,* a craftsman who made wooden cases and boxes for transporting travelers' possessions.

By taking up this trade, he unknowingly embarked on the path that would lead to the Vuitton family's destiny. In 1854 he decided to strike out on his own, and at the age of thirty-three hung up his shop sign on the front of 4 Rue Neuve-des-Capucines (now Rue des Capucines): "Louis Vuitton, layetier-emballeur" (luggage maker and packer). That was only the start; Vuitton was an ambitious man. Soon afterward he opened a workshop on the Rue du Rocher near the Gare Saint-Lazare, where his first series of flat-topped trunks was produced in 1858. The following year he built larger workshops in the suburb of Asnières. In 1871 he opened a second store in Paris, on Rue Scribe. Not long afterward he appointed his son Georges as its manager.

The Louis Vuitton company was swept along by the industrial revolution and the wave of societal changes that accompanied it. Travel was one symbol of those changes: As the modern world took shape, mobility was becoming increasingly possible. The train and the steamship were opening new horizons and making long journeys feasible. In the final decades of the nineteenth century the automobile was just getting under way; it would soon take the first privileged travelers on the road for vacation, a brand-new concept.

Georges Vuitton was only twenty-three when he took over from his father in 1880 but he immediately demonstrated the same desire to expand the business, seeking to develop it abroad. In 1885 he opened a store in London. Soon the company developed the distinctive fabrics and designs that would personalize its products forever: the checkered Damier canvas, created in 1888, and the Monogram motif in 1896.

In 1887, just before the birth of the automobile industry, teams of horses were still used to pull vehicles carrying people and goods. In the early twentieth century horse-drawn carriages gave way to motorized vans such as this 12 HP Clément-Bayard (above). By 1929 the Louis Vuitton stores in Paris, Nice, Cannes, Vichy, and London were provided with delivery vans built on a Citroën C4 chassis (right).

28-40 HP F.I.A.T.
E. LOSTE, 9, RUE DE LA PAIX

CARROSSERIE E. BOULOGNE & FILS, 148, RUE DE COURCELLES
FITTER WITH TWO TRUNKS & ONE SAC CHAUFFEUR BY **LOUIS VUITTON**

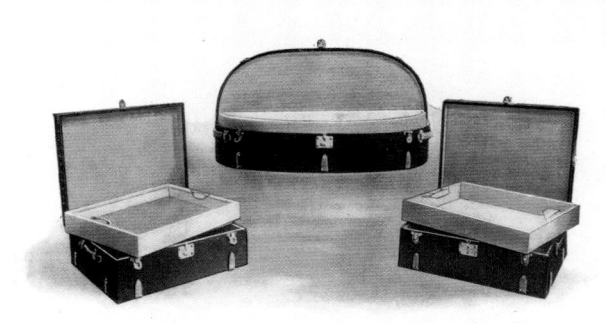

MALLES DE PAVILLON

TAILLES
LES PLUS COURANTES
- 110 × 50 × 27 cent.
- 100 × 50 × 27 —
- 90 × 45 × 27 —

TRUNKS FOR THE TOP

THE MOST POPULAR SIZES
- 43½ × 20 × 10½ inches
- 39½ × 20 × 10½ —
- 35½ × 18 × 10½ —

28 HP PILAIN - LIMOUSINE DE VOYAGE SPECIALLY BUILT
BY KELLNER & SES FILS, 125, AVENUE MALAKOFF, PARIS FOR **LOUIS VUITTON**
WHO EQUIPPED IT AS DESCRIBED ON PAGES 9, 12, 17 & 21

L'équipement de cette voiture se compose de :
1º Sur le Pavillon : le célèbre "Sac Chauffeur" dans lequel se trouvent deux pneus de rechange, et le petit sac intérieur pouvant recevoir des chapeaux ; plus deux malles pour vêtements.
2º Sur le porte-bagage arrière, deux autres malles.
3º Sur les marchepieds, deux coffres à outils (page 12).
A l'intérieur, sous le siège avant : un déjeuner pour 4 personnes et une glacière (page 21) ; sous le siège arrière, un nécessaire de toilette et une pharmacie de route (page 17).

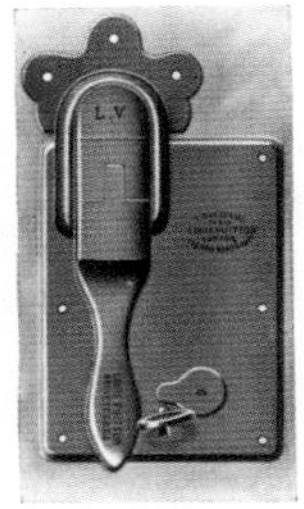

Les malles auto de **LOUIS VUITTON** sont fermées par ses boucles et serrures brevetées.

All **LOUIS VUITTON'S** motor trunks are closed with his patent clasps & locks.

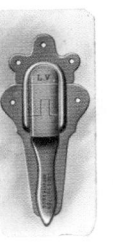

THIS **LIMOUSINE DE VOYAGE** IS FITTED WITH :
On top : L.V.'S "Sac Chauffeur" into which are two spare tyres, and the inner case ready for ladies hats, also two trunks for clothing.
On rack : two other trunks.
On steps : two tool chests (page 12).
Inside, under front seat, a lunch case for four persons, and a glaciere (page 21).
Under back seat : a dressing case & a pharmacie de route (page 17).

MESSRS. CORMIER & CODONI'S PRIVATE CAR
SPECIALLY BUILT BY HENRI LABOURDETTE, 35, AVENUE DES CHAMPS-ÉLYSÉES, PARIS
ON A 24 HP DE DION-BOUTON

COMPLETED BY TWO **LOUIS VUITTON** TRUNKS
THE REAR ONE AS PART OF THE BODY

L.V.'S MOTOR BAG

AUTOMOBILE RUGS GARANTEED PURE SHETLAND
MADE SPECIALLY FOR **LOUIS VUITTON**

40 HP SERPOLLET

CARROSSERIE BAIL JEUNE FRÈRES, 51, AVENUE VICTOR-HUGO, PARIS
TWO TRUNKS & ONE SAC CHAUFFEUR BY **LOUIS VUITTON**

L.V.'S PHARMACIE DE ROUTE

L.V.'S LUNCH CASE WITH COFFEE SERVICE
(FOR FOUR PERSONS)

DÉJEUNER AVEC CAFÉ POUR QUATRE PERSONNES

120 HP PANHARD

RACING CAR
CARROSSERIE E. BOULOGNE & FILS, 148, RUE DE COURCELLES, PARIS
WITH LOUIS VUITTON'S PATENT SAC CHAUFFEUR
— 18 —

Le SAC CHAUFFEUR de LOUIS VUITTON protége les pneus contre le soleil, le vent, la pluie et leur assure une longue durée.

LOUIS VUITTON'S patent "SAC CHAUFFEUR" contains spare tyres and protects them against sun, dust and rain. The inside one can be used for hats.
SEE PAGE 47, THE MODEL TO FIT IN THE TYRES
— 19 —

60 HP SIX CYLINDER NAPIER CHASSIS

UNDER THE STEPS, WITH SLIDES TO BRING THEM FORWARD
Two chests for tools, one for luncheon & another for medical requirements.
Two trunks for clothing, hats, & shirts. One under front seat & the other under back seat.

BODY BY H. J. MULLINER, LONDON
ALL FITTINGS BY LOUIS VUITTON

SOUS LES MARCHEPIEDS AVEC COULISSES LES SUPPORTANT
Quatre coffres dont deux à outils, un pour le lunch et un pour la pharmacie.
Deux malles pour vêtements, chapeaux et chemises, une sous le siège avant et l'autre sous celui arrière.
— 40 —

A TOOL CHEST TO FIT ON STEP BY LOUIS VUITTON
UN COFFRE A OUTILS POUR LE MARCHEPIED
— 41 —

28 HP MERCEDES

BODY BY LAWTON & Cº, LONDON
TWO TRUNKS & ONE SAC CHAUFFEUR BY LOUIS VUITTON
— 46 —

LE "SAC CHAUFFEUR" DE LOUIS VUITTON (PAGE 19)

Indispensable à toute voiture de tourisme, se fait de deux modèles, l'un permettant d'utiliser l'espace intérieur des pneus, l'autre, ayant en plus l'avantage de les contenir et de les protéger contre la pluie, la poussière. Tout assurant ainsi un surcroît de durée.

Fait de toile imperméable, il peut contenir les vêtements du mécanicien, les chambres à air, les parapluies de chauffeur, etc.

Sur le pavillon, il devient une excellente malle pour chapeaux de dame.

D'autres modèles spéciaux, ayant le couvercle doublé de caoutchouc, offrent aux touristes une cuvette de toilette ou un grand tub.

LE "SAC CHAUFFEUR" DE LOUIS VUITTON FERME A CLE

MODEL TO FIT INSIDE SPARE TYRES
SEE PAGE 19 THE MODEL TO CONTAIN THE TYRES

LOUIS VUITTON'S "SAC CHAUFFEUR" (PAGE 19)

Absolutely needed on all touring cars is made of two styles, one fitting in the center of the tyres, gives a most convenient receptacle for waterproofs, air chambers, &c, or a trunk for the chauffeur.

On top it may be a splendid lady's hat box. Its conveniences are illimited.

The other, large enough to contain two tyres, adds to the above advantages, their protection against sun, rain & dust, assuring thus a longer service to the tyres.

Made as a telescope, its top part, when lined india rubber can be used as a washing tub.

LOUIS VUITTON'S "SAC CHAUFFEUR" IS WATERPROOF AND CAN BE LOCKED
— 47 —

70 HP ROCHET-SCHNEIDER

BODY BY LAMPLUGH & Cº, RUE ERNEST-COGNACQ, LEVALLOIS-PERRET
TRUNKS & SAC CHAUFFEUR BY LOUIS VUITTON
— 48 —

TRUNKS TO FIT ON THE RACK

MALLES POUR PORTE-BAGAGES
— 49 —

This extract from the Louis Vuitton catalogue not only shows the diversity of the articles offered but also suggests the breadth of partnerships the company had with the numerous coachbuilders who incorporated Louis Vuitton accessories into their vehicle designs.

At the 1907 Salon de l'Automobile in Paris, Louis Vuitton's exhibit booth displayed a limousine built on an HKV base.

At the same 1907 Salon, Mercedes showed a limousine with Louis Vuitton trunks loaded on the roof.

75 HP C. G. V.

Carrosserie par KELLNER & FILS. — Malles et Campement de LOUIS VUITTON
The C.G.V. with all the Camping & ready to start

In 1908 Louis Vuitton created a range of equipment and accessories that turned the 75 HP CGV into a remarkable touring sedan known as the camping car.

Founding

In 1897 Vuitton introduced its car trunks. Covered in leather or the company's own scratchproof fabric, Vuittonite, they were "absolutely" watertight, as the advertisements proclaimed. At this time the art of automotive design was still based on the heritage of the horse-drawn carriage. The automobile retained its predecessor's terminology, aesthetics, and manufacturing techniques. Indeed, the same craftsmen worked equally well with both types of vehicle: saddlers, blacksmiths, wheelwrights, carpenters, cabinetmakers, trimmings manufacturers, painters, and so forth. For a long time cars' aesthetic rules were founded on traditional conventions for carriages, such as the bend in the bodywork, the curved back, and the running board at the base.

For these early cars, Louis Vuitton designed trunks that could be placed either on top of the vehicle or on the board at the rear. In 1905 the company published a catalogue showing a complete range of car trunks of various dimensions, which had the advantage of being light because they were not weighed down by ornamentation. They were covered in the famous Vuittonite fabric, dyed to match the bodywork. The trunks' shape could be adapted to fit the cars' curves. The trunks were intended primarily for touring cars—the sedans or limousines that were capable of long journeys.

The catalogue also offered *sacs chauffeurs* (drivers' bags), round boxes attached to the side of the car; they contained not just the spare tire but hats, and they could also be used as washbasins. Louis Vuitton took every opportunity to display his products at the Salons de l'Automobile (auto shows) that had since the turn of the century become great meeting places for fashionable society and the business world. They took place at Paris's Grand Palais, which stands between the Seine River and the Champs-Élysées, opposite the Petit Palais. The two buildings, both built in 1900, were originally known as the Palais des Beaux-Arts (Palace of Fine Arts) and the Palais d'État (Palace of State).

The Grand Palais reflects the taste for eclecticism that prevailed at the time. This enormous stone confection has a metal framework concealed behind a heavy facade that bristles with Ionic columns. The Salon de l'Automobile was held there from 1901 on. There were six hundred exhibition stands, each more sumptuous than the last—overflowing with greenery and draperies, and ornamented with pillars and porticoes. Louis Vuitton took part in the show by collaborating with artisans of bodywork.

The trunk maker worked in partnership with numerous coachbuilders (who made only the auto bodies) in the Paris area, including Lamplugh, Rothschild, Boulogne, and Felber, as well as with British firms such as Mulliner, Hooper, and Lawton. All the automakers (who built the cars' mechanical chassis) also used Louis Vuitton accessories, including Hotchkiss, Fiat, Mercedes, Panhard-Levassor, and De Dion–Bouton.

The Louis Vuitton company formed a particularly close link with the coachbuilder Georges Kellner. Together they created the first "camping car," which was shown at the 1908 Salon. Based on a Lorraine-Dietrich chassis, the touring sedan was transformed into a bona fide mobile home. It was outfitted with a washbasin and a three-sectioned mirror, which were hidden in the rear door, a closet holding four suitcases, a toiletries case a trunk for clothes, and another trunk for hats. One bed fitted on the top of the car, another was improvised at the back of the vehicle, and a table could be stretched out alongside the chassis, under a canopy. It was a haven of luxury and comfort, but also of practicality.

In 1909 Georges Vuitton's twin sons, Pierre and Jean, produced their own car to showcase the company's products. Their elder brother, Gaston-Louis, was Georges Vuitton's heir; he had run the company with his father since March 1907, when it was renamed Vuitton and Son. Pierre and Jean designed an ultralight body with clean, sporty lines for a Stabilia chassis. Thus began an exclusive line of cars that was manufactured near Paris from 1908 to 1930, first at Neuilly-sur-Seine and then at Asnières.

The Louis Vuitton company publicized its products throughout the world in all manner of ways, often linking them to events highlighting the art of travel. Vuitton items equipped both the Spyker that took part in the incredible Peking-to-Paris auto race in 1907 and the Thomas Flyer torpedo that drove from New York to Paris via San Francisco, Vladivostok, and Moscow in 1908. These grand adventures proved that Vuitton luggage could be practical and resilient as well as elegant.

Fabrics bearing the famed "LV" monogram were also used for strictly utilitarian vehicles, such as ambulances. A veritable field hospital was fitted out on a 28 HP Decauville chassis, in collaboration with the coachbuilder

In 1909 the brothers Pierre and Jean Vuitton had special bodywork built on a Stabilia chassis. They themselves designed the car's low, sporty lines and added a tent for the two occupants.

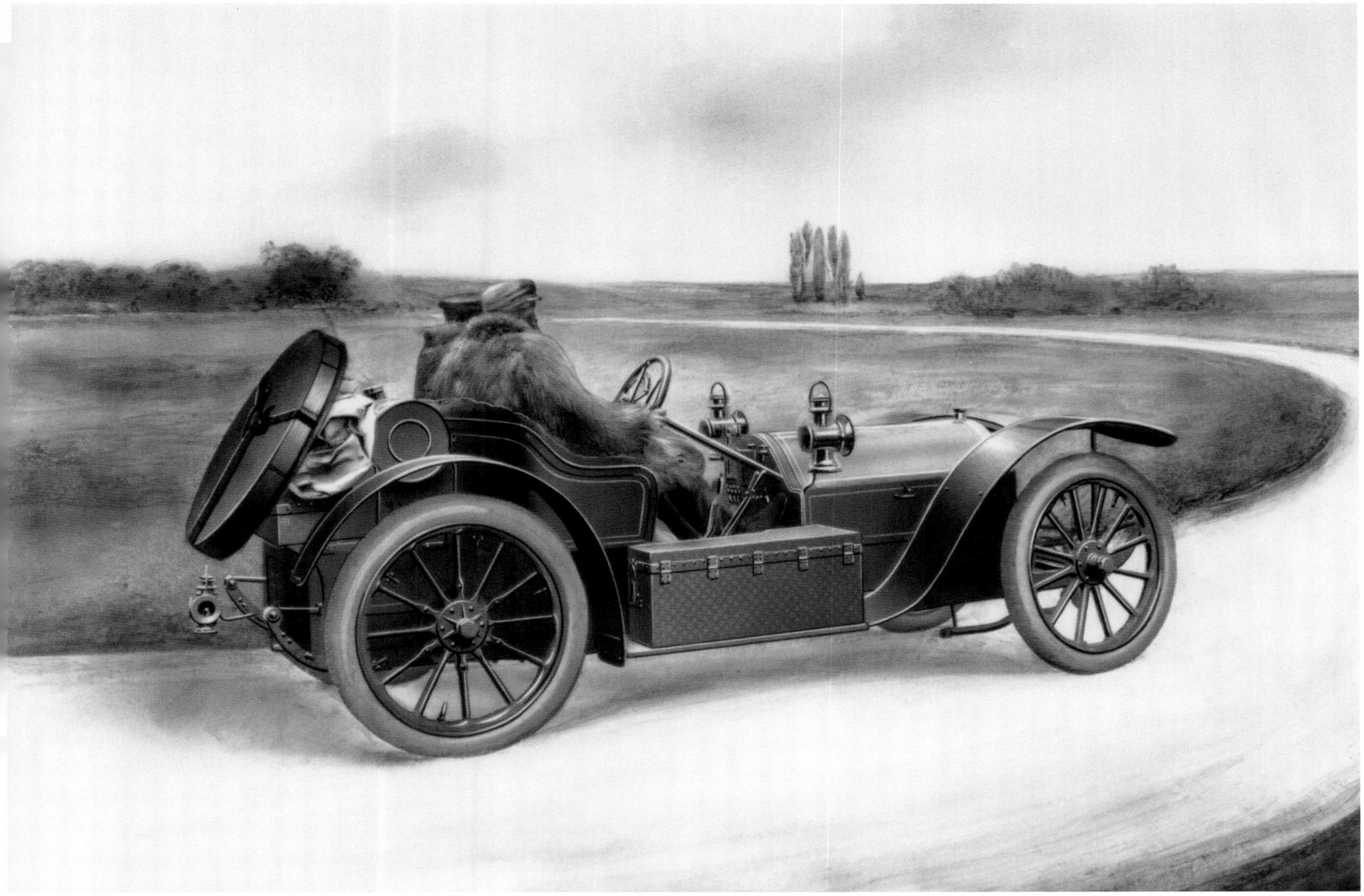

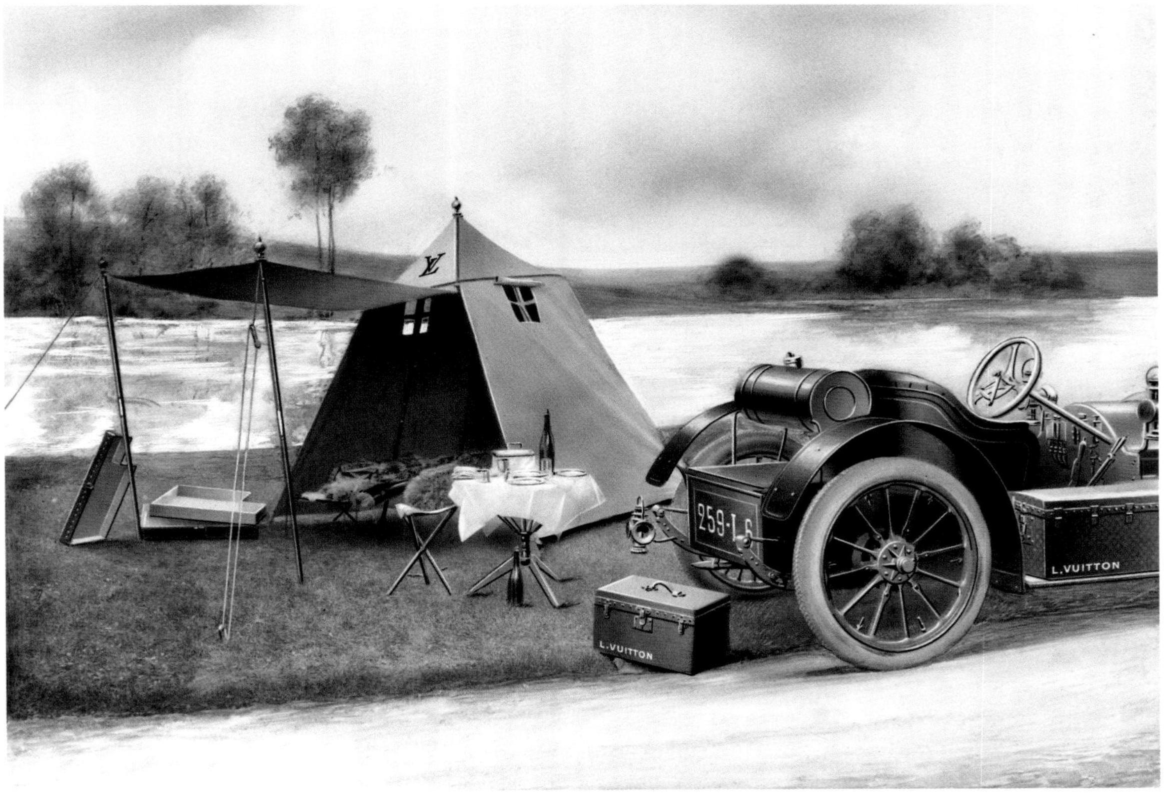
L.VUITTON
L.VUITTON

Uomini e macchine del Raid New York-Parigi.

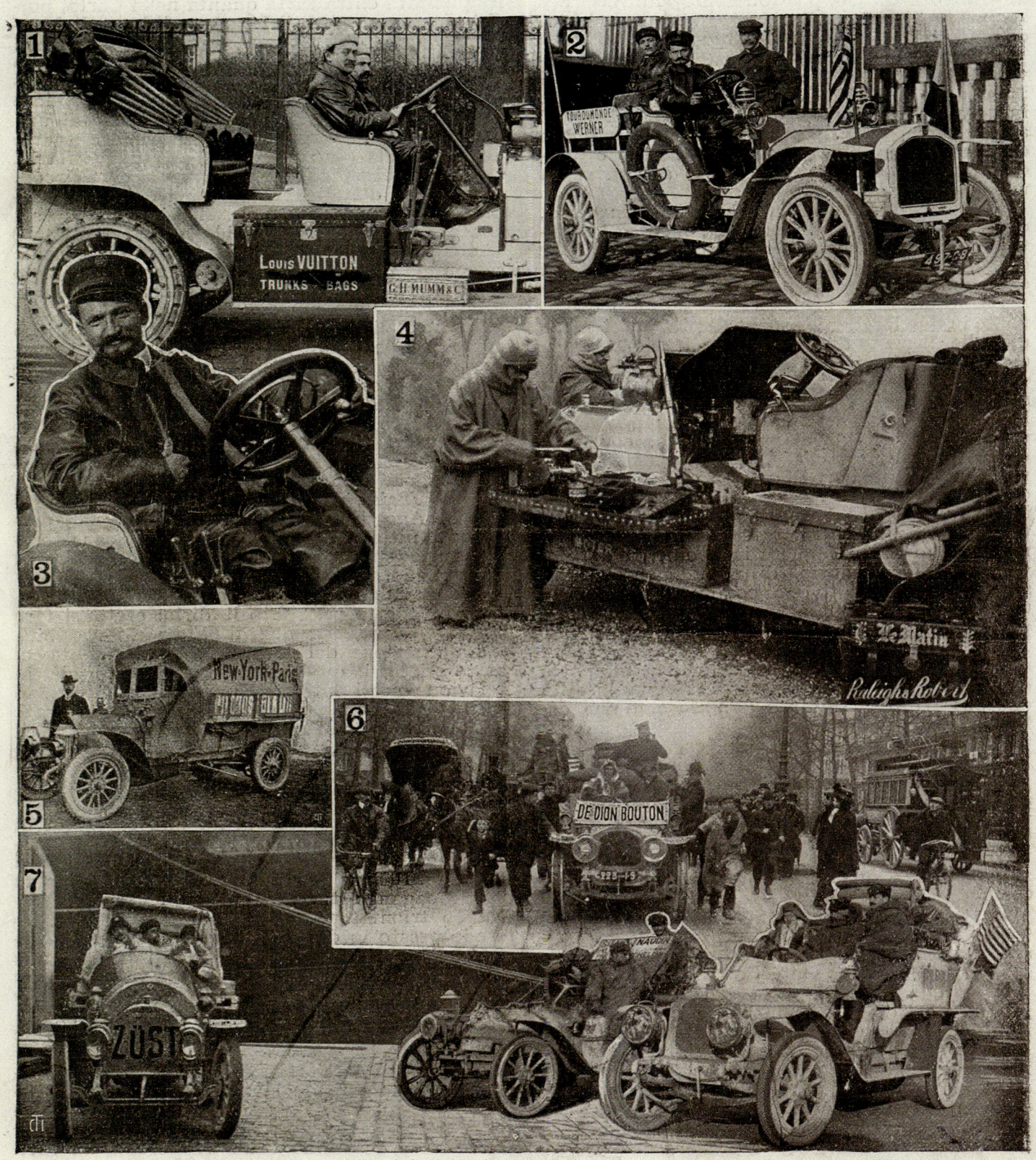

(Fot. Croce e C.)

I concorrenti del Raid New York-Parigi stanno ora compiendo la traversata dell'America. — Presentiamo uomini e macchine:

N. 1. Goddard con la Motobloc (francese). — N. 2-3. Le Louvier con la Werner (francese) che tentava il giro del mondo da secessionista staccandosi dall'organizzazione del Giornale *Le Matin*. Le Louvier sembra però si sia già ritirato. — N. 4. Goddard ed il meccanico della Motobloc durante una riparazione su strada. — N. 5. La Protos di Berlino (germanica) col ten. von Koeppern. — N. 6. La De Dion Bouton (francese) alla partenza da Parigi (al volante Saint Chaffray). — N. 7. La Züst (italiana) con l'ing. Sirtori ed Antonio Scarfoglio all'imbarco sulla Lorraine. — La vetturetta Sizaire et Naudin (francese) con Pons e la Thomas (americana).

KELLNER'S FIELD HOSPITAL on a 28 HP DECAUVILLE

It can carry two wounded on L. VUITTON'S shutters & four seated, or 4 laying down

Deux blessés couchés sur brancards L.V. et quatre assis ou quatre couchés

— 37 —

AMBULANCE MILITAIRE de KELLNER & SES FILS sur 28 HP DECAUVILLE

Garnie de quatre brancards LOUIS VUITTON
Sur le marchepied la pharmacie, avec l'eau dans des glacières et le Filtre breveté Lambert, concessionnaire HENRY, 40, rue Louis-Blanc, Paris.
Sur le pavillon deux malles pour les docteurs

KELLNER'S field hospital on a 28 HP DECAUVILLE
Fitted with 4 LOUIS VUITTON'S shutters and, on top, two trunks to carry the doctors equipment. On the step the Pharmacie with HENRY'S PATENT "Filtre Lambert"

In 1908 a fantastic run from New York to Paris via Moscow gave Louis Vuitton the opportunity to promote its products (opposite), which equipped a Thomas Flyer torpedo.

The military ambulance (above) developed by the coachbuilder Kellner & Son in 1906 was furnished with accessories from the Louis Vuitton catalogue. It was built on a 28 HP Decauville.

2561

This Rolls-Royce Phantom II, first produced in 1929, was equipped with an Autoski trunk in black cowhide.

Kellner & Son. The ambulance was functionally sound but perhaps somewhat overrefined: Even the four stretchers bore the initials "LV."

The company continued to expand the range of automotive accessories: Toolboxes, toiletries cases, iceboxes, picnic hampers, vases, perfume bottles, and powder compacts furnished the interiors of sedans and coupes with exquisite refinement.

On the eve of the First World War the product catalogue was further enhanced by the additions of a sumptuous wardrobe and the Excelsior, a large trunk with a fold-down front containing several suit hangers. Parisian high society discovered the new line of products in a flagship store Georges Vuitton constructed on the Champs-Élysées in 1914.

The war years were marked by economic disruptions, but with peacetime business gradually began to pick up again. Paris was shrouded by a strange atmosphere, and the Treaty of Versailles had left the European signatories with a bitter taste in their mouths. Georges Clemenceau found himself at the head of an impoverished and deeply wounded nation. But not yet a year after the armistice, the resurgence of the automobile industry was symbolized by the opening on October 9, 1919, of a new Salon de l'Automobile, the first since the war and the fifteenth in all. A statue of a tank surmounted by a winged Victory sat imposingly before the Grand Palais.

The automobile industry had lain dormant for more than four years, and its revival, as symbolized by the 1919 Salon, coincided with a fresh start for many businesses that had been involved in wartime industries and were looking for new openings. Airplane manufacturers such as Gabriel Voisin shifted over to car manufacturing, and André Citroën turned his armaments firm on Paris's Quai de Javel into a modern automobile factory. Citroën was an indefatigable pioneer who innovated on every front, taking his inspiration from American methods of production, technology, marketing, and publicity.

It was he who launched the first organized car trips across Africa, beginning with the crossing of the Sahara in 1922 and the African expedition, better known as the Croisière Noire or Black Expedition, which traveled from the north of the continent to the south, in 1924. These were humanistic and scientific adventures that aroused considerable popular interest at a time when the spirit of colonialism was still strong. The expeditions combined a praiseworthy desire to go off and meet other peoples with the flawed urge to conquer or convert them. The sculptor Henri Bouchard and the painter Alexandre Iacovleff went along as the expeditions' official artists, immortalizing the great characters involved.

A yearning to discover new worlds was at the time keenly felt by many, particularly artists. Cosmopolitanism was in the air, and the arts were being stimulated by the tremendous surge of energy created by the intermingling of cultures. Artists from around the world swarmed into Paris, setting up studios from Montparnasse to Montmartre and giving rise to the so-called School of Paris, a term reflecting the city's prominence as a center of modern art. Chagall, Zadkine, Foujita, Archipenko, Van Dongen, and Modigliani were all drawn to the capital from their homelands, enlivening it and being stimulated by it in turn.

At the same time, the automobile was allowing explorers to take off for the distant corners of the world, often outfitted with Louis Vuitton trunks, cases, and other specialized items. Citroën commissioned Louis Vuitton to equip the half-tracks for the 1924 Croisière Noire from Algeria to Madagascar. In 1931 the luggage maker's services were called on again for the Trans-Asiatic Expedition through central Asia.

Although the introduction of mass production brought the democratization of the automobile during the 1920s, coachbuilders continued to custom manufacture luxurious cars, and Louis Vuitton's superb cases were still being strapped to the backs of Rolls-Royces and Hispano-Suizas. Indeed, the great French coachbuilders who had gained renown before the First World War, such as Alfred Belvallette, Henri Binder, Georges Kellner, Louis Gallé, and Henri Labourdette, remained highly successful. Their chauffeur-driven cars were decorated like exquisite boudoirs, motorized hideaways done up in the spirit of Art Deco designers Paul Iribe and Louis Süe. The interiors featured the opulent detailing seen in fine home furnishings, such as eggshell inlays, sharkskin scales, and rosewood marquetry.

There was a ready market for such a riot of luxury. High society savored the magic of travel. The prestigious Orient Express, run by the Compagnie Internationale des Wagons-Lits, had linked London to Istanbul since 1883 with opulent trains; within a few decades, there were more ways to traverse the globe in great comfort and grandeur. Several large

Thanks to the Excelsior car trunk, the automobile could be used for "grand touring," as this June 1925 advertisement in *Fémina* proclaimed.

"EXCELSIOR"
LA FAMEUSE MALLE-AUTO
DE
LOUIS VUITTON

est le complément indispensable de la voiture de grand tourisme dont la puissance et la rapidité auraient été étudiées en pure perte si la malle-auto "Excelsior" ne permettait de trouver impeccables en arrivant à l'étape : smoking, vêtements et linge de rechange. Son étanchéité absolue est garantie par un double joint croisé, pneumatique et feutré, étudié sur un devant abattant à panneau unique supprimant tout jeu. La composition intérieure permet de l'adapter à tous les besoins ; le modèle ci-dessus comporte un porte-habits pour robes et vêtements, deux mallettes à linge, une trousse garnie pour homme et une trousse garnie pour dame. Enfin ses lignes harmonieuses épousant le galbe de la carrosserie lui assurent un succès toujours grandissant et une réputation de perfection devenue sans contredit. Louis Vuitton envoie gracieusement la brochure de la malle-auto sur simple demande.

PARIS — 70, CHAMPS-ÉLYSÉES

CANNES	NICE	LILLE	LONDON
10, RUE DES BELGES	12, Av. DE VERDUN	34, RUE FAIDHERBE	149, NEW BOND St

ÉTUDE SANS FRAIS DE PLANS ET DEVIS

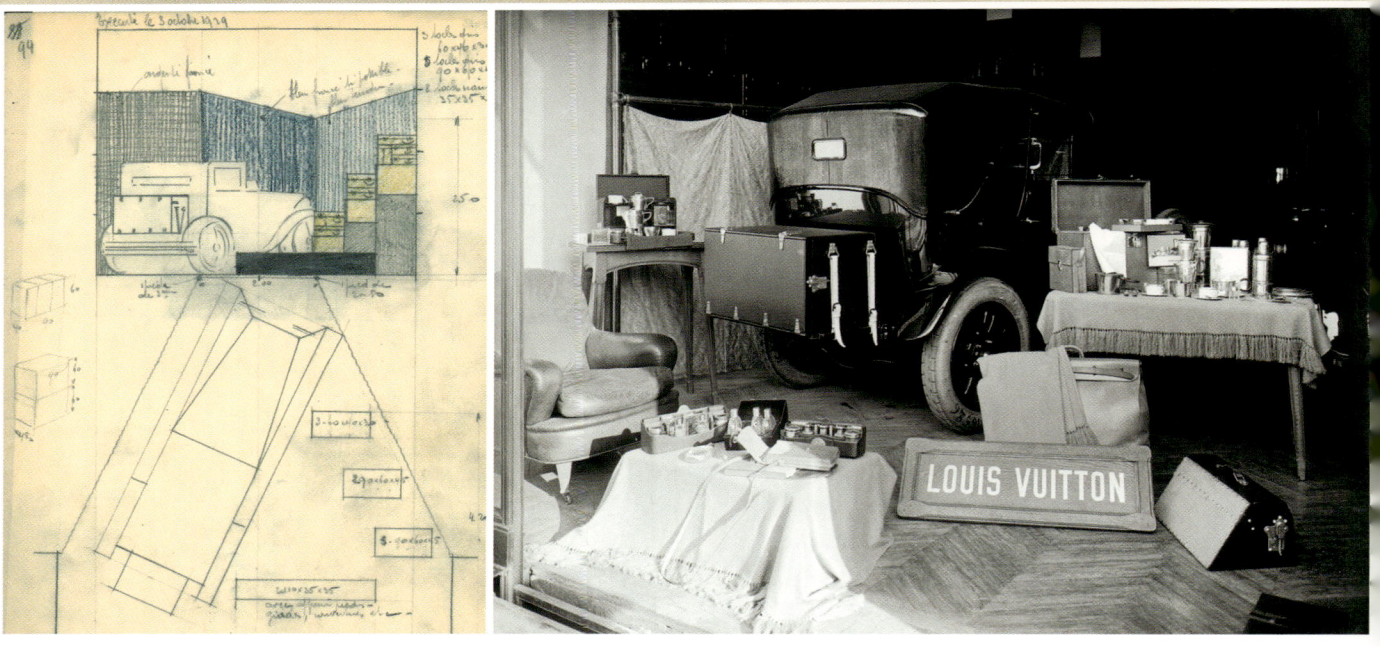

Throughout the 1920s the automobile was a fixture of Louis Vuitton's store on the Champs-Élysées in Paris. Cars can be seen behind stacks of luggage in these images from 1929 (top) and 1924.

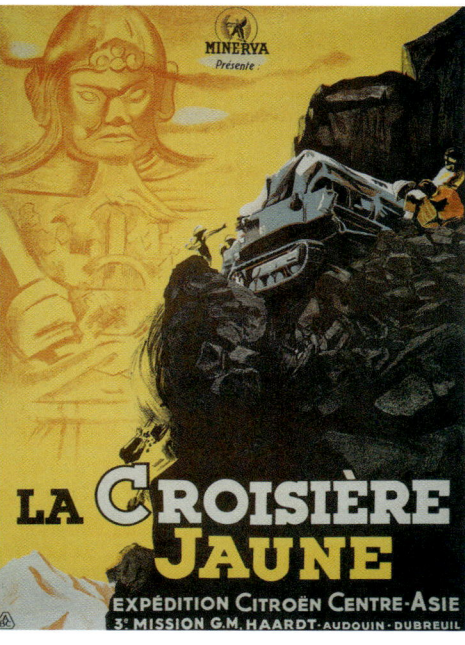

Louis Vuitton played a part in the adventurous automotive excursions organized by André Citroën, including the Croisière Noire (Black Expedition) across Africa in 1924 and the Croisière Jaune (Yellow Expedition) across central Asia in 1931.

steamships shared the Le Havre–New York line, which was run by the Compagnie Générale Transatlantique; the elegant *Île-de-France* joined the fleet in 1927. The first commercial airlines came into being, putting the whole world within reach. And all the developed countries could boast a web of road networks. In France, Parisians could drive all the way south to the Riviera on the famous Route Nationale 7.

Tourism had developed rapidly in the first decades of the twentieth century. The elite visited new spas and beach resorts along the Opal Coast of Flanders, the coasts of Normandy and the Basque country, and the Côte d'Azur. (They also discovered winter sports. André Citroën spent winter ski holidays with his friend Charlie Chaplin at Saint-Moritz; he also introduced him to the pleasures of the half-track.) Luxury hotels sprang up all along the fashionable coastlines. The Hôtel du Palais in Biarritz, the Negresco in Nice, the Normandie in Deauville, and the Lutécia in Paris were temples of sumptuousness and la dolce vita. Superlative automobiles such as Hispano-Suizas and Bugattis fit right into such settings. Just as the moneyed classes were discovering tourism, automakers were developing fast, comfortable automobiles that could undertake long journeys: The high-performance touring car had arrived.

Wall Street's sudden economic crash in 1929 dealt a fatal blow to the luxury industry, with the crisis soon reaching Europe. French car production took a breathtaking dive. Standardization became the norm, very expensive custom-made bodywork became rare, and firms specializing in the most luxurious makes of car faced grave difficulties. Some manufacturers shifted into the aeronautics industry or commercial car production, while other companies merged. Some renowned manufacturers disappeared entirely.

After the economic upheaval, the automobile evolved. Its shape changed, with the bodywork becoming aerodynamic and all-enveloping, with the luggage compartment incorporated within the body of the car. So ended the era when beautiful travel cases hung from the baggage racks, and so ended the collaboration between Louis Vuitton and the coachbuilders—at least for a few decades. At the turn of the millennium, in an era of contemporary design, the collaboration between the car industry and the luggage maker would begin anew.

The 1910 catalogue (at right) touted travel and, of course, offered specialized trunks: a *coffre étau* outfitted with tools for small repairs, a *déjeuner auto* or picnic hamper for lunch breaks, and even a *malle aéro* to attach to the sides of a hot-air balloon basket.

Louis Vuitton continued to produce and promote specialized car trunks until the end of the 1920s. They can be seen (at far right) here in the illustration by Bernard Boutet de Monvel for an article in *Harper's Bazaar*, dated May 1926, and in an advertisement from 1930.

MALLE AÉRO
INSUBMERSIBLE, ASSURE LA FLOTTABILITÉ DES NACELLES EN CAS DE CHUTE EN MER. FERMETURE RIGOUREUSEMENT ÉTANCHE.

DÉJEUNER AUTO
POUR DEUX, QUATRE, SIX, HUIT PERSONNES. TRÈS RECOMMANDÉ POUR L'AUTOMOBILISME & LE CAMPING

COFFRE ÉTAU
CHAQUE OUTIL A SA PLACE & L'ÉTAU SE MET AUTOMATIQUEMENT EN POSITION EN OUVRANT LE COFFRE.

MALLES AUTO
COMME NOS SACS CHAUFFEUR ELLES ALLÈGENT LES CARROSSERIES ET RENDENT LEURS LIGNES PLUS HARMONIEUSES.

HARPER'S BAZAR

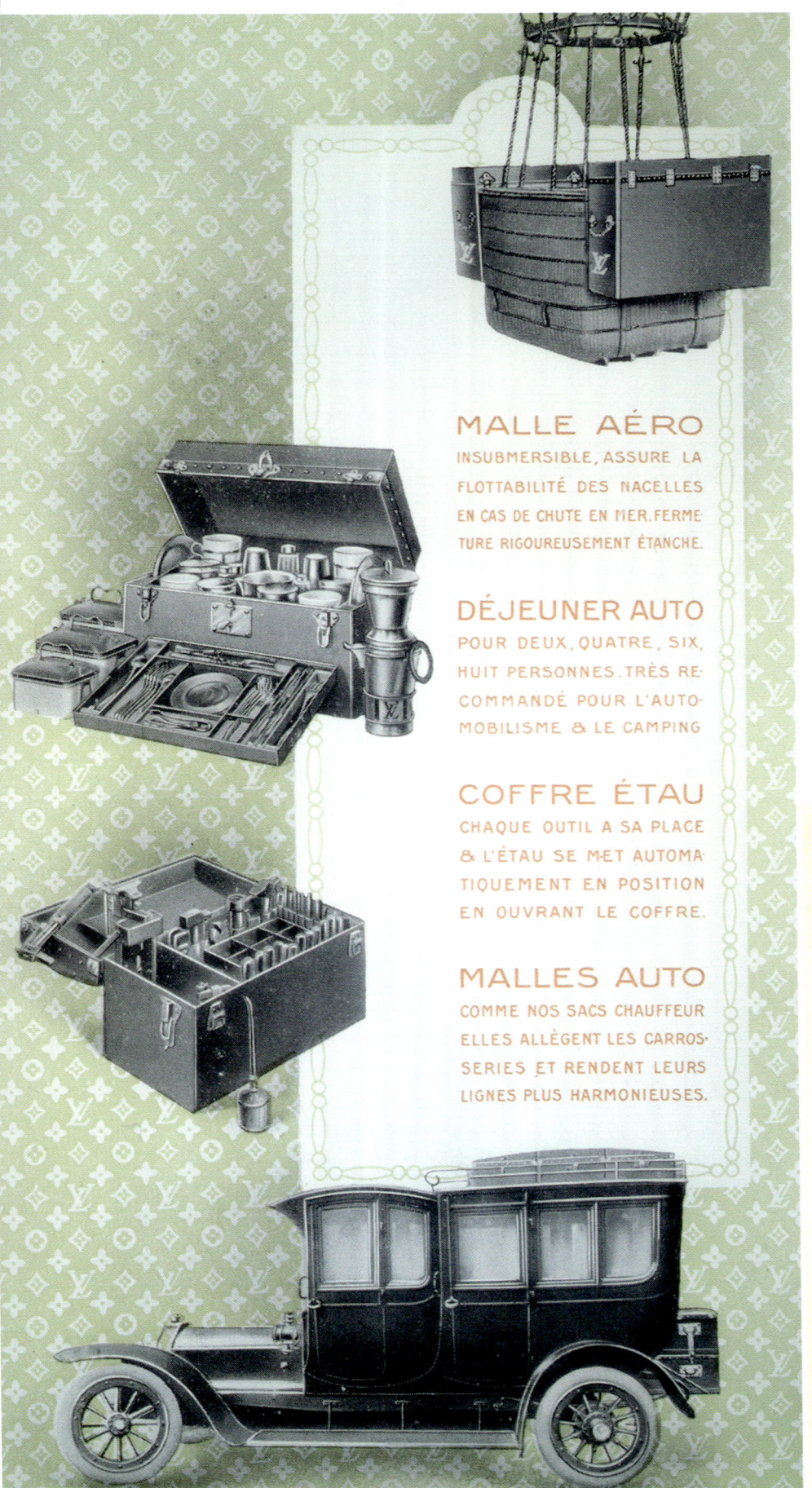

Luggage on this page from VUITTON

Wayside tea from a Vuitton tea-case of sole-leather; the lady wears a beige tweed coat trimmed with giraffe from Fourrures Max.

peach, almond, lemon, and palely rose clothes. This year, the fruit is no longer refreshing; it is stale; and there is a new note of strength, of contrast, vivid and daring, which is like a trumpet call to one's joy in color. This color must be used with taste and with intelligence; otherwise the result is disaster. That is why both white and natural kasha keep their place in the sun—they make such good backgrounds for it. Last year's conception of the purest elegance—everything matching—is superseded this year by clever combinations, in which violent contrasts are the characteristic note, as dissonances are characteristic of modern music. To match everything slavishly is too easy—it becomes unintelligent to do it any longer. It looks too perfect, too like an old-fashioned fashion-plate; our country clothes, at least, should have a less monotonous intention, an unpremeditated air, which is really carefully careless and the result of study.

We were inspired by fruits last summer; this year we have taken flowers for our point of color departure; but not faint, pale exotics; the robust and wholesome blooms of the perennial border in the cottage garden. High in favor are the pure reds—not the purplish wine colors, but the red of the field poppy as well as the dusky tone of the clove carnation; cornflower blues which blend so well with dark marine and midnight blue, and all the blues that we find in Chinese porcelain; the clear greens of vigorous leaves and plant stems, and of fresh spring grasses. These are the shades in favor, not necessarily for entire costumes, which might be too nerve-shattering, but used with distinction, restraint, and discrimination. I must not forget the decided rose pinks, which have certainly not left the mode; they too have the strength and sweetness of roses from a country garden. But the flag colors, after all, are the smartest for resort wardrobes; so you may gratify your patriotism freely.

Both white and the pale neutral fawn of natural wood make a wonderful foil for these courageous shades; so they remain. But the "eatable" browns, gingerbread and spices, have retired for the summer. There are dead

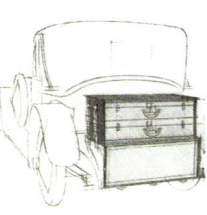

An automobile trunk from Vuitton contains suit-cases for Monsieur and for Madame, in a varnished leather case.

EN COMMANDANT VOTRE VOITURE, COMMANDEZ UNE MALLE-AUTO VUITTON. LE RAYON D'ACTION DE L'AUTO ACTUELLE DÉPEND MOINS DE LA PUISSANCE DE SON MOTEUR QUE DE LA CONCEPTION DE SON CONFORT ET DES BAGAGES QU'ELLE EMPORTE. C'EST EN VERTU DE CE PRINCIPE QUE LOUIS VUITTON RÉALISE DES MALLES-AUTO IMPECCABLES COMPLÉMENTS INDISPENSABLES DE LA VOITURE DE TOURISME.

LOUIS VUITTON
PARIS 70 CHAMPS ELYSEES
NICE 12 AV. DE VERDUN. CANNES 10 R. DES BELGES
VICHY RUE DU PARC. LONDON 149 NEW BOND STREET

Travel

2

Glorious classic cars long to be back on the road again, to take off on delightful getaways, and to satisfy their true vocation: travel.

2

For some lovers of classic cars, it is unthinkable that the objects of their passion should stand forever silent and motionless, as if inside a museum. They could never simply gaze upon their treasures, reducing them to mere collectibles. Such enthusiasts argue that the cars were made to move, that these machines have the right to relive their past glories and see how they measure up against one another, as they did in their prime. So throughout the year sporting events are held, both on the closed circuit and the open road, featuring some of history's most unforgettable automobiles. One of the oldest and finest retrospectives takes place in Italy in the spring.

This event was revived in 1977 along the route of the Mille Miglia, a legendary race from Brescia to Rome and back that was held from 1927 to 1957. Once among auto racing's most extraordinary events, the race had been banned following a tragic accident in which a group of spectators lost their lives.

The modern version of the Mille Miglia is considered safer than the original, since the competitive element has been eliminated, but it is just as spectacular, thanks to the quality of the drivers. After a revival in 1977, then again in 1982 and 1984, the sporadic event's popular success encouraged its organizers to put it on an annual schedule. Since 1986 it has brought a sense of wonderment every year to the Piazza Vittorio in the center of Brescia, where nearly four hundred racing crews gather. Its success has inspired similar events elsewhere.

These great tours of classic cars are like living history. They delight onlookers along the roads while allowing the rally's participants to feel like the champions of yesteryear. The great enthusiasm they generate encouraged Louis Vuitton to associate its name with some wonderful escapes along the world's roadways.

34 From Singapore to Kuala Lumpur Louis Vuitton Vintage Equator Run 1993

April 9–11.

Louis Vuitton organized its first classic car rally amid the luxuriant landscapes of Southeast Asia, on the border of Malaysia.

On January 31, 1907, the daily newspaper *Le Matin* threw out a challenge to automakers in search of glory: "Who is prepared to go by car from Peking to Paris this summer?" Five intrepid teams took up the challenge and set off from Peking on June 10. Two months and 10,000 miles (16,000 kilometers) later, Prince Don Scipione Luigi Marcantonio Francesco Rodolfo Borghese, at the wheel of his Itala, was the first to arrive in Paris.

A century later the Orient still works its magic on the traveler seeking enchantment. The spectacular emergence of new economic forces in Asia is fascinating. New markets are opening up for the automobile industry, stimulating a keen curiosity about classic cars and automotive history. For its first rally's location, Louis Vuitton chose the Federation of Malaysia and arranged the support of the MSVCR (Malaysia and Singapore Vintage Car Register). Consequently, almost a third of the competitors were recruited from among local collectors.

After a night's rest in the colonial splendor of the Raffles Hotel, drivers of almost seventy cars and two motorcycles, all made before 1960, took off from Padang, near the Singapore Cricket Club. Among the participants were two well-known and experienced French enthusiasts, each at the wheel of a highly respected Grand Prix Bugatti: Maurice Sauzay in his immaculate 35 and the historian Antoine Prunet in his fiery 37. The program also included no fewer than eleven MG models, with the complete range of the famed Midget, a profusion that can be explained by the fervent involvement of the MG Car Club in organizing the event. The oldest car was a 1914 Mercer that had no hood and was driven by a courageous, robust American collector.

After three days of driving through the magical Malaysian landscape, on dusty roads through Malacca, Negri Sembilan, and Selangor, in the shade of palm trees and rubber plants, the rally made a triumphant entry into Kuala Lumpur.

A strong contingent of MG Midgets participated in the Equator Run, thanks to the support of the local MG enthusiasts' club. Shown here is a 1939 TA from Singapore.

A 1939 Citroën 11 BL convertible was brought out of storage in Switzerland to get lost in the Malaysian jungle.

Like the American Jim Proffit, seen at the wheel of his 1914 Mercer, the entrants were at the controls throughout the run.

Two French collectors, Antoine Prunet (in the blue car) and Maurice Sauzay, brave a monsoon at the wheels of their Bugattis, a Type 37 and a Type 35 respectively.

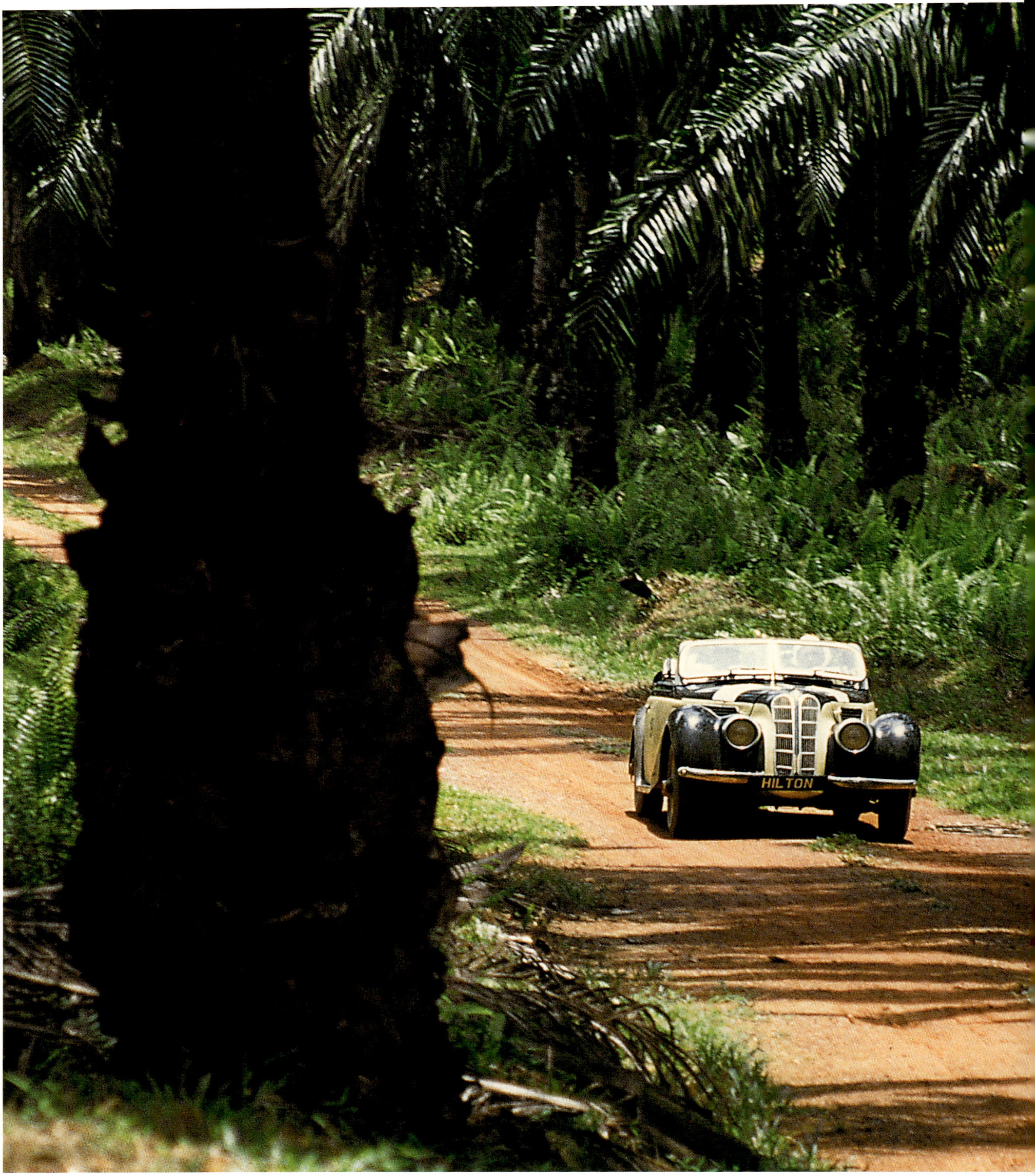
HILTON

Driven by an American collector, a 1936 BMW 327 courses along in the luxuriant forest.

40
Around Lake Geneva
Tour du Léman Louis Vuitton Trophy 1995–97

With the lake lapping in the background, this auto tour paid tribute to the unforgettable early days in the history of the automobile.

Swiss automakers are becoming rare, even in the context of the International Motor Show held in Geneva, Switzerland, every year. Only a few craftsmen keep alive the tradition that brought forth great Swiss makes such as Pic-Pic, Turicum, Zedel, and Martini. Those names, all but forgotten, are honored at the Tour du Léman, an extraordinary rally Louis Vuitton sponsored from 1995 to 1997, and preserved by the Pierre Gianadda Foundation, which operates a museum in Martigny.

Just over an hour from Geneva, at the junction of the roads to the Forclaz and Saint Bernard passes, Martigny is a must-see destination for those interested in art, archaeology, and the automobile. The Pierre Gianadda Foundation delightfully combines exhibits on all three. Léonard Gianadda built the museum next to a fourth-century Roman amphitheater as a tribute to his brother Pierre, who died in an accident. The building, opened in 1978, was constructed around the remains of a Celtic shrine. In its sculpture garden the works of Henry Moore, Constantin Brancusi, and Eduardo Chillida stand out against a backdrop of mountains covered with the vineyards of the Valais. In the museum's basement is a collection of automobiles offering the complete panorama of Swiss car manufacturing.

It is a stone's throw from Lake Geneva, on whose banks the French town of Évian retains the slightly faded charm of old spa resorts. The spring water here, sold since the early nineteenth century, has made the name Évian famous across the globe, but it was fashionable visitors like Marcel Proust and Jean Cocteau, as well as major gatherings of diplomats, that gave the town its pedigree. Its thermal baths, casino, and luxury hotels keep alive the memory of a century of opulence and pleasure.

During the rally an icy northern wind might create waves on Lake Geneva, making it look like an ocean, sending the usually peaceful waters crashing against the banks with uncommon violence, and causing the medieval French village of Nernier, on the lake's south shore, to shiver. The gleaming cobblestones of Nernier's narrow streets reflect the glorious past that gives the Tour du Léman its inexpressible charm. As required by the rules, all the distinguished automobiles in the event date to the turn of the twentieth century.

Competing on its home soil at the Tour du Léman was a limousine made by Piccard-Pictet, a Geneva-based firm that operated from 1910 to 1924.

1995
Tour du Léman, Louis Vuitton Trophy

September 15–17. In its third year, the classic car rally around Lake Geneva took on a prestigious new partner—Louis Vuitton—which crowned the rally, open only to cars built before 1905, with the Louis Vuitton Trophy. The cars set off from Bastions Park in Geneva on a three-day journey, traveling on the first day through Nyon, Rolle, Morges, Lausanne, and Montreux. On the second day the procession crossed the French border, then stopped for the night in Évian. On the final day, after a stop at the Château de Ripaille in Thonon-les-Bains, the old-timers ended their journey at the Parc des Eaux-Vives in Geneva, after a run of 112 miles (180 kilometers).

1996
Tour du Léman, Louis Vuitton Trophy

September 13–15. For this year's rally, the automobiles were joined by other pioneers of locomotion. Seven aircraft built in the 1930s had flown down from the nearby airfield in Prangins to roar around the skies above the canton of Vaud.

On the second day, in Montreux, the Boeings, de Havillands, and Stampes made way for the *Pécadille,* a steamboat that was built on the banks of Lake Geneva in 1897. Nearly a dozen old boats sailed around the lake, while back on the road the Éclair made an appearance; this 1895 Peugeot was the world's first car to be equipped with tires produced by the brothers André and Édouard Michelin.

1997
Tour du Léman, Louis Vuitton Classic

September 12–14. In its fifth year the Lake Geneva rally was renamed, becoming one of the Louis Vuitton Classics—part of the advance preparations for the centenary of the first car race, which took place on this spot in Switzerland in September 1898. The rally paid tribute to the first men to drive faster than 60 miles (100 kilometers) per hour. To mark the occasion, an astoundingly accurate replica was built of Camille Jenatzy's 1899 electric car, Jamais Contente—a missile-shaped automobile that was the first to top 60 miles per hour. On April 29, 1899, at Achères, near Paris, it achieved the then breathtaking speed of 66 miles (106 kilometers) per hour. The original car is reverently conserved at the Musée de la Voiture et du Tourisme (Museum of the Car and Tourism) in Compiègne, France.

The Tour du Léman was limited to cars produced before 1905, which demonstrated how auto bodies descended directly from horse-drawn carriages.

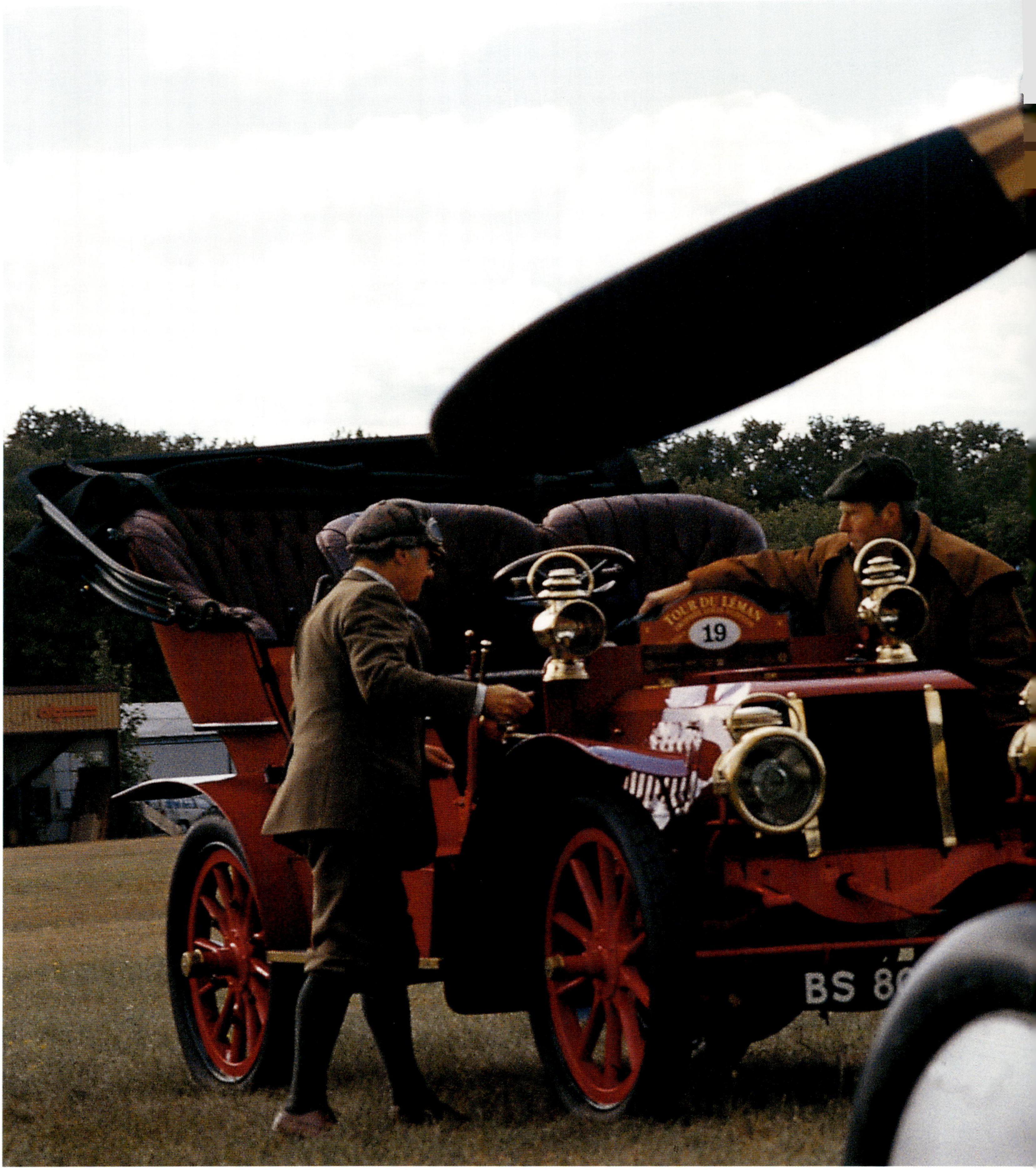
TOUR DU LEMAN
19

On the banks of Lake Geneva, early aviation and early automobiles crossed paths.

46
The Italian Renaissance
Louis Vuitton Italia Classica 1995–97

The legendary Italian motor cars were just waiting to be revived so they could rediscover their terrain and reconnect with their outstanding inherent nature. The Italia Classica fulfilled all their expectations, with four runs on different routes, the last two under the Louis Vuitton banner.

From Modena to Modena via Portofino: This was the itinerary set for the fourth Italia Classica. The names of its destinations are deeply evocative. Modena, at the heart of Emilia-Romagna, was home to the Ferrari family, while Portofino is on the Levant Riviera, a lush inlet that inspired Guy de Maupassant with an "impression of bliss."

In Modena, Enzo Ferrari is more famous than Luciano Pavarotti, another native of the area. Ferrari's memory has overshadowed even that of the Este dynasty, the ducal princes who first raised Modena's profile in the Middle Ages. The name Ferrari is worshipped like no other by automobile enthusiasts, and Modena is their promised land, where they can pay homage to the "cavallino rampant," the prancing stallion that is Ferrari's venerated symbol.

The town is quiet—delightfully provincial, as visitors accustomed to the buzz of big cities often say with a bit of disdain. Historic Modena grew up around the Piazza Grande in the shadow of its cathedral, the Duomo, whose mass of milky marble rises before the Ghirlandina Tower, which overlooks the town. The city center is crisscrossed by narrow, colorful streets that have survived since the seventeenth century. Running through Modena is the Via Emilia, the ancient Roman road from Rimini to Placentia that Consul Marcus Aemilius Lepidus built in the first century B.C.E. The province took its name from that road.

For a few hundred yards the Via Emilia becomes Largo Garibaldi. The huge, dignified building here is the Ferrari family home. Not far away was the first address on the Viale Trente Trieste occupied by the Scuderia Ferrari, founded in 1929 to organize car races. Further along, on the Viale Ciro Menutti, is the headquarters of Maserati, Ferrari's historic rival. Over the years the Modena region has attracted many mechanics of genius. Stanguellini was headquartered in Via Schedoni, Alessandro de Tomaso had his factory in Viale Virgilio, the Scuderia Serenissima was in Via Nicolò Biondo, and Iso Rivolta lived over in Formigine.

Today the names of all these legends shine out from the list of cars taking part in the Italia Classica.

The participants gather on the church square in Borgo San Felice.

1995
Louis Vuitton Italia Classica

September 19–24. The first Italia Classica, in 1991, had an itinerary centering around the Villa Medici. The second, in 1993, ran through the Dolomites, taking in Palladian villas between Venice and Cortina. Then, in 1995, Louis Vuitton associated its brand with the rally. It was open to authentically pedigreed cars that had competed in a championship race among well-known makes before 1971. Thus only the highest-performance, most sophisticated machines took part in this Tuscan event. Of those that participated, the range of Alfa Romeos was particularly impressive.

The village of San Felice, about nine miles (fifteen kilometers) from Siena, is perched at the top of a hill, surrounded by Chianti's vineyards, and protected by a ring of cypress trees. On the first day of the rally the cars drove on the roads around San Felice. The following day they headed for the coast and the port of Piombino, where the convoy embarked for Elba. The next day was devoted to a tour of that harsh, mountainous, magnificent island. The competitors finally returned to San Felice along a road further to the south, passing through Castiglione, with a stop at the castle in Poggio alle Mura.

1997
Louis Vuitton Italia Classica

September 16–20. A highlight of the fourth Italia Classica was a concours d'elegance organized on Modena's Piazza Grande. This provided a break during a run that began with a drive across the Apennines to the coast, ending at Forte dei Marmi, near Massa. On the second day the itinerary took the participants to Portofino, returning in the evening to Forte dei Marmi. The following day the competitors went off in the opposite direction, heading south toward the Ornellaia estate, where they were received by Marquis Lodovico Antinori, whose name graces a famous Tuscan wine. They drove back to Modena on roads evoking memories of the Mille Miglia and passed through Abetone, where several generations of drivers have made the walls shake while testing out new Ferraris. The day ended after a visit to the Cavallino stables in Maranello—a kind of homecoming for cars like Yoji Oyama's 166 MM, which took part in the Mille Miglia in 1950, Harry Leventis's 250 GTO, and Nicolaus Springer's 860 Monza.

Alain de Cadenet

The man behind this old Provençal name is in fact an enthusiastic, talented British sportsman. Between 1971 and 1986 Alain de Cadenet took part fourteen times in the Twenty-Four Hour Race at Le Mans. He could be seen at the wheel of models of all brands, including Ferrari, Duckhams, Grid, Cougar, and Porsche, but above all at the controls of superb prototypes bearing his own name—a series based on the Lola chassis that he began producing in 1974. It was while driving a "De Cadenet" that he achieved his best result in the race, finishing in third place in 1976. He also won events in the World Endurance Championship, as both a driver and manufacturer, at Monza and Silverstone in 1980. After hanging up his racing helmet Alain de Cadenet concentrated on his collection of sports cars, which he has never stopped driving as hard as they will go!

Antoine Prunet

Another key figure in the world of collectible automobiles, Antoine Prunet in 1983 cofounded the magazine *Automobiles Classiques* with Arnault de Fouchier and remained its editor in chief until 1998. A well-informed enthusiast, expert, and author of several essential books on the history of Ferrari, he initiated the Bagatelle concours in 1988, modeling it on the one at Pebble Beach, California. He called on Christian Philippsen to help select the participants and jurors. Antoine Prunet is also a collector who took part in several of the Louis Vuitton runs. In June 2007 he was one of the experts on the jury at the concours d'elegance held at Maranello, Italy, to mark Ferrari's sixtieth anniversary.

An elegant Lagonda Rapide proves the merits of its name on the roads of Tuscany.

The historian and journalist Antoine Prunet seems keenly focused at the wheel of his Bugatti Type 37 (no. 37232).

Two Jaguars on the roads of Tuscany, a C-Type intended for racing followed by an E-Type, which is more of a touring car.

This pale green Ferrari 250 GTO (no. 3505/GT) was delivered to a British owner in 1962.

These two Ferrari 250 GT Berlinetta Competiziones won fame at the Tour de France Automobile starting in 1956.

Resting by the harbor in Portofino, this Maserati Sport 2000 (no. 2179) with superb 1955 bodywork by Zagato is owned by David Sydorick.

One of the first touring Ferraris was this 166 Inter coupe made in 1950.

With its crew in uniform, this Alfa Romeo 1900 Super Berlina has rediscovered its original purpose.

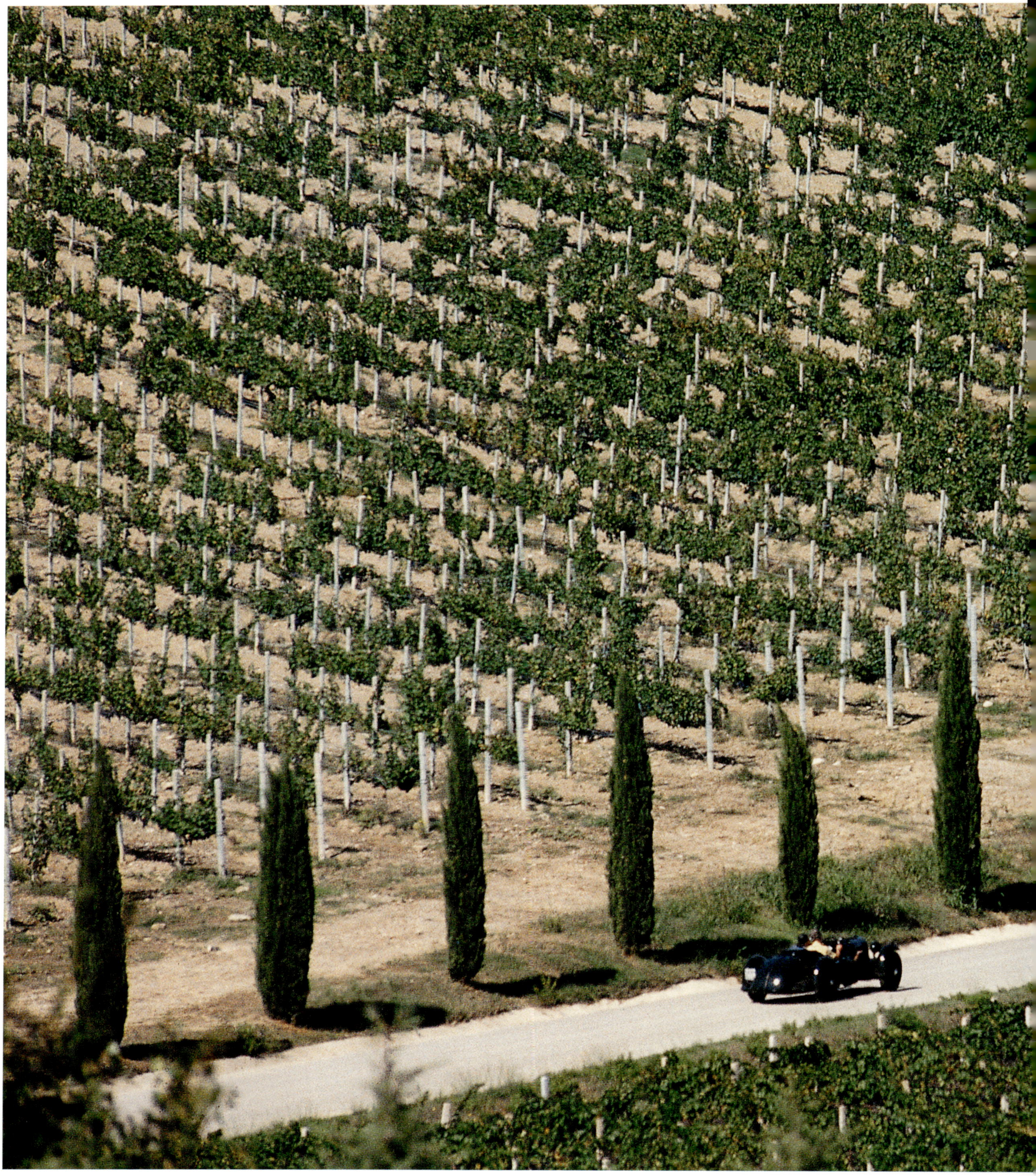

An Aston Martin dashes past a row of cypress trees and the vineyards of Chianti.

56 The Charms of Asia Louis Vuitton Classic China Run 1998

May 25–30.

It is Sunday in Dalian, a port city in northeast China nestled in a peninsula between the mainland and Korea. Dalian is like other cities in Asia—that is, like cities nowhere else.

There is diabolical traffic, noise, frenzy, crowds, run-down buildings covered with an overabundance of calligraphy. But like all metropolises, Dalian has its secret gardens, its backyards, its alleyways where small traders and craftspeople crowd together, and a true street culture. Everything happens outdoors here: Scowling seamstress sew on the sidewalk, cobblers and locksmiths ply their trades, gloomy-faced gamblers set up tables to play checkers or cards, oblivious to the passers-by, and lines of vendors offer their fruit, spices, and teas.

The event's participants include a colorful range of automobiles, a procession of fifty cars from seventeen countries and representing every era. Next to an enormous 1903 Mercedes, which has a chain transmission and is spitting oil, are five Rolls-Royces: two vintage Silver Ghosts and a trio of Phantoms. There is a pride of Jaguars of every type: SS, XK 120, XK 140, and XK 150. A Hong Qi limousine, manufactured in China in the 1960s, is enjoying a new lease on life as a collectible object.

The first stage of the itinerary, to Yingkou, travels through a landscape that seems almost Mediterranean, crossing a plain surrounded by salt banks left by the ocean. The scenery changes on the second day, when the road runs along marshes bristling with oil wells, paddies, and a rocky mountain that has been worked over by quarriers. When they happen upon a village, the driving teams take a break and puff on their cigarettes. It does not take long to get the feel of a region by hanging around its markets. From the gestures, stalls, abundant produce, flavors, and fragrances, you can sense how daily life is lived in these rural areas. In the evening a bivouac of Mongolian yurts is set up by a lake.

The next day the road turns into a track. Covered with mud and dust, the fine old cars seem to have forgotten about concours d'elegance and gala evenings once and for all. The scenery that unfolds between Jianchang and Chengden is majestic. The day ends at the summer residence of the Qing emperors at Chengde. The itinerary for the following day shows that the China Run will head for the Great Wall at Shisalin. This is a dream for all travelers to China: to see for themselves this wildly ambitious structure, to set foot on the monumental folly built by those who thought they could hold back invasions from the north. Stretching across the middle of nowhere, the Great Wall now does nothing but provide shelter for shepherds. After driving along the sacred road that passes the tombs of the Ming dynasty and leaving Mingyuan, the convoy enters Beijing—escorted by the police, congratulated by the onlookers, and fêted on Tiananmen Square.

The winner of the run is a Jaguar XK 150. After such an astounding experience, does it matter?

This 1958 Ferrari 250 Testa Rossa (chassis no. 0718) did not have far to travel for the China Run, as it is owned by the Hong Kong–based collector Brandon Wang.

An MG Midget TD from Brazil makes its way through an amazed and enthusiastic crowd.

The English collector Timothy Scotts has no qualms about sending his 1903 Mercedes 60 HP out on China's demanding roads.

René Metge

Behind the banter is a big-hearted firebrand, fine tactician, and subtle diplomat. Organizing adventurous excursions to far-flung places, he works quietly and efficiently in the background. A lover of open spaces and distant horizons, René Metge made his name by winning the Paris–Dakar rally several times, in a Range Rover in 1981 and 1984 and in a Porsche in 1986. Then this versatile driver added to his achievements in endurance races and Supertourism events. He has masterfully organized rallies around the world, always exhibiting an interest in and respect for the cultures of the countries involved. He was the sporting and technical director of the Paris–Algiers–Dakar rally in 1988 and 1989. In 1992 he organized the first Paris–Moscow–Beijing rally, and from 1995 to 2001 he oversaw the various Master Rallies across Asia. René Metge also designed the itineraries for Louis Vuitton's China Run and Bohemia Run.

For many years the Hong Qi was the car used by Chinese officials. Now it is back on Tiananmen Square in Beijing.

The China Run encountered the Great Wall at Shisalin.

This Jaguar XK 150 S coupe belongs to Chia Quee Khee of Singapore.

This Bugatti Type 44 by Harrington is masterfully driven by Jean-Paul Mouton, a French collector and regular participant in concours and rallies.

The beautiful and rare Alfa Romeo 1900 Super Sprint Zagato owned by American collector Jack Croul adapts well to the dusty Chinese tracks.

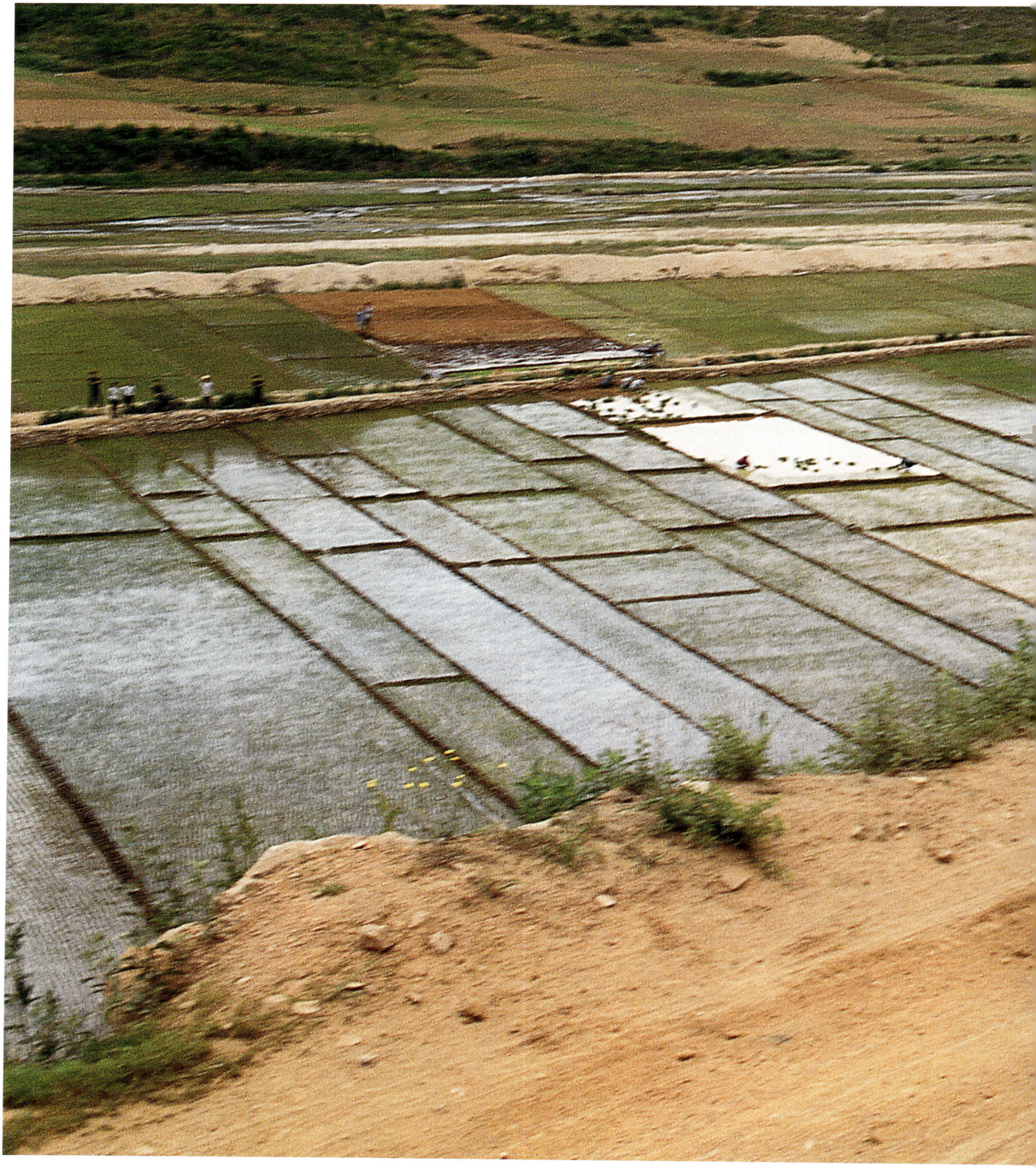

The Australian crew of a Jaguar XK 150 enjoys the view of paddies between Jianchang and Andashi.

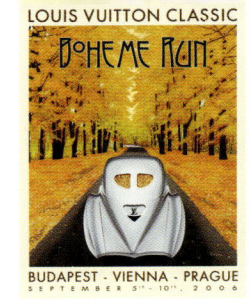

From Budapest to Prague via Vienna
Louis Vuitton Classic Bohemia Run 2006

September 5–10.

The atmosphere in Vienna's Café Schwarzenberg is warm and muffled, with mahogany paneling and crystal chandeliers. It's easy to imagine the ghost of Otto Wagner sitting here with a *kleiner Schwarzer* in front of him. Sipping that small black coffee is a ritual for the Viennese.

Wagner (1841–1918) was one of the innovators of Vienna's architecture. Throughout the city are the traces of his stylized art: metro stations and buildings ornamented with purple flowers and gilded friezes, remnants of Jugendstil or Art Nouveau, which, as Thomas Mann wrote, was characterized by a "guileless worship of line, decor, form, and sensuality."

Even at the beginning of the twenty-first century, the ghosts of the late nineteenth century haunt this city, on which other inventive styles have been superimposed. The Secession movement arose from discord among Austrian artists, including the painter Gustav Klimt. One of the Secession's leading members, Klimt, with his reassuring beard and endearing wrinkles, looked rather jovial. He vociferated against all kinds of academicism, but for some the Secession itself had its limits. With his taciturn air and pinched mouth, the architect Adolf Loos was Klimt's opposite. He left the Secession to pursue a more severe, purist aesthetic.

The participants in the Bohemia Run spent a night in this contradictory city and found that they had similar disagreements pertaining to the world of applied arts. Quarrels broke out between the supporters of baroque decadence, who were carried away by Saoutchik's Pegaso Z-102, and the lovers of classic elegance, who had eyes only for the graceful BMW 507.

Eight years had passed since the China Run, the last great excursion to which Louis Vuitton had lent its name. This one was worth the wait. The destination, in the heart of Europe, was novel: The trip took in three capitals, three cultures, three destinies that have intersected periodically through the trials and torments of history. The landscapes, from Budapest to Prague via Vienna, reflected the musical tonalities of Bartók, Mahler, and Janáček.

Among the familiar characters here were the smiling Christine Bélanger, director of the Louis Vuitton Classics, the formally elegant Christian Philippsen, head of the selection committee, and René Metge, the chief on-course race official, with his mischievous grin. Those three people have been involved in every automobile event sponsored by Louis Vuitton.

The Bohemia Run took place in two stages, the first one from Budapest to Vienna. About fifty cars set off from Roosevelt Square. They were divided into seven categories, each of which boasted some great rarities. The Gran Turismo class included an Alfa Romeo 1900 Super Sprint by Zagato; it had been sent by David Sydorick, an avid collector of everything the Milanese Zagato produced. Under the banner of "the art of travel" was a Tatra 603, the emblematic sedan of Communist party dignitaries in Eastern Europe in the 1960s—an unusual car, with an air-cooled eight-cylinder rear engine.

Most recognizable of all in the crowd were the well-known collectors: Arturo Keller, who came from Mexico with his Mercedes Benz Type S built by Castagna; the California-based Peter Mullin, with an extremely rare Talbot Lago "teardrop" built by Joseph Figoni; Jim Hull, also from California, with a green Delahaye with bodywork by Henri Chapron; as well as the amiable and dedicated French collector Jean-Paul Mouton, who is inseparable from his Bugatti 44 torpedo, created in Great Britain by Harrington. These men live their passion and at the same time share it with the countless spectators at these unforgettable excursions.

Bugatti produced only forty-two cars of the 57 S type, but that does not prevent collector Antonius Meijer from barreling along in his extremely rare Atalante, with 1937 bodywork by Gangloff.

Shown at Fertöd Castle, in Hungary, is one of the Ferrari 250 GT Berlinettas that came out in the summer of 1959. They marked an intermediate stage in the model's evolution, heralding the future with a short chassis (94 inches [2.4 meters]) but retaining a long wheelbase (102 inches [2.6 meters]).

The 1959 Cadillac Eldorado Convertible marked the height of the passion for tailfins in the United States.

Firmly planted on its thick tires, the broad Cobra 427 takes up the whole road. This 1960s reptile was an American adaptation of the slender British AC Ace.

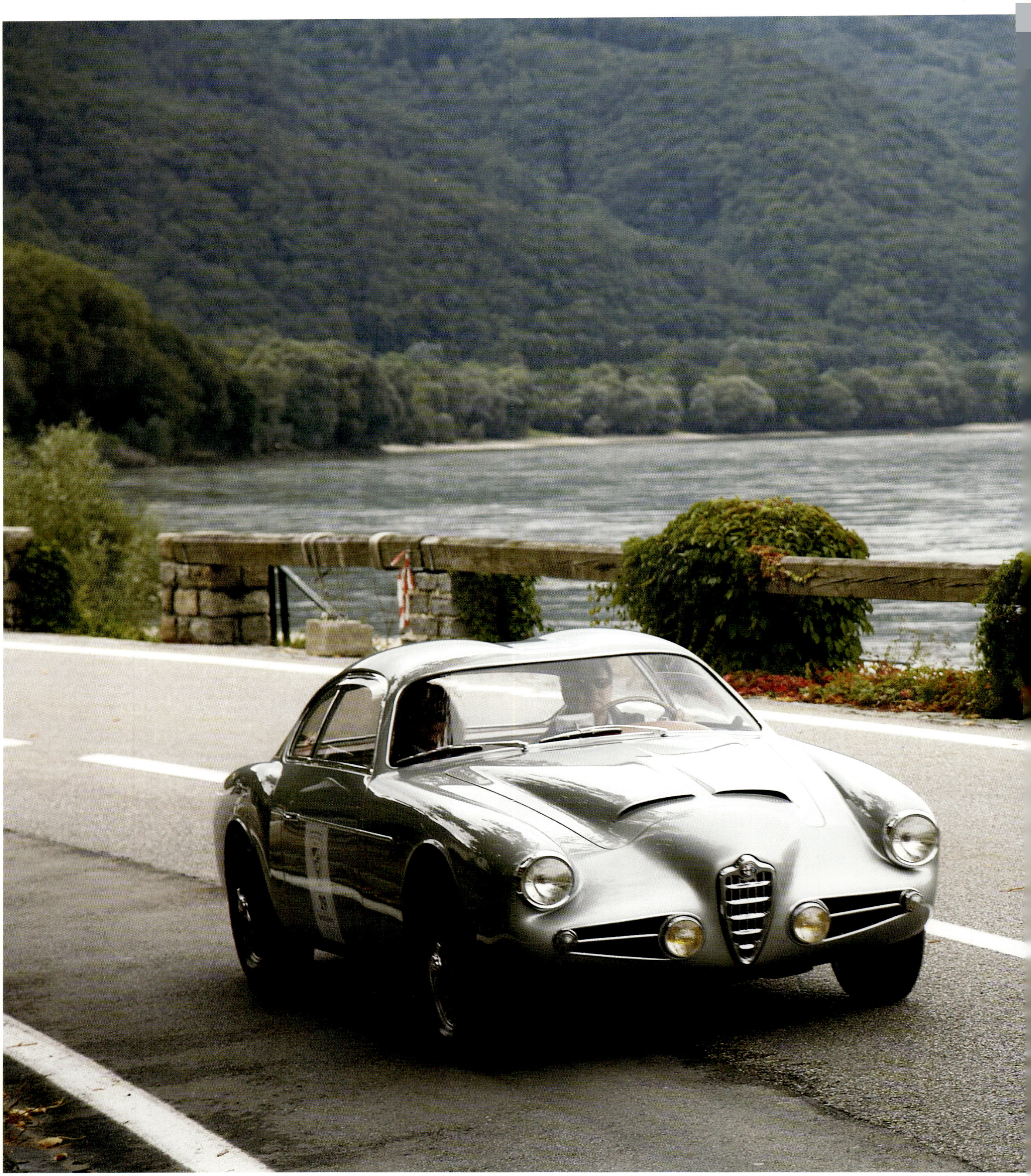

David Sydorick's Alfa Romeo 1900 Super Sprint is one of eighteen cars of this type Zagato made in 1956.

3

Elegance

Reflecting the creativity of their age, automobiles show themselves off in the sunlight of a concours d'elegance.

3

Coachbuilders and couturiers worked together throughout the 1920s in a lavish outpouring of creativity. Sharing a well-heeled clientele and cultivating the same values as practitioners of applied arts, the two professions joined up naturally at the concours d'elegance.

These gatherings—contests of automotive beauty and workmanship—took place at venues familiar to the elite. Racecourses were especially popular: Auteuil, Longchamp, Saint-Cloud, and Vincennes in the Paris area, but also the Parc des Princes and the Bagatelle polo grounds on the city's outskirts. In every region of France, the smartest vacation spots were proud to host concours d'elegance in the summer months. The grounds of casinos and luxury hotels in resorts like La Baule, Enghien, Vichy, Deauville, Biarritz, and Monte-Carlo made excellent settings for exhibitions of elegance of every kind. Couturiers such as Schiaparelli, Worth, and Lanvin would display their collections in association with coachbuilders like Franay, Binder, or Gallé.

Each year several concours were organized, the most important of which quickly became the one launched by *L'Auto*, a daily sports paper that was a predecessor of *L'Équipe*. The spirit of competition added some spice to the proceedings. The automobiles were grouped together by categories—closed or convertible cars, conventional or innovative ones—and a grand prize was awarded at the end. Women were used to show off bodywork, just as they displayed haute couture to its best advantage, a paradox at a time when women's position in society was beginning to evolve. The final touch was added by superb specimens of extraordinary breeds of dog—wearing frilly costumes, no less.

The Americans were the first to revive this kind of event in the early 1950s. The concours at Pebble Beach, on the California coast, served as a model for the show that was first held at the park of the Château de Bagatelle, near Paris, in 1988.

74 Parisian Classics from Bagatelle to Saint-Cloud 1989–2003

The fine adventure of Louis Vuitton's concours d'elegance in the Paris area began in the park of the Château de Bagatelle, on the outskirts of the city, and ended at the gardens of Saint-Cloud.

As soon as she arrived at Bagatelle, the maréchale d'Estrées set the tone for indulgence. She turned the charming residence—built in 1720 by her husband, Victor-Henri d'Estrées, on the edge of the Bois de Boulogne—into a center of dissolute behavior. All the gallants of the court crowded into their home. The young Louis XV himself was one of the maréchale's guests; she was an effective go-between, said to be "seductive and not at all shy." After the maréchale's death, the marquise de Monconseil took up where the maréchale had left off, organizing entertainments and rendezvous with the same fervor but at such a hectic pace that eventually she was ruined. She allowed the building to fall into ruins as well.

The property changed hands a few times before being taken over in 1777 by the comte d'Artois, who built an extravagant new folly—the current château— designed by François Bélanger. Until the French Revolution Bagatelle continued to be the setting for the most licentious gatherings of the ancien régime's high society. In the boudoirs, the walls and ceilings were covered with gilt and mirrors; luxury and lust were united in a parabola of pleasure. During Napoléon's reign Bagatelle was turned into a hunting lodge. At the time of the Restoration the château was returned to the comte d'Artois, but by then he had become devoutly religious. He removed all traces of debauchery, took down the most risqué paintings, and handed the estate to his son, the duc de Berry. In 1885 it was purchased by Lord Seymour, an English aristocrat who made a number of alterations to the château and laid out the park. There was now room for peacocks, water lilies, and ... automobiles.

The magazine *Automobiles Classiques,* founded in 1983, mounted its first concours at Bagatelle on September 11, 1988. The magazine's founder, Arnault de Fouchier, was inspired by the Pebble Beach Concours d'Elegance in California, held regularly since 1950. The first event included a special exhibition of dazzling Rolls-Royces that had once belonged to maharajas. It was also notable for the early involvement of Ferrari, which fully responded to the call of Antoine Prunet, editor in chief of *Automobiles Classiques,* who was responsible for selecting the participants. Christian Philippsen, the head of the organizing committee, contributed his own elegant 1957 250 GT Cabriolet.

From 1989 on, the Louis Vuitton company associated its name with the Bagatelle concours.

2002. Former racing stars stretch out languidly before the Trianon. In the foreground are a Delahaye 135 S and an Aston Martin Speed Model that did battle in 1936.

1989
Automobiles Classiques and Louis Vuitton

Parc de Bagatelle, September 9–10. It is impossible not to think of the licentiousness of Bagatelle's early history when you look at the sensual mauve Delahaye built by De Villars; its streamlined form was tailor made for taking off to the Riviera on adulterous adventures. And then there's the extremely rare Alfa Romeo 8C 2300 coupe-spider built by Touring for the 1932 concours at the Villa d'Este: Behind its dark windows you can almost see the disquieting figure of Princess Soldatenkov, who drove the car that year.

Louis Vuitton celebrates the automobile, the art of travel, and the art of living not only as the event's new sponsor but with its exhibition of old trunks, filled with dreams, adventures, and crazy schemes, and a collection of sketches and paintings that make a link between woman and the car. Also on display are sublime automobiles, products of a collaboration between Ferrari and Pininfarina. To close the event, the Delahaye 135 MS built by De Villars will lead the parade of Italian beauties.

Yves Carcelle

A brilliant graduate of the École Polytechnique and a rigorous administrator, Yves Carcelle held high positions at several major companies before joining the LVMH group in 1989. The following year he took over the reins at the Louis Vuitton company and began redeveloping the venerable firm's image, internationalizing and modernizing it while underscoring its great past; he saw to it that luxury was infused with creativity, quality with innovation. Yves Carcelle engaged contemporary artists and leading architects from around the globe, and Louis Vuitton's new buildings were lauded as landmarks. He encouraged Louis Vuitton's involvement in concours and rallies, recognizing that, like Louis Vuitton, the automobile reflects its times, symbolizes the art of living, and boasts a proud heritage as well as ongoing innovation.

1990
Automobiles Classiques and Louis Vuitton

Parc de Bagatelle, September 8–9. This is truly a year of superlatives! All six Bugatti Type 41s—better known as the Bugatti Royale—are united in front of the Trianon: a rare gathering until now achieved only at the Pebble Beach concours. These cars, usually dispersed around the globe, represent the ultimate in extravagant luxury. They are wrapped in myth that grew out of their monumental failure. Ettore Bugatti wanted to offer the VIPs of the world the longest, most expensive, most powerful car imaginable, but its introduction proved to be poorly timed. The Bugatti Royale came out just after the crash of 1929—and there were only six buyers! Its extravagant proportions provided the consulting designers a vast canvas, and they produced eleven bodywork designs for the six chassis. Two of the Royales were refurbished with new bodywork over time.

The jury rewarded another diva of the history of the automobile: the Ferrari 330 P4 Spider, which was world champion in 1967 and is considered one of the most desirable racing cars of all time.

Christian Philippsen

It is rare indeed for a major automobile event to take place without Christian Philippsen. His distinguished figure can be seen at international auto shows, concours d'elegance, and rallies across the globe. An eminent specialist in history and design, he is a respected automobile consultant. With Antoine Prunet he organized several exhibitions of artists influenced by machinery, to promote art and the automobile. Christian Philippsen has helped select competitors and organized the juries for most Louis Vuitton rallies and concours. He also maintains extensive ties to the world of publishing. He was responsible for publishing Albert Uderzo's "Astérix" comic books and developing the related theme park north of Paris. Since 2005 he has been publisher of *Automobile Year*, an invaluable reference work on the world of cars published annually since 1953.

1991
Automobiles Classiques and Louis Vuitton

Parc de Bagatelle, September 7–8. The "cars of the stars" are touted on the Bagatelle poster, for which the illustrator Razzia, an artist associated with all Louis Vuitton events, has painted a charming, enigmatic Clark Gable. The theme is the movies, with an exhibition of automobiles that stars of the silver screen have invested with their aura. All convey the glamour of Hollywood: Clark Gable's dazzling yellow Duesenberg, Marlene Dietrich's austere Cadillac, Rita Hayworth's immaculate Delahaye, and Ingrid Berman's silver-gray Ferrari. They share an exuberance, a sense of spectacle, and a penchant for panache. All these cars are exceptional, custom made to suit the unique desires and whims of their owners.

Under the impassive gaze of the peacocks and mallards, the jury deliberates over the very dissimilar entries. How to choose between sportiness and sophistication? It's not easy to decide between an Aston Martin DB 4 GT, made by Bertone in 1961, and an Alfa Romeo 8C 2900, which took part in the Twenty-Four Hour Race at Le Mans in 1938, or between a Hispano-Suiza that competed for the Georges Boillot Cup in 1922 and a Talbot Lago Grand Sport produced by Henri Chapron in 1948. In the end the prize went to the Talbot Lago, which was both sporty and sophisticated enough to win the most votes.

1989. This extremely rare Alfa Romeo 8C 2300 coupe-spider by Touring won the Best of Show at the 1932 concours d'elegance held at Villa d'Este.

1989. This is one of the twelve Delahaye 135s that Figoni & Falaschi built from a design by the illustrator Geo Ham in 1936.

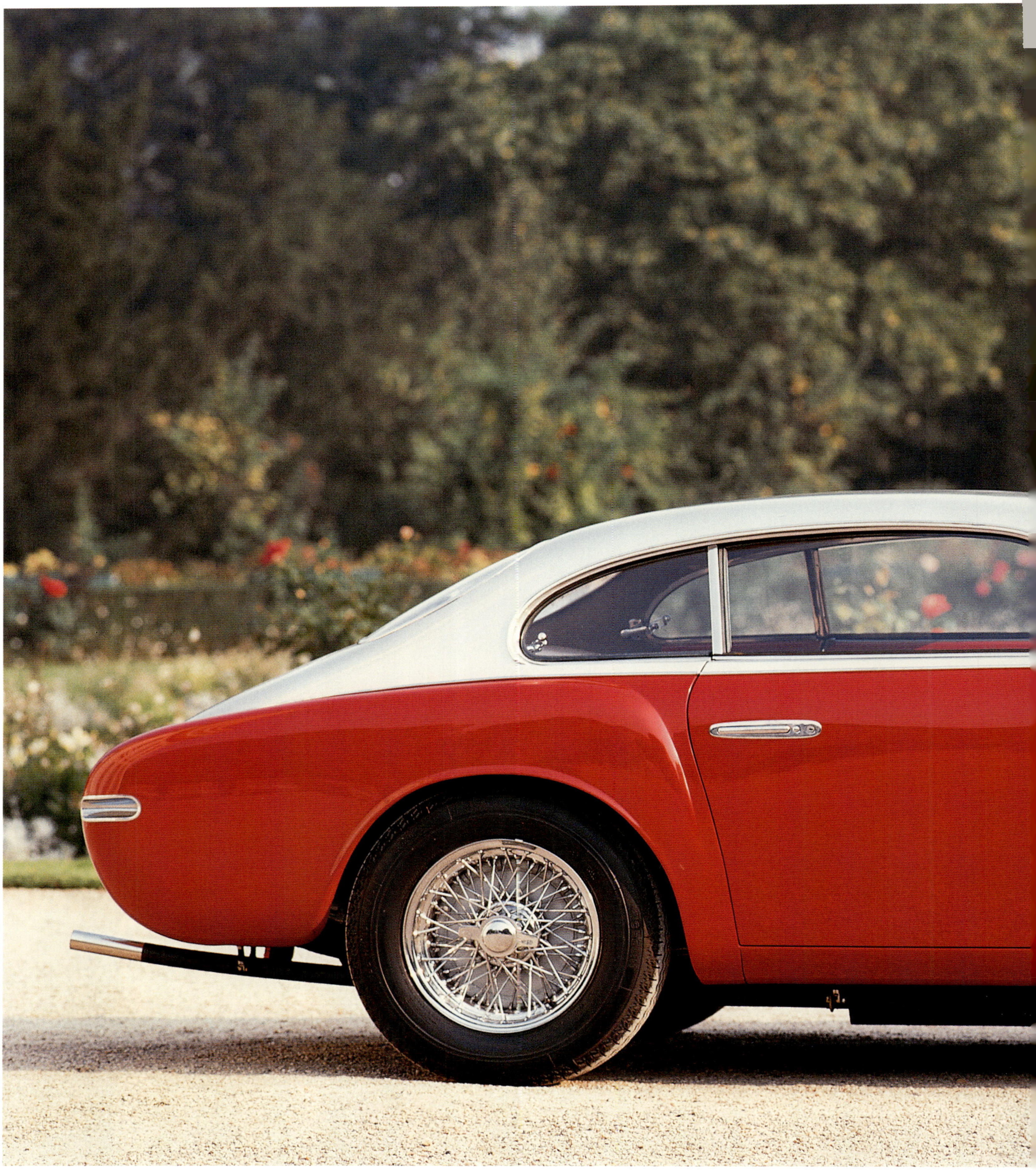

1989. The Ferrari 212 Inter (no. 0111/ES) has a low body built by Vignale after an original design by Giovanni Michelotti.

1989. Unlike many Alfa Romeo machines, this 8C 2900's body was built in the Alfa Romeo factory instead of being sent to an outside auto-body maker.

1989. This is one of the rare Duesenberg Model Js built in France, in this case by Kellner in 1929, in the torpedo style known as *scaphandrier* (diver).

1990. Belgium's King Leopold III adapted this Grand Prix Bugatti 59 for road use. It still bears its original patina.

1990. The six Bugatti Royales made a very rare joint appearance at Bagatelle. Here is the Kellner coach (no. 41141).

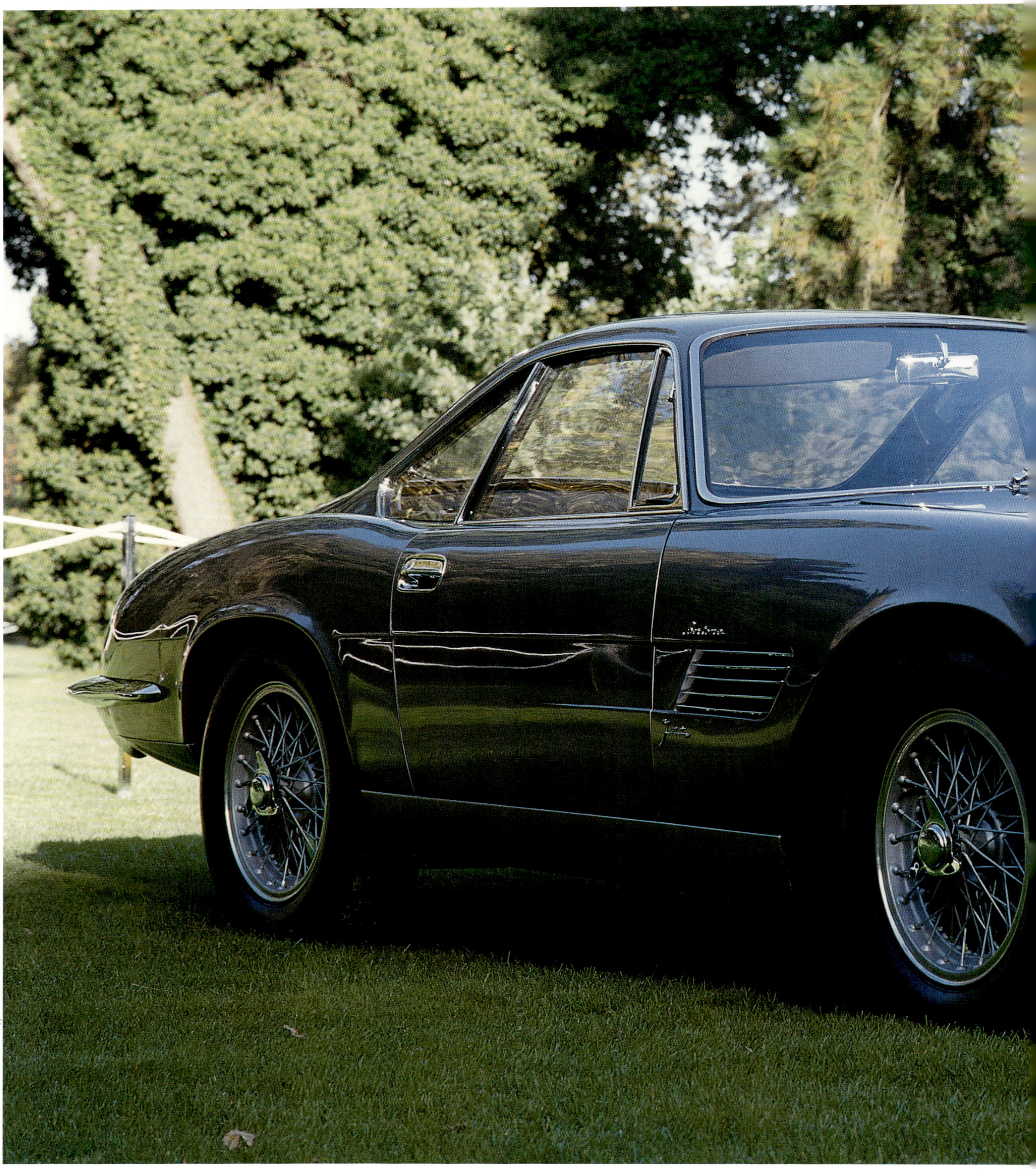

1991. The Jet was a unique creation, produced in 1961. Bertone built the body after a design by Giorgetto Giugiaro on an Aston Martin DB 4 GT chassis.

1992
Automobiles Classiques and Louis Vuitton

Parc de Bagatelle, September 12–13. The fifth concours at Bagatelle is inspired by true royalty. The posters for the event advertise a display of the "automobiles of princes," outstanding vehicles that have transported monarchs or are tucked away in the garages of royal courts in Europe and elsewhere. That is how Prince Rainier's Hispano-Suiza finds itself parked next to the Rolls-Royce Phantom IV that H. J. Mulliner made for Princess Elizabeth in 1950, before she became queen of England. Another, more exotic Rolls-Royce, this time a Twenty, was adapted for racing in 1926 for the demanding maharaja of Bharatpur in 1926. The one with the loudest roar is the one-seater in which Prince Birabongse Bahnutej (using the diminutive, Prince Bira) raced under the colors (yellow and blue) of Thailand. In the end the judges reward a car with a less princely pedigree: a Talbot Lago SS made by Figoni & Falaschi, more extroverted than last year's winner.

Arnauld de Fouchier

This is the man responsible for reviving the concours d'elegance in France. Head of the EPA publishing house, Arnauld de Fouchier founded *Automobiles Classiques* magazine in 1983 and soon thereafter decided to associate its title with a concours. He organized one near Paris, modeling it after the Pebble Beach Concours d'Elegance—at that time the only event of its kind in the world. With the help of Paris officials and the expert advice of Antoine Prunet, his magazine's editor in chief, and Christian Philippsen, the magazine's "No. 1 subscriber," who had suggested the project, Arnauld de Fouchier hosted the first Automobiles Classiques concours at Bagatelle in 1988. Visitors were immediately enchanted, including the directors of the Louis Vuitton company, who decided to lend their support for the 1989 concours. The magazine that started the Bagatelle concours then changed hands several times, while Arnauld de Fouchier left the automobile world to devote himself to his other passion: mountaineering.

1993
Automobiles Classiques and Louis Vuitton

Parc de Bagatelle, September 11–12. French bodywork reflects the two divergent trends that influenced art in the years between the wars: the conservative and the progressive. The first exploited a conformism inherited from the period before the First World War and was full of historical references; the second expressed a modernity that looked toward a future rich in scientific and technological progress. Both are on display at the concours. Cars such as a Rolls-Royce handled by Kellner in the 1920s and a more recent Delage by Henri Chapron show the conservative side of the French makes, as well as their remarkable elegance. On the other hand, the Voisin racing car, known as Laboratoire and designed for the ACF Grand Prix in 1923, illustrates the nonconformism of the avant-garde designers, one of whom was without a doubt Gabriel Voisin. In another vein, Ettore Bugatti, with his son Jean, developed an unusual style uninfluenced by any trend, as can be seen in his Type 50.

Notwithstanding this feast of Continental style, Best of Show was awarded to an eminently British product: a Bentley Speed Six made by H. J. Mulliner in 1930.

1994
Automobiles Classiques and Louis Vuitton

Parc de Bagatelle, September 10–11. Rolls-Royce, Bugatti, Ferrari? None of these: This year the jury's favorite does not belong to the coterie of firms with the finest reputations and the most media coverage. The prize goes to an obscure Italian manufacturer of modest but extremely modern sports cars. By rewarding the Cisitalia 202 MM, the judges have disrupted the established order with a subtle selection that favors reflection over convenience, emotion over bluff, and substance over style. A classic car does not have to be a huge, chrome-covered vehicle.

The jury's choice is very much in the spirit of this year's event, whose keynote is speed. On display in the courtyard, four explosive machines symbolize the obsessive quest for pure velocity—which the Italians were first to exalt—that has characterized the twentieth century.

As usual there are also concept cars illustrating contemporary trends. Renault is showing its Argos roadster, an important indicator of future styles, Pininfarina has its three environmentally sensitive Ethos prototypes on display, and Ghia exhibits its Lagonda Vignale, which has an Art Deco flavor.

1992. After a 1937 career as a racing car, this Alfa Romeo 8C 2900 was stripped, then given new bodywork two years later by Pinin Farina.

1992. Two Voisin C27s were produced in 1934. Figoni & Falaschi gave one of them this classical body, which is incongruous for a Voisin automobile.

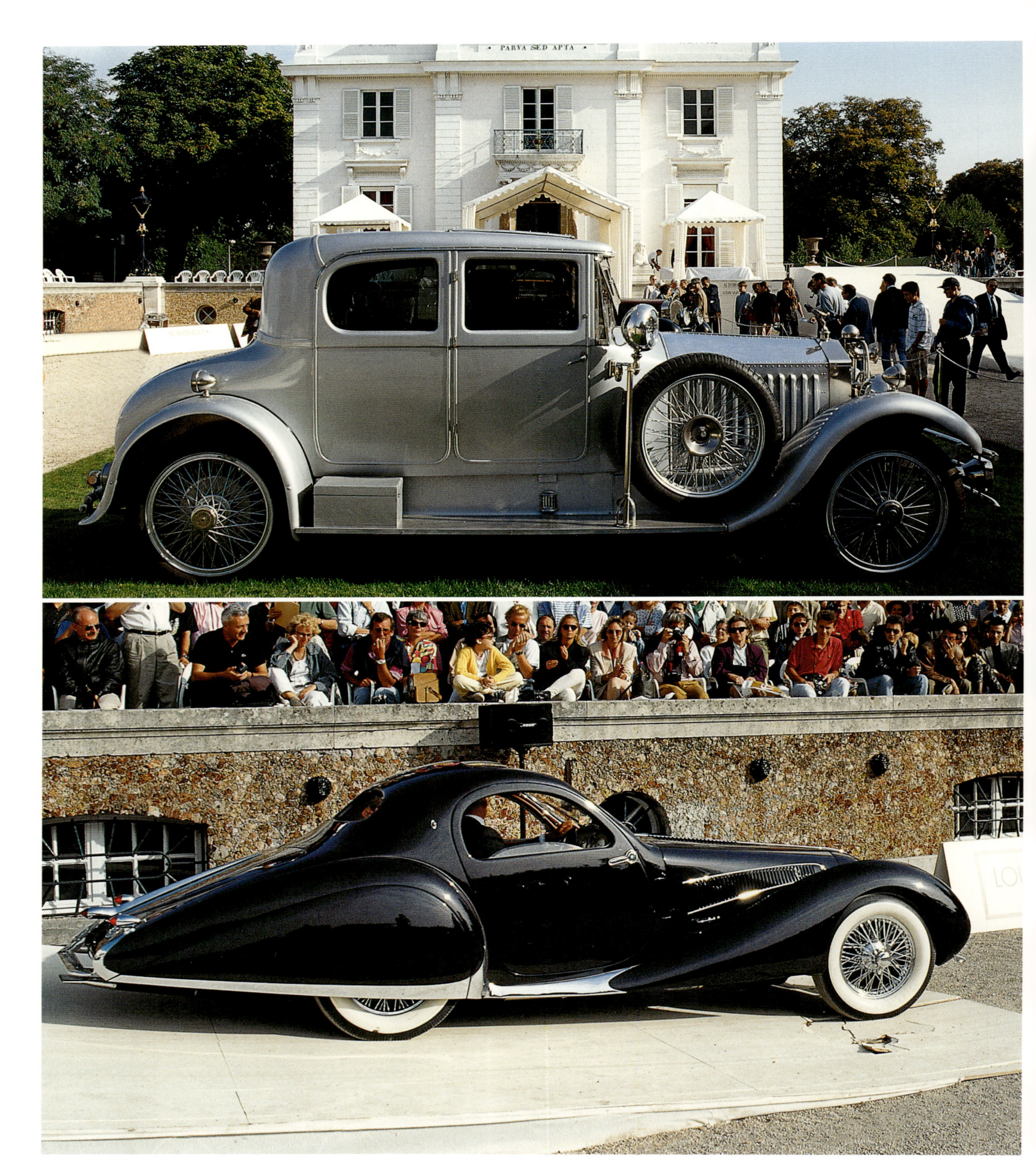

1992. This polished aluminum sedan, based on a Rolls-Royce Twenty, was created in 1926 for the prince maharaja of Bharatpur by Wylder, a little-known coachbuilder in Surrey, England.

1992. The Talbot Lago SS (Type 150 C, no. 90104) by Figoni & Falaschi deservedly wins the Best of Show.

1993. Discreetly decorated and magnificently proportioned, this Hispano-Suiza K6, designed by Saoutchik in 1935, beautifully illustrates the art of French bodywork, the theme of this year's show.

The experts on the jury at the Bagatelle concours are most often recruited from among collectors and designers—for example, Christopher Bangle, director of design for BMW, pictured at left.

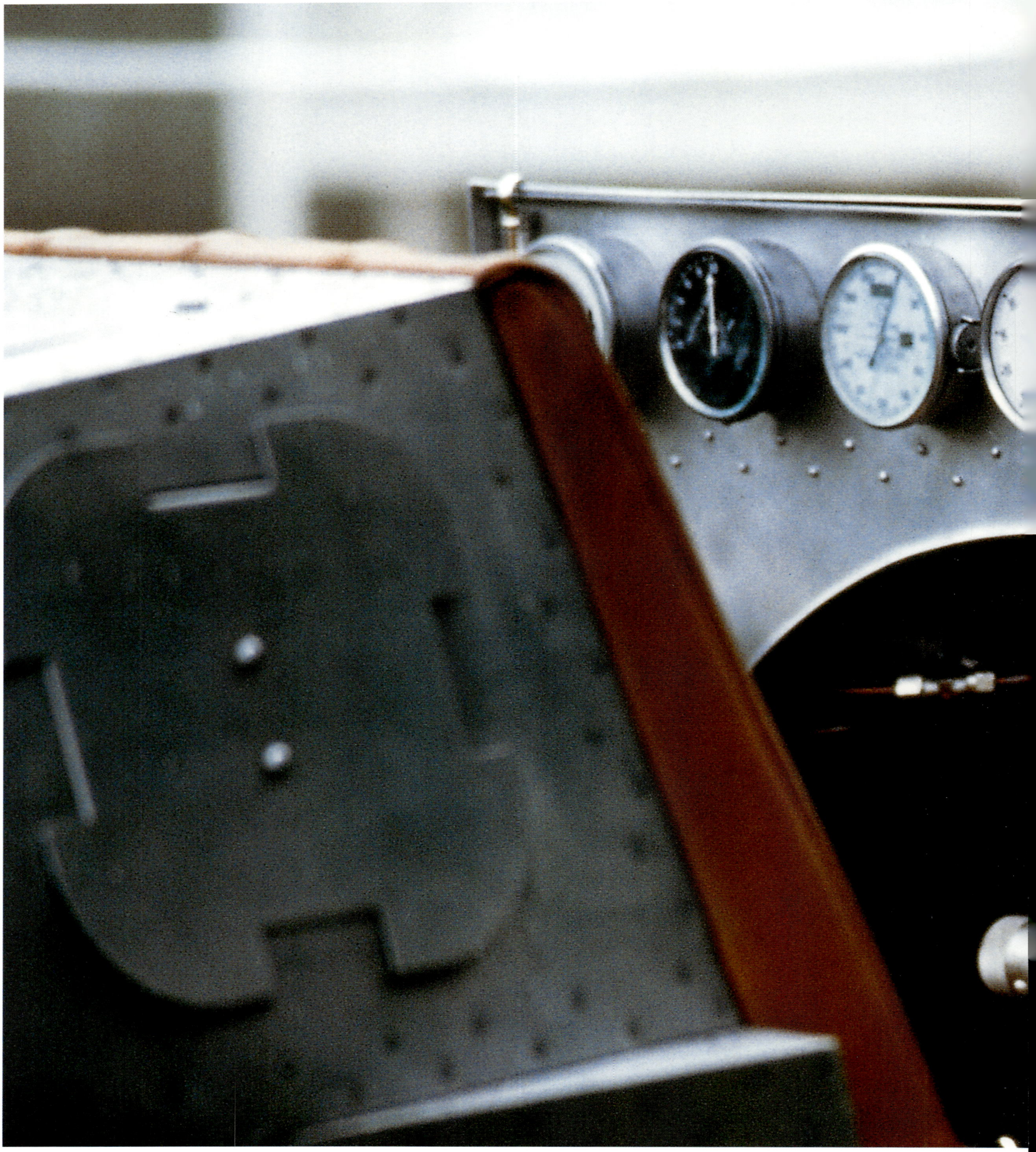

1993. The amazing cockpit of the Voisin Laboratoire. This superb reconstruction of one of the entrants in the 1923 Automobile Club de France Grand Prix was created by Philippe Moch.

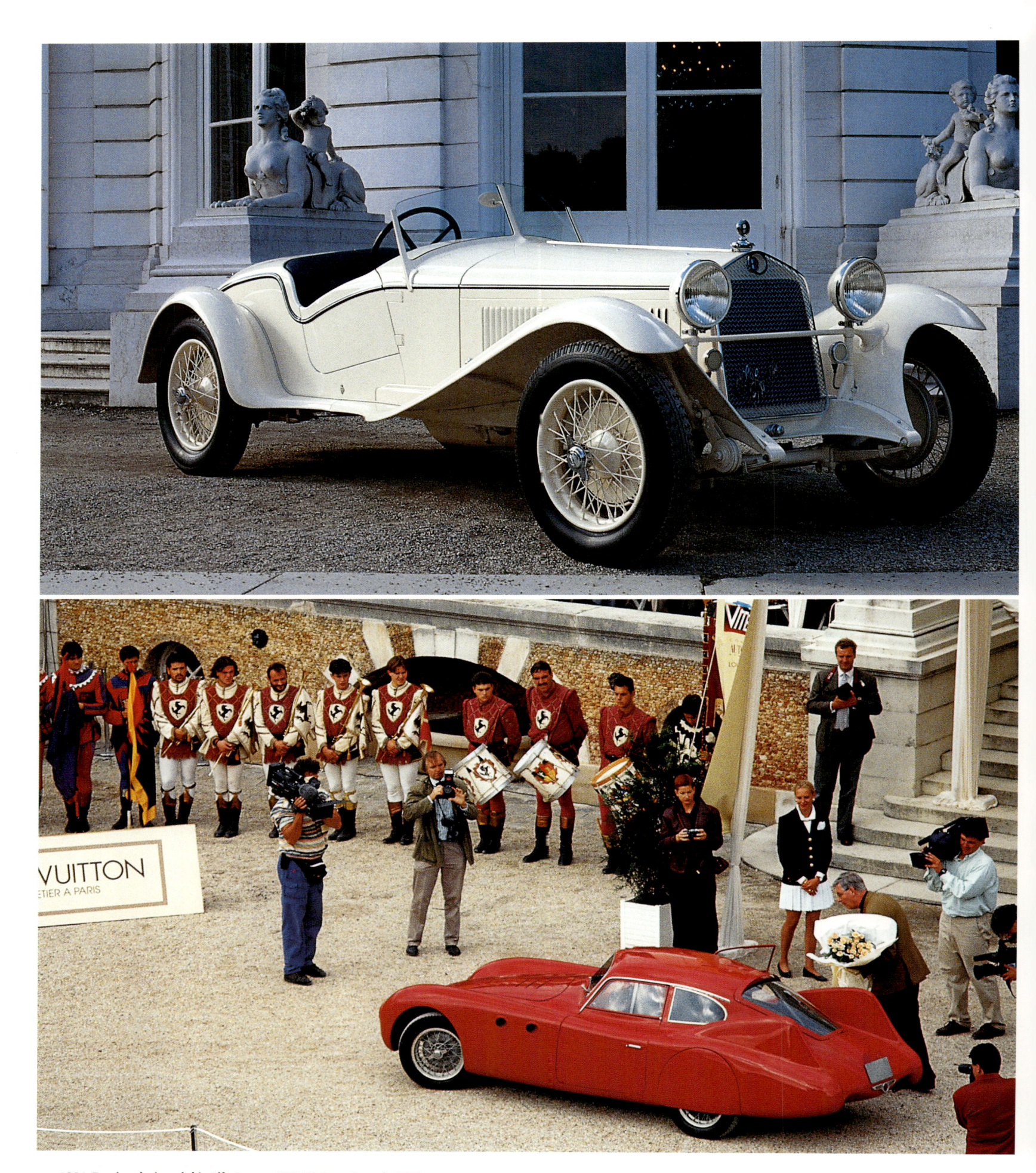

1994. Touring designed this Alfa Romeo 6C 1750 Gran Sport in 1930, in an unusually sophisticated style for a racing machine.

1994. To everyone's surprise, the Cisitalia 202 MM won Best of Show. More high-performance than elegant, it was designed by Mario Savonuzzi for the Mille Miglia in 1947.

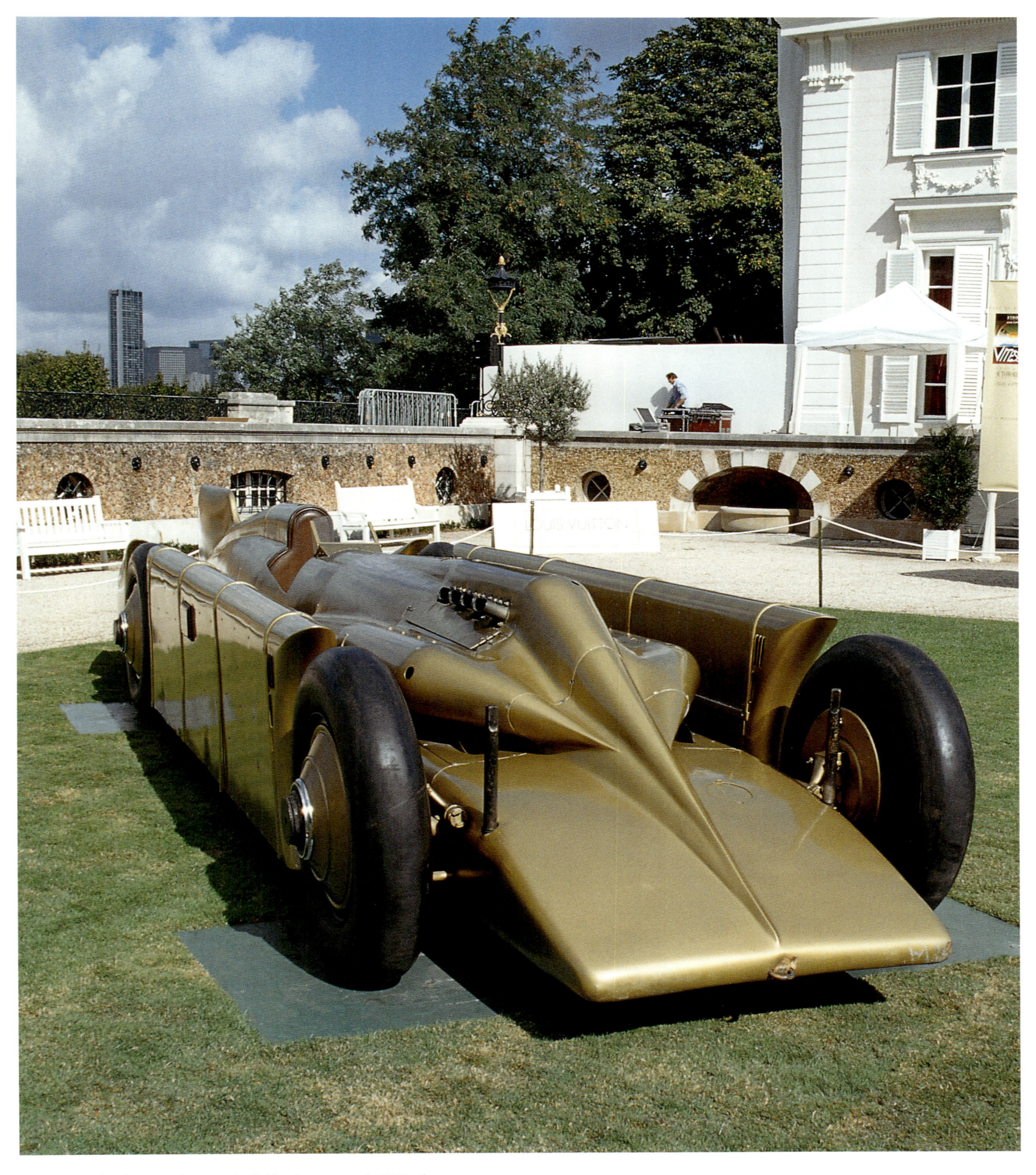

1994. Driven by Henry Segrave, the Golden Arrow exceeded 231 miles (372 kilometers) per hour on Daytona Beach in March 1929!

1995
Automobiles Classiques and Louis Vuitton

Parc de Bagatelle, September 9–10. On this weekend Renault, Ferrari, and Mercedes-Benz are vying against each other at both the Italian Grand Prix and Bagatelle. While Renault attracted visitors to Bagatelle with its preview of the Initiale, Ferrari exulted with its 250 GTO, one of Ralph Lauren's cherished "dear cars."

Meanwhile, Mercedes-Benz won Best of Show with an impressive 500 K Spezial-Roadster that just edged out the more discreet Alfa Romeo 6C 2500 by Touring. Unlike the scenario of 1994, this year exuberance won the day over discretion, majesty over modesty.

In the courtyard was a gathering of "dear cars"—in other words, very, very expensive automobiles that are adored by their owners. Among them was the W196 Mercedes-Benz that was unrivaled at the 1954 World Championship in the hands of Juan Manuel Fangio. Even more stellar was a copy of the lunar rover that was sent to the Moon in 1971.

1996
Automobiles Classiques and Louis Vuitton

Parc de Bagatelle, September 7–8. This year the show expanded beyond Bagatelle to a course within the Paris city walls. The concours gets under way at daybreak, in the shadow of the Palais de Chaillot. The participants set off from the Trocadéro fountains and drive along the banks of the Seine, glowing pink in the dawn light, then turn onto the Champs-Élysées, parade along Avenue Foch, and cross the Bois de Boulogne before making a triumphal entry into Bagatelle's park. The Ferrari that Phil Hill drove on the Reims circuit in 1953 has made the streets of the capital vibrate.

This year the jury includes Andrée Putman, the high priestess of French interior design, whose arrival attracts much attention. Her candor and judiciousness surprise her seasoned colleagues. Together they pay tribute to Touring, which wins five prizes, including Best of Show for a 1937 Alfa Romeo 8C 2900 B Spider. Arrayed before the Trianon, the extraordinary cars display their diversity: A turbine-driven Fiat (1954) languidly sits next to an Abarth with bodywork by Pinin Farina (1957), which stands beside the Whale, an outsized monster designed by the artist Paul Arzens (1937).

1997
Automobiles Classiques and Louis Vuitton

Parc de Bagatelle, September 6–7. A small Austin wears a black ribbon, discreetly tied. The British are mourning Diana, princess of Wales, who died tragically in Paris the previous weekend. The upcoming confrontation for the Best of Show award is unusual in that it is a contest between two equally iconoclastic vehicles, a Bentley and a Ferrari. In the eyes of the queen's subjects, the Bentley Mark VI represents a sort of crime of lèse-majesté. Rather than ennoble it with a British brand, the owner who commissioned it preferred to grace the car with French bodywork—and by a not particularly renowned commercial firm into the bargain. The nerve! All the same, the result is sumptuous. The builder, Facel, endowed the car with an astonishingly pure, modern line, less stiff and unnatural than many of the auto bodies designed by Bentley's British compatriots. The Ferrari is no less unexpected. Unlike almost all the road cars of this make, which since 1952 have been sent to Pininfarina for their bodywork, it was designed by Giorgetto Giugiaro for Bertone. At the end of the day, its voluptuous curves were victorious.

Shiro Kosaka
This elegant Japanese gentleman is a great admirer of Italian bodywork. Shiro Kosaka created a museum near Mount Fuji, the Abarth Gallery, that not only pays tribute to Italian design but is named after a sports car maker who operated in Turin in the 1950s and 1960s. The Abarth Gallery houses an impressive selection of cars bearing the Abarth escutcheon, including one that won a speed record and was a star at the Bagatelle concours in 1995. To enrich his collection, Shiro Kosaka undertook the painstaking restoration of two masterpieces of Italian bodywork: the 1968 Ferrari 250 P5 by Pininfarina and the Alfa Romeo Canguro by Bertone, a 1964 concept car.

Giorgetto Giugiaro
Trained as both a fine artist and a technical designer, Giorgetto Giugiaro was always passionate about cars. In 1955, at the age of seventeen, he joined Fiat, whose technical director had seen his drawings at an end-of-course exhibition. Just four years later, with all the impertinence of a twenty-one-year-old, Giorgetto Giugiaro joined Bertone as head of design, succeeding the enigmatic and brilliant Franco Scaglione. In 1965 he left for Ghia, where he spent two years before founding his own company, Italdesign. In 1999 Giorgetto Giugiaro was named car designer of the century by a group of distinguished industry figures. His son Fabrizio joined the firm in the 1990s, and the two have shared design commissions since.

1995. Marcel Leyat conceived this sort of wingless airplane, known as Helica, in 1922.

1995. Extra mechanics arrive to relaunch the capricious engine of the Talbot 1500, a rare and magnificent machine that competed in the Grand Prix races of 1927.

1996. This year's Bagatelle concours started from the Trocadéro in Paris. Designed in 1937 by architects Jacques Carlu, Louis-Hippolyte Boileau, and Louis Azéma, the building makes a suitable backdrop for automobiles of the same period.

1996. A Buick Series 40A Eight, with bodywork designed by the French craftsman Janoir in 1934, leads the procession along the prestigious Avenue Foch.

1995. **The Mercedes-Benz 500 K Spezial-Roadster, shown by a great Japanese collector, wins Best of Show.**

1998

Automobiles Classiques and Louis Vuitton

Parc de Bagatelle, September 5–6. Bagatelle "between heaven and earth," says the program, and indeed five extraterrestrial machines are standing in the courtyard. They are testaments to the relationship between the aeronautics and automobile industries. They illustrate the beneficial lessons on forms, materials, and technologies that aviation has given the car from time to time. There's the Trossi Monaco, a Grand Prix car featuring a star-shaped engine, and the Firebird III, whose spoilers suggest the science fiction fantasies of the 1950s. Then there's Marcel Leyat's Helica. Designed in the 1920s, the Helica is a sort of airplane without wings. Made of taut canvas, it has the shape of a slender airplane cabin and a propeller at the front, which the driver uses to steer this unstable machine.

The Best of Show award is no more down-to-earth than are those vehicles, since it goes to a Ferrari 375 MM that Scaglietti specially created for Roberto Rossellini. Paul Dupuy, the editor of *Automobiles Classiques* and a member of the grand jury, awards the trophy to the diva's current owner, Jon Shirley.

1999

Automobiles Classiques and Louis Vuitton

Parc de Bagatelle, September 4–5. The dappled stallion brushes past the tables with a Spanish step, then performs a capriole. His rider imperceptibly presses his fingers on the reins, the gesture of a puppeteer, and tickles the flanks with a spur. The fine Andalusian horse bends under the rider's seat and lowers his head to bow by the Delahaye 165 with bodywork by Figoni & Falaschi, which is about to receive the Best of Show award. There is an old bond, and a rivalry, between the automobile and the horse. Mechanics liberated the animal but stole his terminology, his aesthetic, and his artisans. Even today the power of engines is measured in horsepower: a fitting recognition.

There is no lack of panache or horsepower in the Delahaye, which is carried along by a thoroughbred 175. Its career is epic. In the summer of 1939 the vehicle was sent to the New York World's Fair, whose theme was "The World of Tomorrow." War broke out, so the Delahaye stayed put in the United States, lying low in a barn before being rediscovered and restored by the collectors Jim Hull and Peter Mullin.

2000

Louis Vuitton Classic

Parc de Bagatelle, September 9–10. After eleven years the *Automobiles Classiques* show has taken a new title, the Louis Vuitton Classic. Also adding meaning to this year's event, Pininfarina is celebrating its seventieth anniversary with great pomp. Its director, Sergio Pininfarina, has been named head of the jury. An engineer, he has for fifty years lent his expertise to the company founded by his father, Battista, in 1930. He has served as its director since 1966 and has lost none of his verve, humor, or humility. Also on the jury are Leonardo Fioravanti and Lorenzo Ramaciotti, both of whom once ran Pininfarina's research center.

For Best of Show, the jury is enthusiastic about—and divided over—two very different Ferraris bearing the Pininfarina escutcheon: a 400 Superamerica Aerodinamico shown at the Geneva motor show in 1961, and a 250 Mille Miglia from 1953. These two models have nothing in common apart from their make; they illustrate two opposing facets of Ferrari and Pininfarina, a flamboyant style versus a rational aesthetic. One is luxurious, the other sporty. Pininfarina has always been capable of designing to either taste.

During a break Sergio Pininfarina drives an honorary lap at the wheel of the prototype Ferrari Rossa created to mark the new millennium.

Wahei Hirai

Wahei Hirai loves visiting France—not as a tourist, but as a close observer of trends and life-styles. He has spent years of his career in France and in 2000 headed ED2, Toyota's European design center in Sophia-Antipolis, near Nice. He returned in 2002 to Japan, where he reigns over Toyota's worldwide design—a key post, given the profusion of models in the company's global production catalogue. With a presence on every continent and a determination to respond appropriately to its varied clientele, Toyota has greatly increased its number of foreign design studios. Tying all the pieces together, Toyota's headquarters building in Nagoya, Japan, has since 2007 housed a Louis Vuitton store.

Leonardo Fioravanti

Leonardo Fioravanti is among those who breathed a technical dimension into Italian automotive design. He received his diploma in mechanical engineering from Milan Polytechnic before joining Pininfarina's research and development department. He designed numerous Ferraris during his long tenure at Pininfarina and in 1988 was appointed assistant general manager of Ferrari SpA and managing director of Ferrari Engineering. He was later chief of advanced design for Fiat and director of the Centro Stile Fiat. Since 1991 Leonardo Fioravanti has devoted himself exclusively to his own architecture and design company, Fioravanti, and participated in some concours d'elegance.

1998. Created for the 1935 Grand Prix races, the Trossi Monaco was propelled by an aeronautics-style star-shaped sixteen-cylinder engine.

1998. The Firebird III, developed in 1958 by the research center at General Motors, is a wonderful illustration of the link between the automobile and aeronautics. This car is actually propelled by a turbine engine.

1999. **This Delahaye 135 MS was shown at the 1938 Salon de l'Automobile.**
It is a luxury roadster in the classical style mastered by Henri Chapron.

1999. In 1938 Pourtout created this streamlined body on a Delage D8-120 chassis. It is notable for its sleek style and restrained proportions.

1999. The Carabo, designed in 1968 by Marcello Gandini for Bertone, is one of the icons of the wedge-shaped style of the period. It is built on an Alfa Romeo Type 33 chassis.

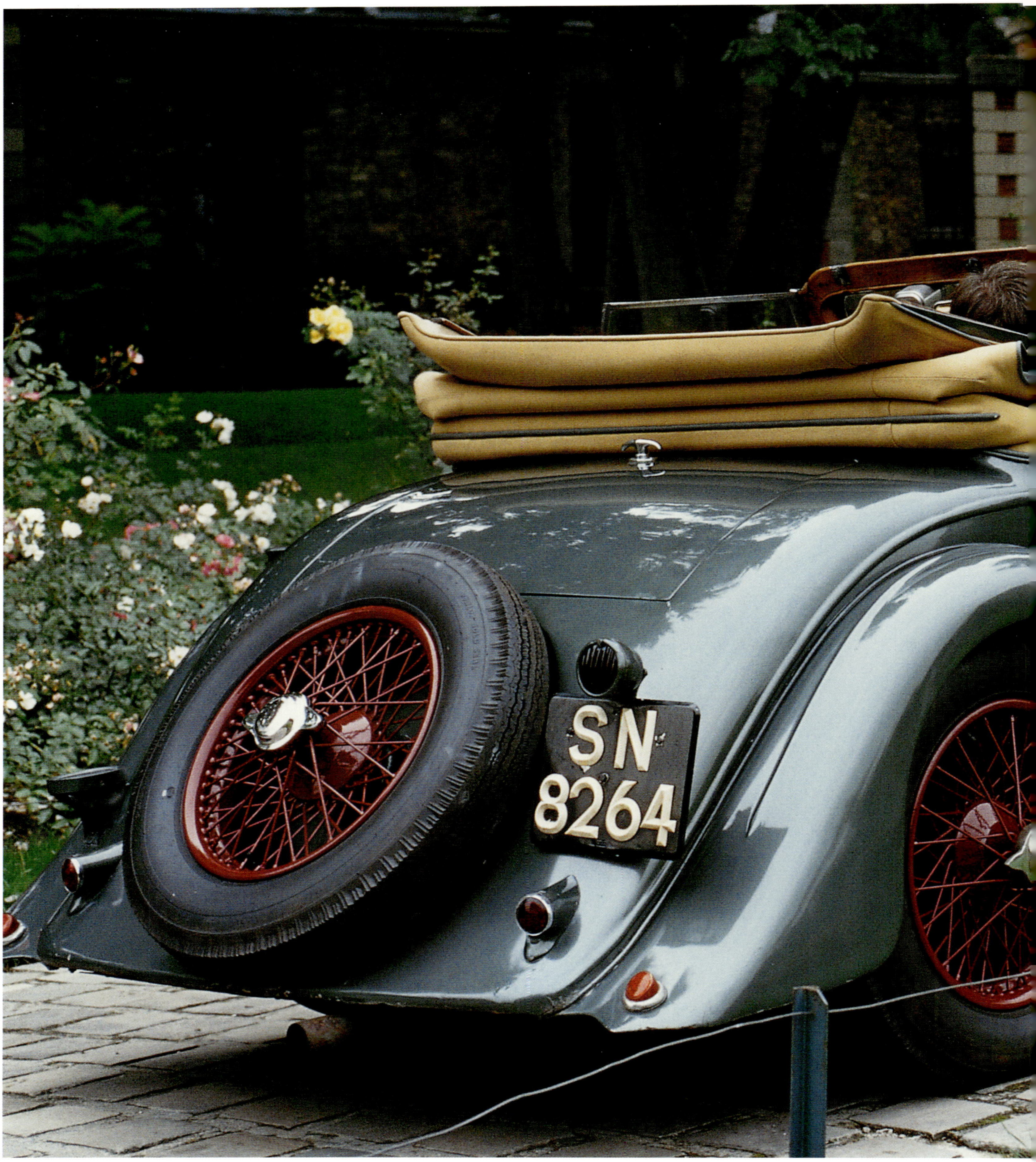
SN
8264

2000. At the entrance to the park at Bagatelle stands a two-liter Aston Martin created in 1937 by Enrico "Harry" Bertelli.

2001
Louis Vuitton Classic

Parc de Bagatelle, September 8–9. Can an automobile be considered a work of art? The Italian futurists launched this debate at the beginning of the twentieth century. The auctioneer Hervé Poulain, with his great love of speed and professional interest in beauty, had the excellent idea of combining his passions by having artists paint his racing cars. The first of these was a BMW, a multicolored comet painted by Alexander Calder, that took part in the Le Mans Twenty-Four Hour Race in 1975. There was precedent for such a blend of art and automobile: In 1967 several painters chose ordinary cars as their canvas. One of these was a Matra that Sonia Delaunay painted with geometric motifs. It is on exhibit at Bagatelle, alongside a BMW painted by Roy Lichtenstein (1977), a Venturi covered in layered tiles by Arman (1994), and a McLaren decorated by César (1995). Hervé Poulain added an extra element of drama by organizing a race of the Art Cars. Even when they are not sublimated by a painter's work, cars can be masterpieces of applied art. Such is the case with the BAT 7, which wins Best of Show. It is a poetic creation designed in 1954 by Franco Scaglione for Bertone. The curves at the back spread out and then contract like the wings of a frightened bird.

Hervé Poulain

Humane, erudite, urbane, witty, appealing, mischievous, talkative, and generous: Hervé Poulain, a spirited professional auctioneer, is all of these. But he is also the founder of a significant artistic movement that embodied the idea that, as the artist Arman put it, the car was "the object of the [twentieth] century." That is, he initiated the remarkable series of Art Cars, machines enhanced by the genius of artists, sculptures made sublime by movement and dramatized by racing. He conceived the project as an artwork that acquires meaning and value from use. Hervé Poulain has often served on concours juries and on several occasions orchestrated charitable auctions at the Bagatelle shows.

2002
Louis Vuitton Classic

Parc de Bagatelle, September 28–29. The Old World dreams of "American beauties," whether because of their pioneering character (like that of Ford's 1911 Model T, the first car made on a production line) or their outrageous extravagance, like that of Cadillac's 1959 Eldorado Biarritz, with its rear fender fins as sharp as a fighter jet's tailplane.

While American automobiles impress, Italian ones captivate. This year, a whole category is dedicated to the Ferrari 250 GTO, a legendary car celebrating its fortieth birthday. It was created in 1962, the year the World Championship of Makes was opened to Gran Turismo cars and not just sports cars.

Efficient, even unbeatable, the 250 GTO has gone down in history for both its record of achievement in competition and its minimalist, logical, technological aesthetic. Seven of the existing thirty-six cars have been brought together here.

Even so, the Best of Show award goes to an infinitely more discreet creation, a 1939 Alfa Romeo 6C 2500 with very sober bodywork by Touring.

Andrée Putman

Although she was destined for a career in music, Andrée Putman became a grande dame of French design. In 1978 she founded Écart, which distributed her own lines of furniture as well as reproductions of emblematic items in design history. She increasingly devoted herself to interior design, outfitting an extensive range of offices, hotels, and stores. She discovered the automobile in 1987, when working on a remarkable exhibition of Ferraris at the Fondation Cartier, then in Jouy-en-Josas near Versailles. Despite her impressive credentials, she served with humility on the Bagatelle jury, asking advice of the experts serving with her.

2003
Louis Vuitton Classic

Domaine National de Saint-Cloud, September 6–7. The Louis Vuitton Classic has crossed the Seine, leaving Paris for a new setting in the national park at Saint-Cloud. Saint-Simon described the château that once stood here as a "home of delights." It was used in turn as a princely, royal, and imperial residence. Empress Eugénie gave it great luster, but the château was destroyed in 1870, during the Franco-Prussian War. Fortunately the gardens and fountains keep alive the memory of its magnificence.

This last Louis Vuitton Classic concours in the Paris area features some pearls. There is one of the extremely rare Stout Scarabs that were produced about 1935, an important yet little-known landmark in the history of locomotion. Although not particularly graceful, the vehicle was very much ahead of its time; with its single-passenger interior and its balance between capacity and clutter, it prefigured the modern single-seater.

The Bentley Speed Six, which wins Best of Show, has a story too. Its streamlined bodywork was created by Gurney Nutting at the request of the driver Woolf Barnato, who had one objective in mind: to beat the Blue Train from Monte Carlo to Calais. Which it did.

2001. This Matra 530, transformed by artist Sonia Delaunay, was shown in a Parisian art gallery in October 1967.

2001. At the initiative of Hervé Poulain, the artist César decorated a McLaren F1 GTR with the design of one of his compressions, or sculptures. This mobile work of art took part in the Le Mans Twenty-Four Hour Race in 1995.

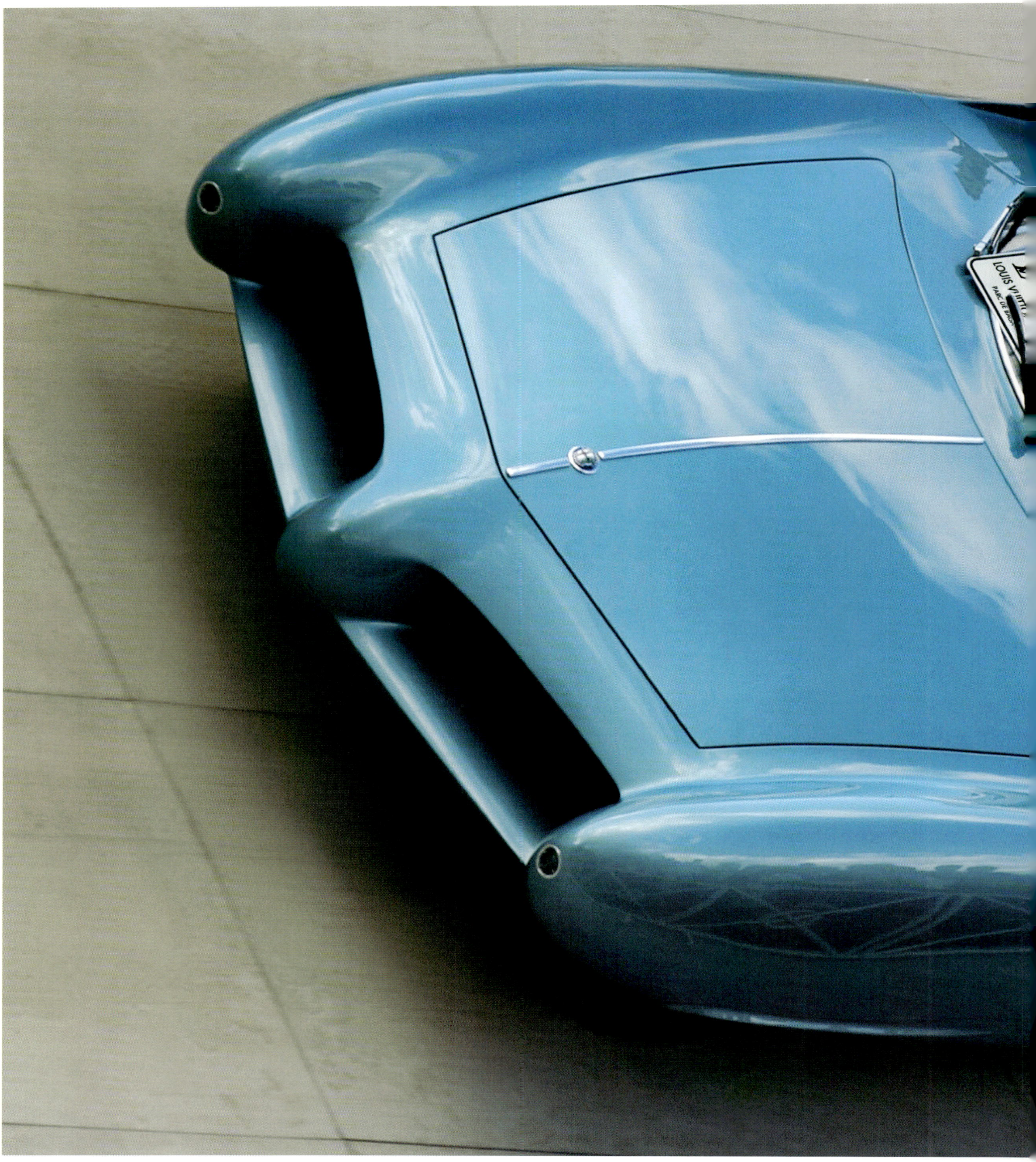

2001. The BAT 7 is one of a trio of prototypes Bertone developed on Alfa Romeo chassis between 1953 and 1955. This is the second, which was shown at the Turin auto show in 1954.

2002. This 1953 Cadillac convertible was the first to bear the name Eldorado.

2002. This Ferrari 342 America by Pinin Farina was delivered brand new to Leopold III, king of Belgium, in 1952.

2002. The Ferrari 555 Super Squalo was an aerodynamic experiment that did not achieve success during the 1955 Formula 1 season.

2002. Mercedes-Benz dominated the World Championship in 1954 and 1955 with the W 196 one-seater.

2003. This Talbot Lago SS "teardrop" has been magnificently reconstructed by a restoration workshop in Tours. Its lines were designed in 1937 by Figoni & Falaschi.

2003. The classical elegance typical of Henri Chapron can be seen in the outlines of this 1937 Delahaye 135 MS.

2003. The eclectic aircraft manufacturer William Stout designed this Scarab in 1935. With its monolithic proportions and huge interior, it prefigured today's minivans.

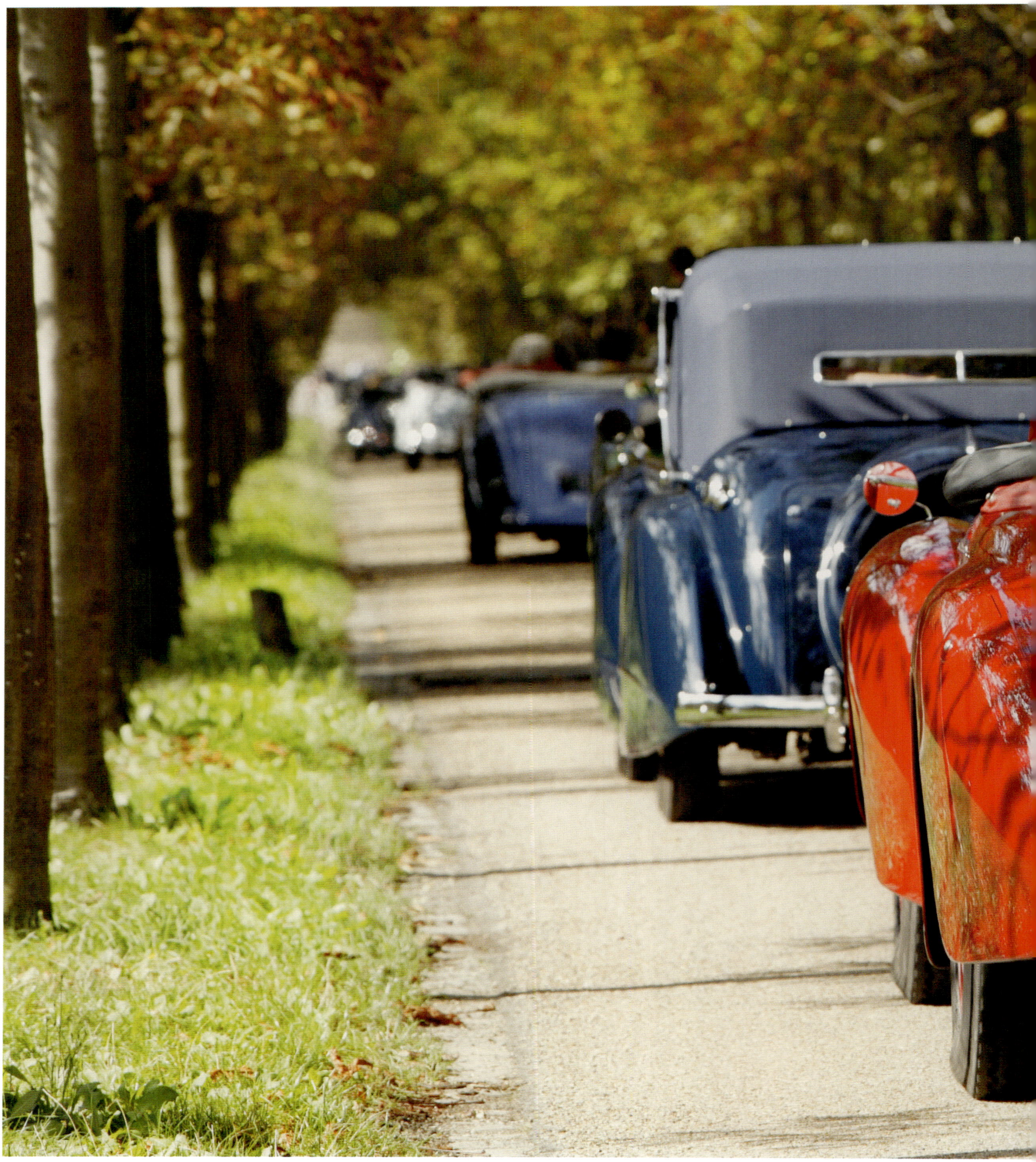

2003. **At the end of the weekend, a Bentley convertible leaves the park at Saint-Cloud to return home to England.**

112 Concours in and around London
Stowe, Hurlingham, Waddeson Manor 1990–2004

The London area was the hub of British elegance, with events held at Stowe, the Hurlingham Club, and Waddesdon Manor.

The British have an unusual concept of the automobile industry these days: They concentrate on producing either marginal or exceptional types of car. The manufacture of run-of-the-mill makes is left to the Japanese and American firms, which have conveniently located branches of their production units in the British Isles. On the other hand, in the spirit of Trafalgar, the British have preserved the cream of their national industry by aligning with foreign companies. Jaguar and Land Rover belong to Ford, Rolls-Royce and Mini are part of BMW, Bentley is owned by Volkswagen, and Aston Martin is backed by Arab investors. But the British makes are legends, not just commercial brands.

Stowe, a grand eighteenth-century estate northwest of London, was an excellent location for a concours d'elegance. It was there that architecture joined with the art of landscaping. Today the gardens at Stowe remain a perfect example of the savoir-faire of the Georgian era, while the great house is a homage to the Baroque style. In 1848 the sale of the second duke of Buckingham's collections ended with the building itself being sold. This appeared to be the beginning of the end until, in 1923, the establishment of a private boarding school there saved the estate from being broken up.

After a year at Stowe the Louis Vuitton concours took up residence at London's Hurlingham Club, which was built in 1760 as a fine private home. In 1803 the architect George Byfield expanded it, adding panache, dignity, and classicism, while the landscape architect Humphrey Repton turned the gardens into jewels. The club became famous thanks to repeated visits by the prince of Wales, later King Edward VII, but it was a playground for all kinds of sportsmen. Polo was established there in 1874, tennis in 1877, golf in 1894, and croquet in 1901. Then began the era of the "gentlemen drivers." The Hurlingham Club joined with the Motor Car Club in 1903, and in 1939 the Veteran Car Club of Great Britain put on an exhibition.

All this history paved the way for the Louis Vuitton Concours d'Elegance.

2004. The British love their traditions, which certainly have some poetry about them, as can be seen from this 1901 Panhard & Levassor, driving around the park at Waddesdon Manor.

1990
Louis Vuitton Concours d'Elegance

Stowe, July 28–29. The concours at Stowe was modeled on the one at Bagatelle. Among the familiar faces was that of Christian Philippsen, who headed the jury. Louis Vuitton's primary partner for the event was Condé Nast's *GQ* magazine.

The show's victor was an astounding Mercedes-Benz Type S convertible with bodywork by the Milanese firm Castagna. Made in 1929 for a Californian enthusiast, this car with an endlessly long hood marked the apotheosis of the classical age in the art of bodywork. It was a unique creation, like most of the cars selected for the concours. Among the others were a charming Bugatti 55 made in 1932 by the Boulogne-sur-Seine coachbuilder Figoni, and a dignified 1932 sedan de ville built on a Delage D8N chassis by Fernandez, also based in the Paris area. Its first owner had softened its appearance by having it painted the color of a turtledove.

One of the charms of these shows is that they allow for the discovery of such unique cars, which teach the history of the applied arts and also supply fascinating information about the people behind them. On the final day the prizewinners paraded on the famed Silverstone racing circuit, and the Best of Show winner was invited to attend the Bagatelle concours the following September.

Nick Mason

The only member of Pink Floyd to have lasted throughout the group's history, Nick Mason is clearly a steadfast man. The Birmingham native was only twenty-one when Pink Floyd formed in 1965. When he is not sitting behind his drums he likes to take the wheel of one of his racing cars, which have a host of prestigious pedigrees and glorious achievements. They include a McLaren, a Jaguar, a Porsche, and an outstanding selection of Ferraris. Notably, he is the lucky owner of one of the thirty-six legendary 250 GTOs. Though he has owned it since 1978, he has never been separated from that car; his indifference to the sirens of speculation reveals another side of his steadfastness.

1991
Louis Vuitton Concours d'Elegance

Hurlingham Club, June 8. A change of scene: The concours d'elegance took up residence at the select Hurlingham Club on the banks of the Thames. The jury was again run by Christian Philippsen. Among the respected designers serving were Royden Axe, head of design at Rover, Tom Karen of Ogle, and John Heffernan, formerly of Aston Martin. Retired drivers also weighed in, including Paddy Hopkirk, who drove little Mini Coopers mercilessly at the Monte Carlo Rally, and John Surtees, the world champion for Ferrari in 1964. An academic flavor was added by eminent historians such as Simon Moore, a specialist in the Alfa Romeos of the 1930s. Nick Mason, the drummer for Pink Floyd, lent his special cachet to the occasion.

The concours was divided into six classes: pre-1940 Rolls-Royces, roadsters and torpedoes from 1920 to 1933, coupes and convertibles from 1934 to 1940, postwar coupes, postwar convertibles, and postwar racing cars.

1992
Louis Vuitton Concours d'Elegance

Hurlingham Club, June 13. The world's three most prestigious concours d'elegance will be linked this year. The car that wins Best of Show at Hurlingham will be sent to Bagatelle in France in September. There it will face a new field of competitors, and the winner of that event will cross the Atlantic to be shown to the public at Pebble Beach the following August. At Hurlingham, Best of Show for 1992 goes to an Alfa Romeo 8C 2900.

1993
Louis Vuitton Concours d'Elegance

Hurlingham Club, June 5. London's chic set gathers for a picnic on the lawns of the prestigious Hurlingham Club. Among the members of the jury are Lord Brocket, Stirling Moss, Fiona Fullerton, Victor Gauntlett, James Ogilvy, Lord Kenilworth, and Antoine Prunet. They scrutinize the entrants' original condition, rarity, and elegance before finally awarding Best of Show to the 1929 Alfa Romeo 6C 1750 Super Sport presented by Keith Bowley for Sir Michael Kadoorie.

1990. This 1932 Delage D8N (no. 35301) was given a sedan de ville body by Fernandez & Darrin, a firm in Boulogne-sur-Seine run by the American designer Howard Darrin.

1990. The Ford GT 40 was produced in a limited series (more than seventy cars) between 1965 and 1969. Some were for road use, while others, including this magnificent machine, were intended for racing.

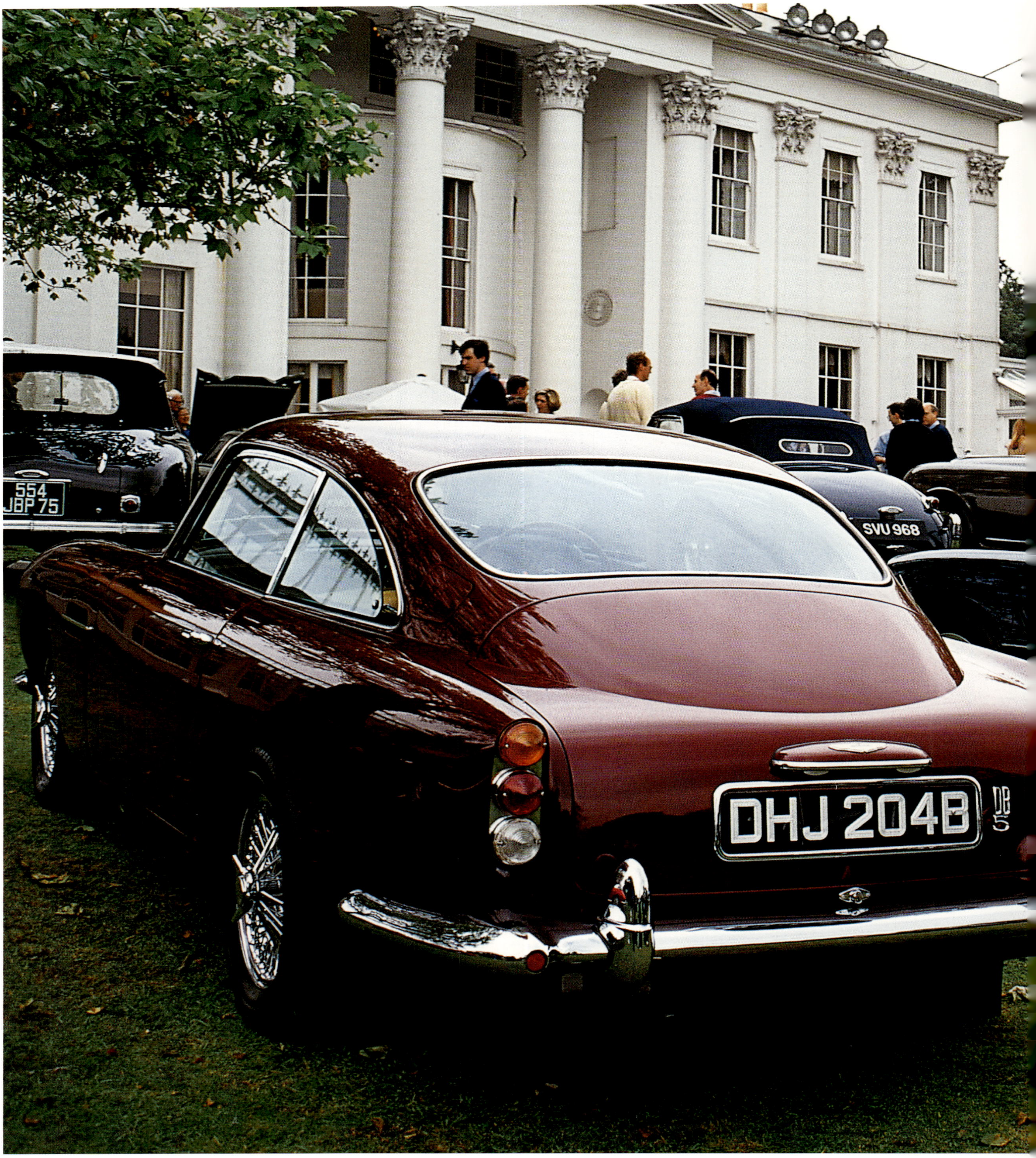
DHJ 204B
DB 5
554 JBP 75
SVU 968

1991. The quintessence of Gran Turismo is represented on the lawns at Hurlingham by a 1964 Aston Martin DB 5 and a 1963 Ferrari 400 Superamerica with a long wheelbase.

1994

Louis Vuitton Concours d'Elegance

Hurlingham Club, June 4. The great attraction of this event was the rare sight of all three Bertone BATs (for Berlinetta Aerodinamica Tecnica) together. These three exuberant prototypes, designed between 1953 and 1955, express the strong influence of aeronautics on automobile styles at the time—and, with their winglike tail shape, they do resemble bats.

The participants were divided into eight classes, one of which was vintage motorcycles. Another class was dedicated to the creations of Zagato, the Milanese auto-body maker. Though the British appreciate the Zagato touch, which has graced some of their own products, the Best of Show award went to a 1934 Rolls-Royce Phantom II Continental designed as a "city sport convertible" by the British Gurney Nutting.

1995

Louis Vuitton Concours d'Elegance

Hurlingham Club, June 3. Touring took pride of place here, and Carlo Felice Bianchi Anderloni, former head of that great Italian company, was a member of the jury. Some of Touring's most unforgettable creations were on show, such as the sleek 1932 Alfa Romeo 8C 2300 Mille Miglia Spider, the flamboyant, long-wheelbase 1938 Alfa Romeo 8C 2900 B, the ultralight 1949 Ferrari 166 MM Spider, and the more rugged Ferrari 195 S Berlinetta Le Mans, which won the Mille Miglia in 1950. They were up against one of Touring's later creations: the Lamborghini Flying Star II, which was shown at the Turin auto show in 1966 and acquired by Jacques Quoirez, the brother of Françoise Sagan. Best of Show went to a 1947 Bentley Mark VI, with wildly baroque bodywork by the French firm Franay.

1996

Louis Vuitton Concours d'Elegance

Hurlingham Club, June 1. This year the jury introduced a class for pre-1904 automobiles. The oldest of all was an 1884 steam car by the French coachbuilders Albert de Dion, Georges Bouton, and Charles-Armand Trépardoux. Others in the class were comparatively youthful cars by Mercedes, Daimler, Mors, and Panhard & Levassor.

A wide range of Maseratis was brought together to mark the company's seventieth anniversary: an extremely rare A6GCS with superb bodywork by Pinin Farina and two A6G 2000s—a slender one built by Pietro Frua and a more hefty version by Zagato. The retrospective was completed by several Grand Prix one-seaters, including Type 26 M, 8 CL, and 250 F, and the finest Gran Turismo models, such as Mistral and Ghibli. The winner was an unusual Isotta-Fraschini with Danish bodywork.

1997

Louis Vuitton Classic

Hurlingham Club, June 7. This concours d'elegance was restricted to guests of Louis Vuitton and members of the Hurlingham Club. These happy few lauded a Rolls-Royce Phantom I owned by Charles Howard, a sports tourer made by Barker in 1929 for a Canadian client. The recognition was a just reward for Rolls-Royce, which has supported the Hurlingham event from the first.

In contrast to the noble serenity of the Rolls were the race cars participating in a new class: the explosive machines of the CanAm Championship. These monsters, with their limitless capacity and astonishing power, competed in a series of challenges held in Canada and the United States in the late 1960s.

1993. **The world's most beautiful automobiles make no impact at all on the croquet enthusiasts.**

1995. In an outstandingly eclectic display, an Alfa Romeo 8C 2900 B (no. 412022), with a spider body by Touring, sits sheltered under an umbrella in front of the Ferrari 250 TR/60 (no. 0772/TR) that won the Le Mans Twenty-Four Hour Race in 1960.

1995. A baroque masterpiece, this Bentley Mark VI was built in 1947 by Franay, a firm in the Paris area.

1997. Originally sold in Portugal in 1956, this Jaguar D-Type (no. XKD 535) has spent some time in the Musée de l'Automobile in Le Mans.

1998
Louis Vuitton Classic
Hurlingham Club, June 6. The British have always had a passion for Bugatti. Two classes were reserved for the make this year: "The Marvels of Molsheim" and "Glory and Dust." The oldest model, dating to 1910, was a Type 15 lent by the National Motor Museum. Alongside a host of authentic Bugattis was a stunning copy of a Bugatti Royale from the Musée National de l'Automobile (National Automobile Museum) in Mulhouse, France. Best of Show went to an Alfa Romeo Type B that raced four times at Indianapolis in the 1930s.

1999
Louis Vuitton Classic
Hurlingham Club, June 5. One of the attractions of the Louis Vuitton Classic concours is the diversity. This year's event has twelve classes, one open to motorcycles. The eleven others reflect different aspects of the history of the automobile, showing cars from various eras, of various styles, and of various uses. For there is no connection—except in the secret places of the heart—between the Ferrari that had its career in Tasmania in 1968 and the Tatra 87, a technological curiosity made in Czechoslovakia just after the Second World War. Nor is there any reason the 1923 racing Delage should compete in the company of the aristocratic eight-liter Bentley, which won Best of Show this year.

2000
Louis Vuitton Classic
Hurlingham Club, June 3. Rather than dividing the program by type of bodywork or era of manufacture, the event's organizers thought up themes for the various classes of competition. So here were gathered cars that have all played a part in the career of the great Italian champion Tazio Nuvolari, ranging from the beautiful Bugatti 59 to the Norton motorcycle and a terrifying Alfa Romeo Bimotore—which, as its name suggests, has two engines, one at the front and one at the back. The winner is a sumptuous 1953 Ferrari 375 MM Berlinetta, an automobile with a considerable sporting pedigree. It was owned by the French collector Jean Sage before being acquired by the English collector Anthony Bamford.

Sir Michael Kadoorie

In 2006 Rolls-Royce celebrated the largest commission in its history: fourteen specially fitted limousines supplied to the Peninsula Hotel in Hong Kong. The initiative came from the hotel's owner, Sir Michael Kadoorie, an affable, chivalrous, cultivated man. At a ceremony marking the delivery of the limousines, he recounted the stories behind his own collection of cars, lingering over an extremely rare 40–50 HP Rolls-Royce that took part in the 1912 race from London to Edinburgh. Sir Michael's collection also includes a Bentley, a Hispano-Suiza, and a Bugatti 57 S Atalante. Sir Michael Kadoorie comes from a Jewish family of Iraqi origin that settled in Shanghai in 1880. Today he reigns over Hongkong and Shanghai Hotels Ltd., which operates eight select hotels around the world.

1998. This Alfa Romeo 8C 2300 lost its original bodywork and was elegantly clad in a Zagato copy.

1998. This Tipo 308 C one-seater was built by Alfa Romeo for the 1930 Grand Prix season.

1999. Just two cars of the Delahaye 165 type were produced by Figoni & Falaschi in 1938. This one went to America for the New York World's Fair and did not return to Europe until the 1990s.

2000. High society gathers at Waddesdon Manor around a Ferrari 250 GT Spider California.

2000. Unusually decorated, the Ferrari 375 MM Berlinetta was built in 1953 to compete in arduous tests of endurance such as the Le Mans Twenty-Four Hour Race and the Mexico City Carrera Panamericana.

2001
Louis Vuitton Classic

Hurlingham Club, July 7–8. The very popular Jaguar E Type was celebrating its fortieth anniversary. Coupes, convertibles, and lighter sports versions were shown on the lawns at Hurlingham, along with other, unexpected classes of car: The British had invited the hot rods to join the party. These once ordinary cars had been transformed into economical sports cars, dreamed up by American rebels who modeled themselves on James Dean. Another category was for cars that hark back to the Red Flag Act, a British law of the late nineteenth century that required every automobile to be preceded by a man on foot waving a red flag. Best of Show was awarded to an entirely different kind of car, the powerful and rare Isotta-Fraschini KM4, built in 1911.

Patrick le Quément

Behind Renault's purposeful strategy and high-calibre creations like the Initiale and the Fluence is the remarkable Patrick le Quément, who gave vigor to the brand's design. Born in Marseilles, he spent his teenage years in Britain; on his bookshelf, David Hockney monographs rub up against volumes on the Beatles. Patrick le Quément joined the car industry with a degree from Birmingham Polytechnic under his belt. He worked for Simca, Ford, and Volkswagen before joining Renault in 1988. An open and adventurous spirit, Patrick le Quément imbued the brand with rigor and inventiveness. Under his influence, Renault Design conveys the complexity and richness of French creativity.

2002
Louis Vuitton Classic

Hurlingham Club, June 8. For its final concours at the Hurlingham Club, the Louis Vuitton Classic paid a well-deserved tribute to the driver James Hunt. Now all but forgotten despite his talent and his record of achievement, he was a chivalrous, charismatic figure, lively enough to take the stuffiness out of the tradition-bound sporting world. Blond, extremely tall, very handsome, and irresistibly appealing, he loved every kind of excess. A golden boy, he drank, smoked, and showed an irrepressible desire to burn the candle at both ends, whether on his yacht or his private jet. He embarked on his short racing career as a way to get revenge: A bus company had rejected him as a driver because he was too tall. But he wasn't too tall to drive the McLaren M23 to victory in the 1976 Formula 1 World Championship, beating Niki Lauda to the wire. In 1989 he left McLaren for the Wolf team, but five years later, at age forty-three, he died of a heart attack.

2004
Louis Vuitton Classic

Waddesdon Manor, June 5. Concept cars often make their world premieres at the Louis Vuitton Classic, and this year's event, held at Waddesdon Manor, near London, provided the setting for another dramatic debut. Waddesdon Manor is a sumptuous residence built in the nineteenth century for the Rothschild family. It is a sort of anachronistic extravagance, designed in the Renaissance style by the French architect Gabriel-Hippolyte Destailleur.

Renault's Fluence concept car barely made it there in time. The truck transporting the prototype, which was produced in Turin by G-Studio's expert craftsmen, arrived at Renault on June 1. There was just time to go under the studio spotlights for a few photos, then off the car went to England for its official presentation at Waddesdon Manor.

But British honor emerged unscathed. The Best of Show award went to a quintessentially British 1934 Rolls-Royce Phantom II built by Carlton.

2001. This Jaguar E-Type Lightweight was given specially streamlined bodywork by Samir Klat and Harry Watson to compete in the Le Mans Twenty-Four Hour Race in 1964.

2001. This 1947 Ford underwent a fine customization by Spike McMurtrie of Jackson, Michigan, a process common in the United States in the 1950s.

2004. Motorcycle riding need not be inelegant, as proven by the owner of this 1961 Norton Manx.

2004. This Aston Martin Ulster is one of the three cars the factory set aside for racing in 1934.

2004. The majestic Rolls-Royce 100 EX prototype heralds the Phantom Drophead Coupé launched in 2007.

130
Classics in the Heart of Manhattan
1996–2000

For a number of years Louis Vuitton brought the finest specimens from American car collections together in the heart of New York City.

An icy gust blows between the skyscrapers. Fifth Avenue is almost deserted. The homeless fellow who spent the night leaning against the door of Saint Patrick's Cathedral packs up his cardboard boxes and rags. Everything will be neat and tidy by the time the windows light up at the Tiffany and Louis Vuitton stores. A fire engine, sirens blaring, rushes past the few taxis that are on the streets at dawn. The roars of a Ferrari ring out between the buildings: At a time of day more customarily devoted to first cups of coffee Jean Sage is revving up the engine of his berlinetta with bursts of its accelerator. It is one of the fifty classic cars taking part in the concours at Rockefeller Center this weekend. The collectors arrive early to remove the tarpaulins that have covered their treasures during the night. Dawn strokes the bodywork, which is still shivering.

In the 1920s a botanical garden belonging to Columbia University flourished here in the center of Manhattan. John D. Rockefeller Jr. leased the space, between Fifth and Sixth Avenues and Forty-ninth and Fiftieth streets, in 1928, with plans to build an opera house there. Then the stock market crash, with its trail of disenchantments, brought a thunderous close to the Roaring Twenties; all projects collapsed. Rockefeller revised his plans and in the 1930s developed on the site fourteen skyscrapers, designed in Art Deco style by Associated Architects. This complex formed the core of what came to be known as Rockefeller Center.

The cars are displayed on Rockefeller Plaza, at the foot of the GE Building, which towers 850 feet (260 meters) above. Encouraged by the success of the concours at Bagatelle and Hurlingham, Louis Vuitton brought the event to New York for the first time in 1996. Many of the world's most exceptional cars are stored away (and occasionally exhibited) in North America. The United States is an inexhaustible source of well-informed car enthusiasts, and the country has become home to the most desirable automotive specimens. The New World's pioneering collectors initially could be naive or excessive, pouring their limitless enthusiasm into inappropriate restorations, but with experience their knowledge matured and their tastes became more refined.

The event has transformed Rockefeller Plaza over the weekend. There's a podium, tiered seating, Champagne, and trophies ready to be handed out. Let the party begin! The growling of engines rises between the towers, and two quarter horses escort the Best of Show winner.

1998. Rockefeller Center provides the Alfa Romeo 8C 2900 B, here in the form of a Touring Spider Lungo, with an appropriately grandiose setting.

1996
Louis Vuitton Classic

Rockefeller Center, September 27–29. From the start the Louis Vuitton Classic in America differed from the others in that it took place over three days, with the judges arriving on the scene on the afternoon of the second day. Headed by Murray Livingstone Smith, the jury this year includes American notables such as Chuck Queener, the talented illustrator, and Jonathan Stein, editor of *Automobile Quarterly*. There are eight classes: cars from before 1931, racing cars, separate classses for prewar and postwar sports cars and touring models, Gran Turismo models, and "woodies."

These delightfully American curiosities, generally produced just after the Second World War, had a rustic appearance because the main part of the body was clad in wood. Among the rarities here is the futuristic Chrysler Thunderbolt, with its streamlined bodywork. It is one of two prototypes created by the designer Alex Tremulis for the New York World's Fair of 1939. The Best of Show award goes to the remarkable Bentley Speed Six that beat the Blue Train from Cannes to Calais in 1930.

Murray Smith

Murray Smith is one of the delightful personalities encountered at concours d'elegance and vintage car rallies: a true car lover. On weekends the businessman turns into a "gentleman driver." He is not the kind of collector to treat his cars like museum pieces; indeed, he travels the world behind the wheel of his most precious cars, and the Louis Vuitton rallies provide an opportunity to exercise his sharp driving skills. He was one of the people behind the launch of the Louis Vuitton Classic concours events in New York.

1997
Louis Vuitton Classic

Rockefeller Center, September 26–28. Concept cars, or dream cars, are the product of creative fantasy. They probe future possibilities, some more imminent and some more realistic than others. Some of them edge into the avant-garde, while others prefigure models that are destined for a commercial future. They express the tremendous responsiveness of the automobile industry to the desires and needs that evolve along with its customers' life-styles.

The first concept cars appeared in America in the early 1950s. Some of them are on display at the concours, such as the Pontiac Bonneville Special and the Buick Wildcat, both straight out of a General Motors Motorama. Also here is a 1939 Bugatti with bodywork by Vanvooren, a concept car in its own way. The French government presented it to Mohammad Reza Pahlavi, the crown prince and future shah of Iran, in honor of his marriage to Fawzia, the sister of King Farouk of Egypt. Much more realistic is the Alfa Romeo 6C 1750 Gran Sport with bodywork by Zagato, which wins Best of Show.

1998
Louis Vuitton Classic

Rockefeller Center, October 2–4. Along Channel Gardens, the planted pathway leading from Fifth Avenue to an open-air skating rink, stands a line of extraterrestrial vehicles. One of these is a model for the revolutionary Dymaxion Car, designed by the architect Buckminster Fuller in 1933: It is a large, monolithic, aerodynamic beast, sitting on three wheels and with an incredible passenger compartment. A little further along is the remarkable Phantom Corsair, a monster featured in the 1938 movie *The Young in Heart,* starring Paulette Goddard and Douglas Fairbanks Jr. A very special Ferrari 375 MM takes one of the leading roles at Rockefeller Center; it is a unique model Roberto Rossellini commissioned from Scaglietti for Ingrid Bergman. Romance often lies behind the most flamboyant creations.

For other cars the emotion is hidden in the patina, giving them an extra measure of soul and feeling. This is true of the Bugatti Type 59, a former Grand Prix car that the king of Belgium bought for his daily use once it had finished its racing career. Its current owner, Anthony Wang, keeps the Bugatti in its evocative original state, retaining all the scars, such as cracked paint and worn leather, left by passing time.

1997. **This racing car, produced by Adler in 1937, is a stunning example of what avant-garde German aerodynamics experts created shortly before the Second World War.**

1998. **This is a model of the remarkable Dymaxion Car developed by architect Buckminster Fuller for the 1933 Chicago World's Fair.**

1999

Louis Vuitton Classic

Rockefeller Center, September 24–26. Reflecting the extraordinary setting in the heart of Manhattan, the organizers of this year's concours at Rockefeller Center seek to reflect the American way of life in the cars on show. So there is a class for "muscle cars," superpowerful machines concealed beneath extremely ordinary exteriors similar to the most undistinguished midsize car. One great American car here is the Thomas Flyer that won the New York–Paris race in 1908.

The Best of Show award goes to a car belonging to an American collector who is himself an icon of elegance: fashion designer Ralph Lauren. His 1938 Bugatti Atlantic (one of only four produced) has no ornamentation at all, so the emphasis is entirely on the flowing lines and the pronounced spine running from front to back (a seam created by riveting the body panels externally).

Ralph Lauren

"These automobiles are moving works of art," declared Ralph Lauren in the catalogue for the 2005 "Speed, Style and Beauty" exhibition at the Museum of Fine Arts, Boston, which included some of his cars. The fashion designer does not regard himself as a conventional collector. "I have never wanted to be a collector," he said. "That was not my goal . . . but I have always loved automobiles." In 1983, at age forty-four, the designer began putting together a collection, which took only five years to amass. That haste reflected the compelling desires of the euphoric 1980s, when interest and speculation around vintage automobiles flourished. Ralph Lauren's ambition was to own the most representative creations from the most legendary brands, and he valued engineering more than bodywork design. Yet Ralph Lauren's cars reflect his own image: timeless elegance.

2000

Louis Vuitton Classic

Rockefeller Center, September 22–24. In its fifth consecutive and final year in New York, the Rockefeller Center event attracts two million spectators. Louis Vuitton is taking advantage of the occasion to display some creations from its own design studio, with three specially fitted-out BMW C1 scooters and a Chrysler PT Cruiser upholstered with the famous "LV" monogram.

Top marks for originality go to a prototype made in France by André Dubonnet, a curious, inventive spirit who lent his name to both an aperitif and a design for an automobile suspension. His prototype, the Xénia, is unusual, with slender bodywork, glazed cockpit, and sliding doors. It was produced just before the Second World War by Saoutchik but did not perform its first run until June 1946, when it marked the opening of the French Autoroute de l'Ouest (Western Highway) at Saint-Cloud.

2000. The Scarab, an American sports car designed by Lance Reventlow in 1958, takes part in the parade on Fifth Avenue. Behind the wheel is Augie Pabst, who drove it in the past.

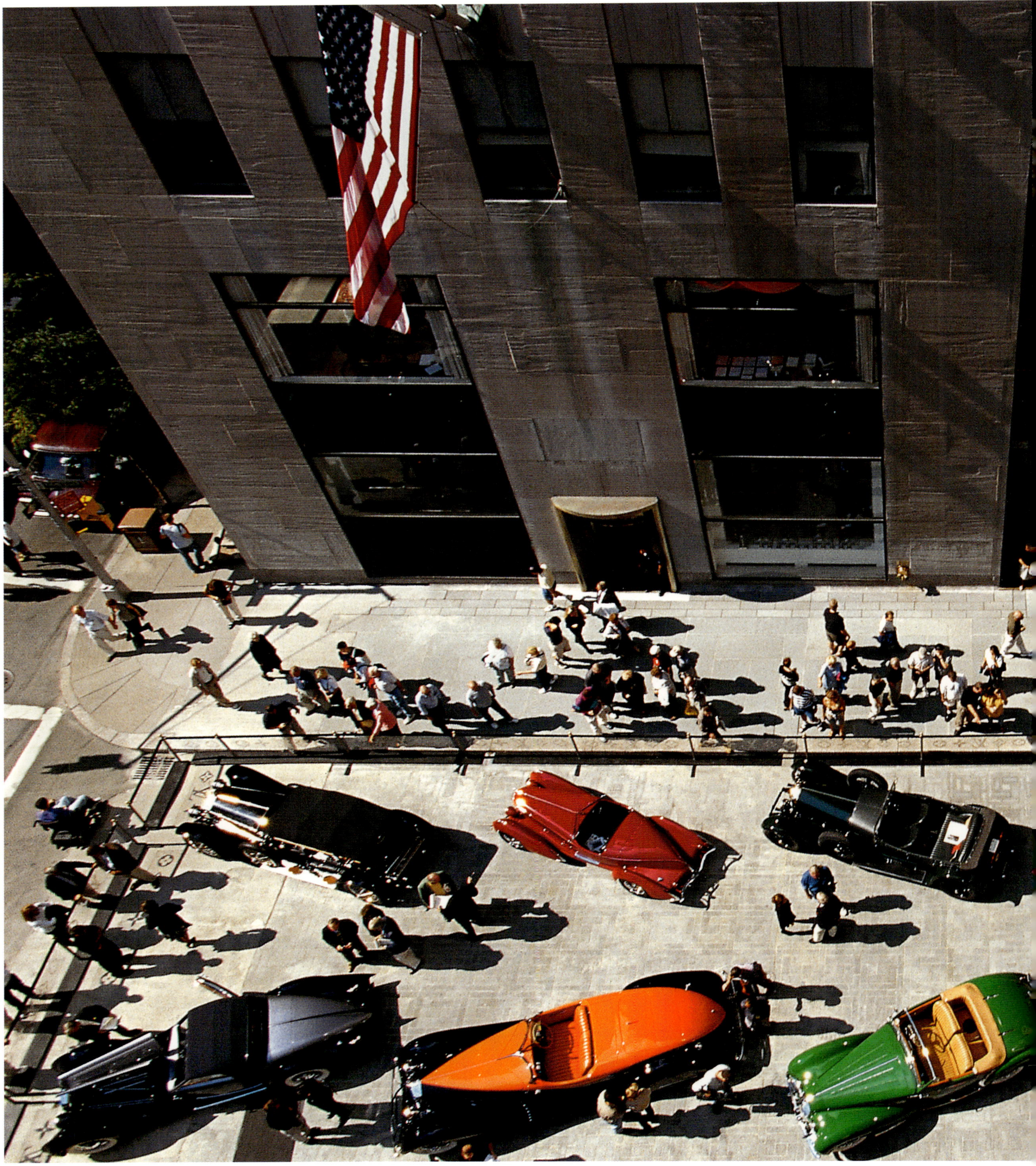

1999. **A breathtaking array of automobiles spreads out beneath the dizzying heights of Rockefeller Center's towers.**

138 Louis Vuitton Rewards Creativity

After staging a prestigious series of concours d'elegance in Great Britain, France, Switzerland, the United States, and elsewhere, Louis Vuitton decided to continue celebrating automotive excellence by introducing two new awards.

The name of Louis Vuitton is clearly and inextricably linked to the world of outstanding automobiles. In 1989 the company began sponsoring the concours at Bagatelle that *Automobiles Classiques* had initiated the previous year and followed the show to Saint-Cloud in 2003. It also hosted magnificent exhibitions in Stowe, London, and New York, and organized expeditions across Switzerland, Italy, Malaysia, China, and central Europe. Its next step in celebrating automotive excellence was to create two awards that are less public than those bestowed before the spectators at the concours but equally prestigious: the Classic Award for the year's best Best of Show winner and the Design Award, given to the best concept car of the year—one that might win Best of Show at a concours in perhaps forty years' time.

The man responsible for this initiative was Christian Philippsen, a well-known and well-informed enthusiast who crops up everywhere in the world of collectible cars. He is the elegant and indefatigable defender of an aristocratic view of the automobile. With Christine Bélanger, who runs the Louis Vuitton Classic events, Christian Philippsen conceived the new awards, one of which entailed a competition among the cars that dominated some of the most famous automotive events of the previous year, including the concours at Amelia Island, Villa d'Este, Meadow Brook, Pebble Beach, Quail Lodge, and the Cavallino Classic.

Through the glass top of this Maserati by Pininfarina are glimpses of the tubular frame—an allusion to the Birdcages of the 1960s.

2006
Classic Award & Design Award
French Bodywork Takes Pride of Place.

The first Louis Vuitton Classic Award went to a sublime Delage, unique of its kind. It shared the honors with a Maserati by Pininfarina, which received the Design Award.

Six cars that had won Best of Show at concours held in 2005 competed for the "best of Best of Show": two Alfa Romeos, a Bugatti, a Mercedes-Benz, and a Ferrari were up against the Delage D8-120. The first qualifying contest in the series was the fourteenth Cavallino Classic, which took place in Palm Beach in mid-January. The winner was the 1955 Ferrari 375 MM Berlinetta Special made by Pinin Farina on a 0490/AM chassis. This berlinetta is ivory with a navy blue roof, and different from the standard 375 MMs because of its prominent spoilers and the oval radiator grill, which would be repeated on various 250 GTs. Shown at the 1955 Turin auto show, this car was bought brand new by Inico Bernabei; it was also seen at Villa d'Este in April 2005 and is currently in the United States, in the collection of Manuel Del Arroz.

The second leg of the series was also in Florida, where the Amelia Island concours took place in March. Another era and another legendary make were saluted here: an astounding Bugatti whose merit lies as much in its history as its elegance. It was made in 1937 on the initiative of André Birth, who owned a Type 51 Grand Prix (Louis Chiron's 51113), which he treated to bodywork in the Atlantic style. The commission was carried out by Louis Dubos. After the war the car emigrated to the United States, where it was involved in an accident. The great collector Jack Nethercutt salvaged the chassis and had a reproduction Grand Prix body added to it. Meanwhile the coupe's original bodywork was fitted on a copy of a 51 chassis—which meant that two cars were each half fake! When Nethercutt acquired the second car, he was able to put the Dubos bodywork back on its original chassis; the coupe became whole again in 2003.

Next came the concours at the Villa d'Este, on the banks of Italy's Lake Como, in April. On its home ground, the Alfa Romeo won the day. This masterpiece, designed in 1964 by Giorgetto Giugiaro for Bertone, had been badly damaged by an American journalist in the 1960s, then abandoned. After lengthy negotiations the Japanese collector Shiro Kosaka purchased the wreck. He had its reconstruction supervised by Tateo Uchida, who was the last designer at the Michelotti studio and is now head of Forum.

The American concours series resumed in August in the elegant setting of Meadow Brook, in Michigan. A flamboyant Mercedes-Benz SSK with bodywork by the American company Murphy was the queen of the show. She had previously been white, but her current owners, Arturo and Deborah Keller, preferred to show her in burgundy.

Finally, two Best of Shows were awarded in the course of a busy week spent around Monterey, California, in August. On the lawns of Quail Lodge, the prize went to a long-chassis Alfa Romeo 8C 2300, which after several metamorphoses has been restored to its original form—that of the Touring torpedoes that took part in the Le Mans Twenty-Four Hour Race. This beauty was shown by John Ridings Lee.

Then, at Pebble Beach, the Best of Show was awarded to the Delage D8-120 S. It is a unique creation, which Pourtout specially fitted out for the personal use of Louis Delâge after its display at the 1937 Salon de l'Automobile in Paris. Most compelling about this car is its remarkable body, which is characteristic of Pourtout's designer Pierre Paulin. It is a very modern coupe with sleek, dynamic, harmonious lines. This little masterpiece of French bodywork now belongs to the superb collection of Samuel J. Mann.

The Delage went on to be selected the year's overall winner, receiving the first-ever Louis Vuitton Classic Award at a ceremony in Paris in February 2006. Also presented at this event was the Design Award, intended to honor a spectacular, even over-the-top, car. The votes were cast for a creation that combines extreme style and superlative machinery: The Maserati Birdcage 75th by Pininfarina was the unanimous winner.

Robert Peugeot

Always keen to recount the epics of his African journeys and racing career, Robert Peugeot is a dynamic epicurian but is above all a pragmatic businessman. He started out in 1975 with PSA Peugeot Citroën in South Africa. The great-grandson of one of the first directors of the company bearing the family name, Robert Peugeot never allowed his lineage to determine his fate; in fact, he spent more of his career at Citroën than Peugeot. In 2004, to the benefit of both brands, he created the Automotive Design Network in Paris, an ultramodern, spectacular creative center housing all Peugeot's and Citroën's designers and engineers.

Jean-Pierre Ploué

Upon assuming his duties as head of the Citroën design center in late 1999, Jean-Pierre Ploué began thinking about the top of the line. He is one of the new leaders of automobile design, and his rise has been meteoric. He joined Renault in 1985, after studying architecture at Besançon and completing his studies at the École des Arts Appliqués in Paris. He first gained recognition for work on the project that led to the Twingo, which debuted in 1992. In 1995–98 he ran Volkswagen's new design center in Catalonia, then served as Ford's head of design in Germany before returning to his native land. Since then, he has given a tremendous boost to design at Citroën.

The Delage D8 120 S by Pourtout is shown on the Champs-Élysées in February 2006.

This futuristic silhouette was designed by Jason Castriota for Pininfarina.

2007
Classic Award & Design Award
A New Crown for Ferrari.

At the second annual awards presentation, a mythical Ferrari 250 GT California received the Louis Vuitton Classic Award, which goes to the finest classic car of the year. The Design Award honored Citroën.

This year's panel of experienced car lovers chose the "classic of classics" from the Best of Show winners of six of the most prestigious concours d'elegance of the previous year: Amelia Island, Villa d'Este, Meadow Brook, Quail Lodge, Pebble Beach, and the Ferrari Club of America Field and Driving in Washington.

Once again Christian Philippsen was in charge of the event. To enhance its international appeal, the organizers decided to hold the awards ceremony at the Geneva International Motor Show in March 2007, where it united the prizewinners of the previous year's events. There the Ferrari 250 GT California was honored with the Classic Award, and the Citroën C-Métisse carried off the Design Award for the most influential concept car of the year.

The 250 GT California is one of the classics in the history of the automobile. The first version, shown at the Geneva motor show in 1960, had a short chassis; in many respects it continued the evolution of the legendary short-chassis Berlinetta. The reduction of the wheelbase by eight inches (twenty centimeters) resulted in the more compact proprortions that gave the California its muscular outline and sharp road performance. However, the Pinin Farina design was similar to that of the long-chassis Californias: in other words, sublime.

The winning model was irreproachable. A navy blue California with red leather seats, it began its career in France in the 1960s, then spent a few years in Switzerland before being acquired in 1996 by Peter S. Kalikow, an experienced collector who is a real estate investor and served as director of mass transit in New York.

The 2007 Classic Award went to a Ferrari 250 GT California, while the Citroën C-Métisse received the Design Award.

4

Applied Arts

4

Bodywork is beginning to achieve the same status as an art form enjoyed by other, more widely recognized, applied arts. At various concours d'elegance, the exhibition of major examples from the 1930s to 1950s has testified to such artistry.

The automobile generally does not receive the same recognition as other consumer products. The inclusion in a museum exhibition of a lemon squeezer by Philippe Starck or a Paul Iribe pedestal table goes unquestioned, but there is inevitably an outcry when a car is accorded the same respect.

How many design exhibitions have ignored the car; how many reference works on the applied arts treat it with utter disdain? Is it too sophisticated an object? Too compromised by commercialism? Too tainted by its industrial origins? Perhaps, but the same judgments could apply to a household implement or a piece of furniture.

The car is a complex expression of the applied arts, as its manufacture brings together a diverse range of crafts and skills. If the car is not itself a work of art, it could be considered art's nearest rival. As the painter Fernand Léger said with perspicacity and foresight at the Collège de France in 1923, "The manufactured object is there, absolute, polychrome, clear and precise, beautiful in itself; and it is the most fearsome competition that the artist has ever faced."

Like the other applied arts, the art of bodywork wavered between two opposite poles—conservative and progressive—during its golden age, the 1920s to the 1950s. The conservative movement focused on historical references, while the avant-garde expressed a modernity that embraced science and technology. The famous 1925 Exposition des Arts Décoratifs in Paris marked the junction of these two tendencies, giving rise to the Art Deco style that paradoxically encompassed both luxuriously burled woods and sleek nickel, swirling complexities as well as pure, simple lines.

Masterpieces of the art of bodywork are represented among various types of cars of various origins. Some are high-performance sports cars; others are rakish status symbols. But they have one thing in common: a unique history, shared with remarkable men and women—engineers who invented the most sophisticated techniques, designers who created the most elegant and audacious lines, craftspeople with inspirational know-how, drivers who fought heroic battles behind their wheels, and, finally, loving, caring collectors.

148
Jean
Bugatti
Bugatti
50-T
1932

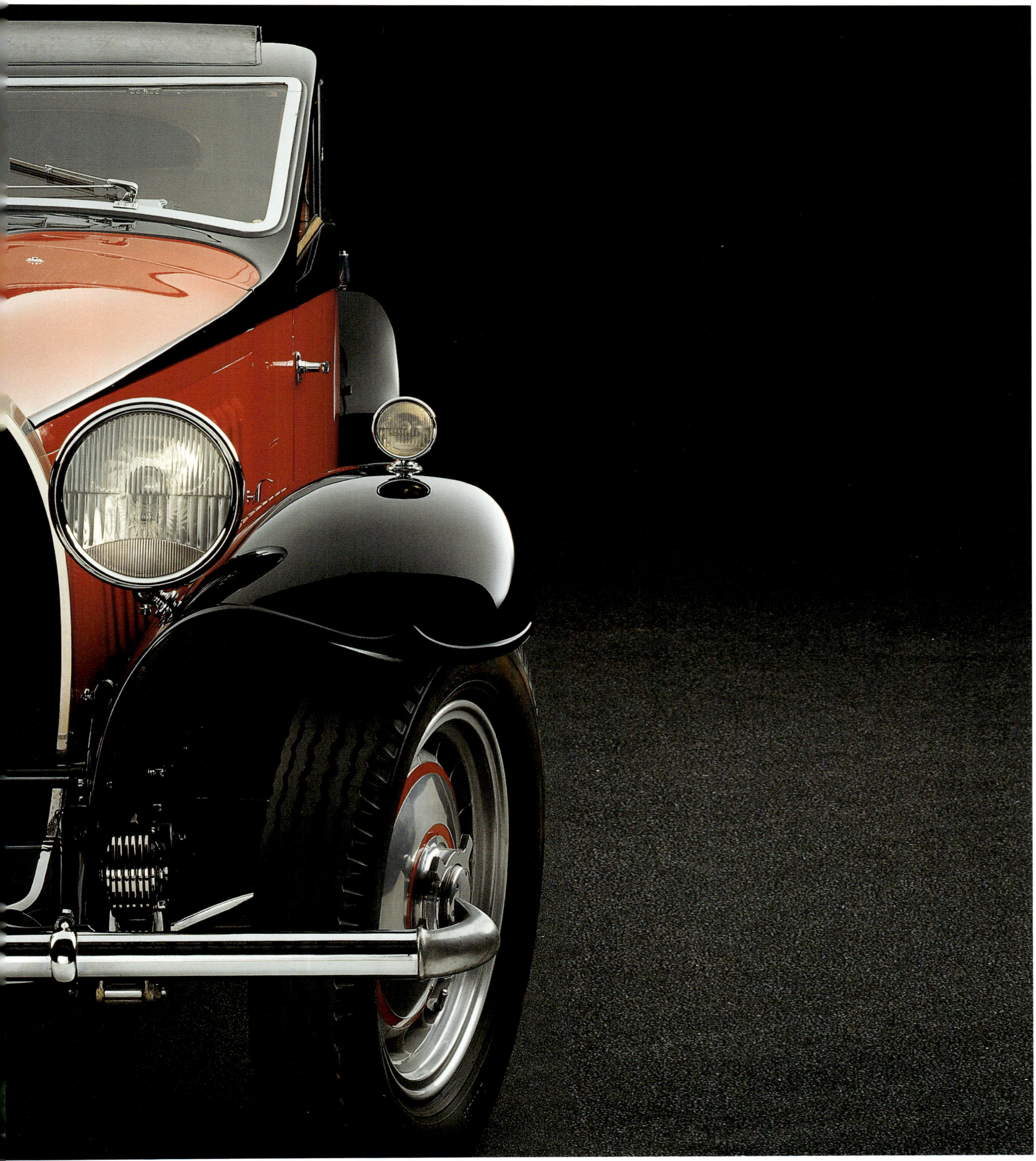

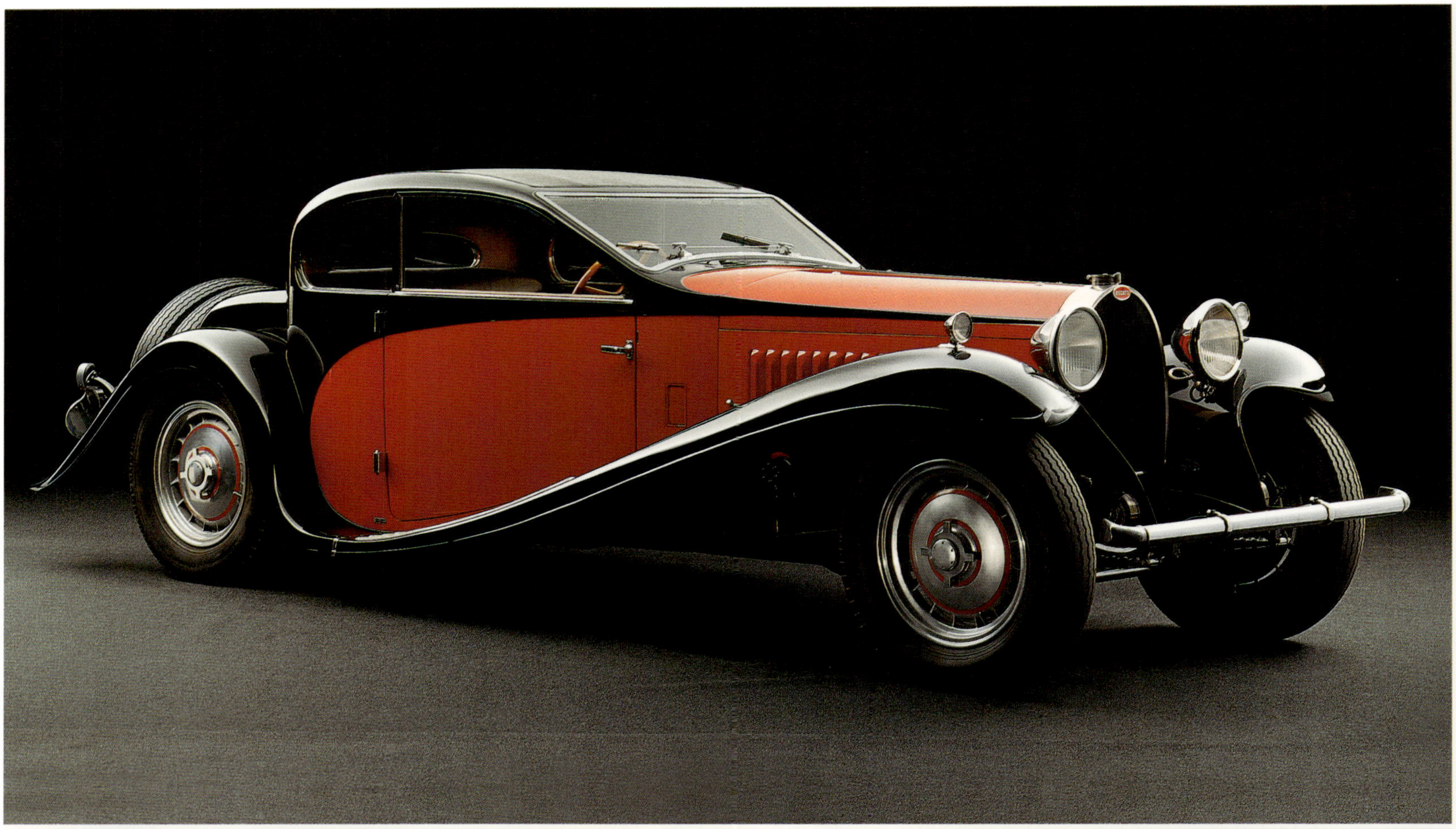

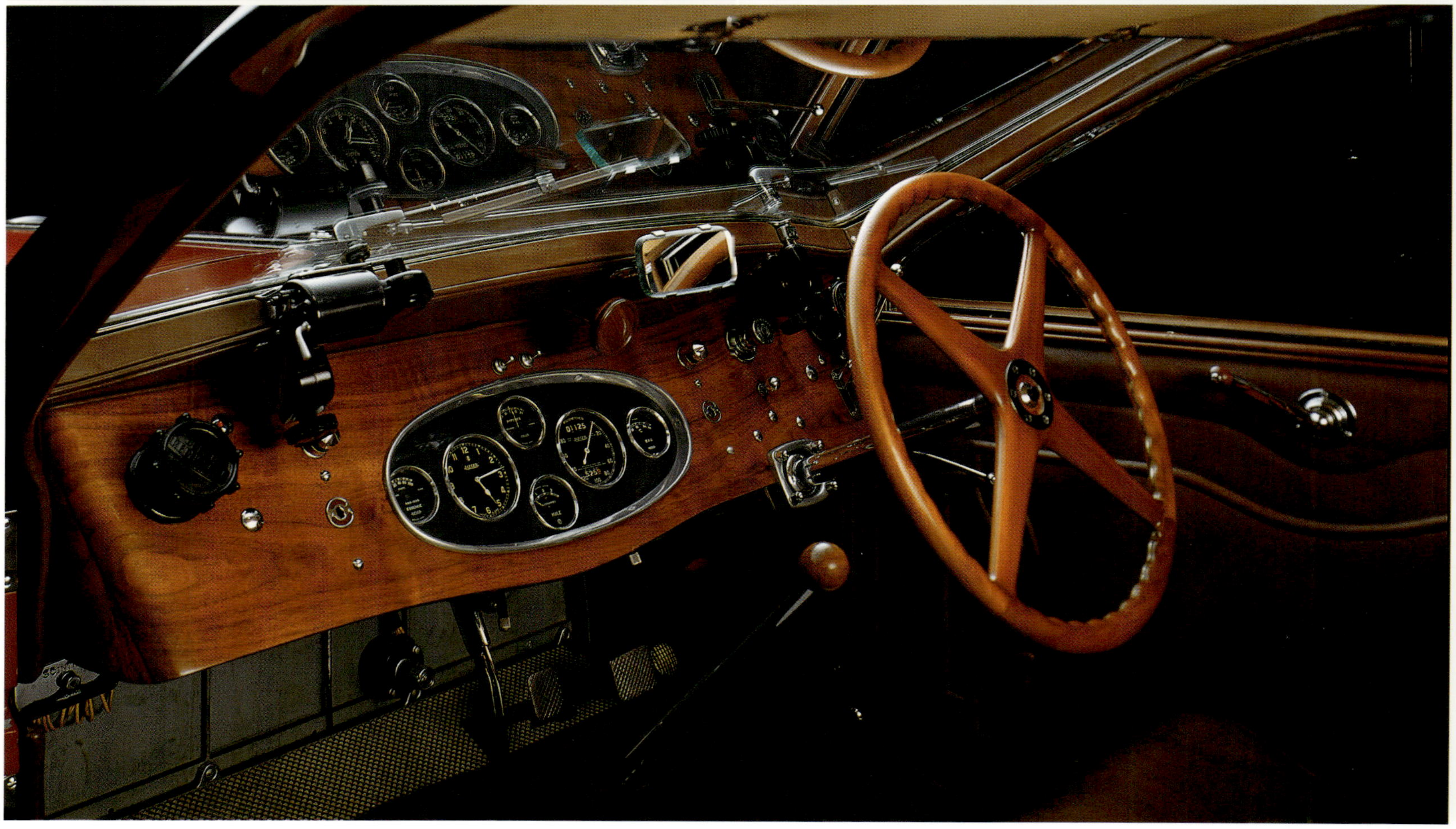

Some versions of the Type 50 (especially the 50-T variation, which has a wheelbase lengthened from 122 to 142 inches [3.10 to 3.60 meters]), have an aerodynamic look. The Type 50-T initially took the anachronistic form of a landaulet (design no. 1038) but was shown at the 1932 Paris Salon as two remarkable coaches: one with a trunk, as seen here, and the other with a streamlined rear.

Between 1930 and 1933 Bugatti produced sixty-five units of the Type 50, the last twenty-three of which had a long chassis (50-T) similar to that of the Type 46. The main technical innovation was Bugatti's use for the first time of a straight-8 engine with a capacity of almost five liters and a double overhead camshaft.

The inimitable design technique of Jean Bugatti found its fullest expression in the Type 50-T Coach unveiled at the 1932 Salon de l'Automobile in Paris.

Since 1927 Jean Bugatti played an active role in running his father's factory. He was the designated heir and beloved son of Ettore Bugatti, the founder of the automobile firm that bore his name. From the start Jean Bugatti was involved in designing bodywork and he quickly developed a personal style, characterized by elegant, sweeping contours that intertwined gracefully. After the sublime bodywork achieved for the chassis of the Type 41 (the Bugatti Royale) and the Type 55 Super Sport, Jean Bugatti's design technique reached its peak with the Type 50-T Coach, which was unveiled at the Paris Salon de l'Automobile in October 1932.

As his style clearly expressed, the designer was a young man, only twenty-three, impetuous, romantic, and sophisticated. Monsieur Jean, as the factory employees respectfully called him, conveyed his talent through sinuous lines that were particularly expressive in the fenders, a magnificent sequence of curves swooping from the front before their contours drifted into space.

Despite the influence of streamlining, a trend then taking root in the United States, Jean Bugatti never indulged in the excesses and simplifications of his contemporaries. He retained his own style and did not respond to that of other designers, although some versions of the Type 50 did suggest a taste for aerodynamics. Even Jean Bugatti's most audacious projects showed restraint. The side windows were shaped like teardrops, extending in a slender point to the corner of the radiator. Another contour was expressed along the hood and reached to the base of the windshield, which tilted at an exceptional angle.

As with many of Jean Bugatti's creations, the interplay of colors contributes to the style's dynamism. Looking at the car in profile we see color starting at the front and spreading out in two swirls, one covering the side, the other surrounding the windows. The different colors are delimited by curves and moldings. Black is contrasted with bright colors, and flat surfaces are contained within skillful arabesques.

152
Figoni & Falaschi
Talbot Lago SS
1937

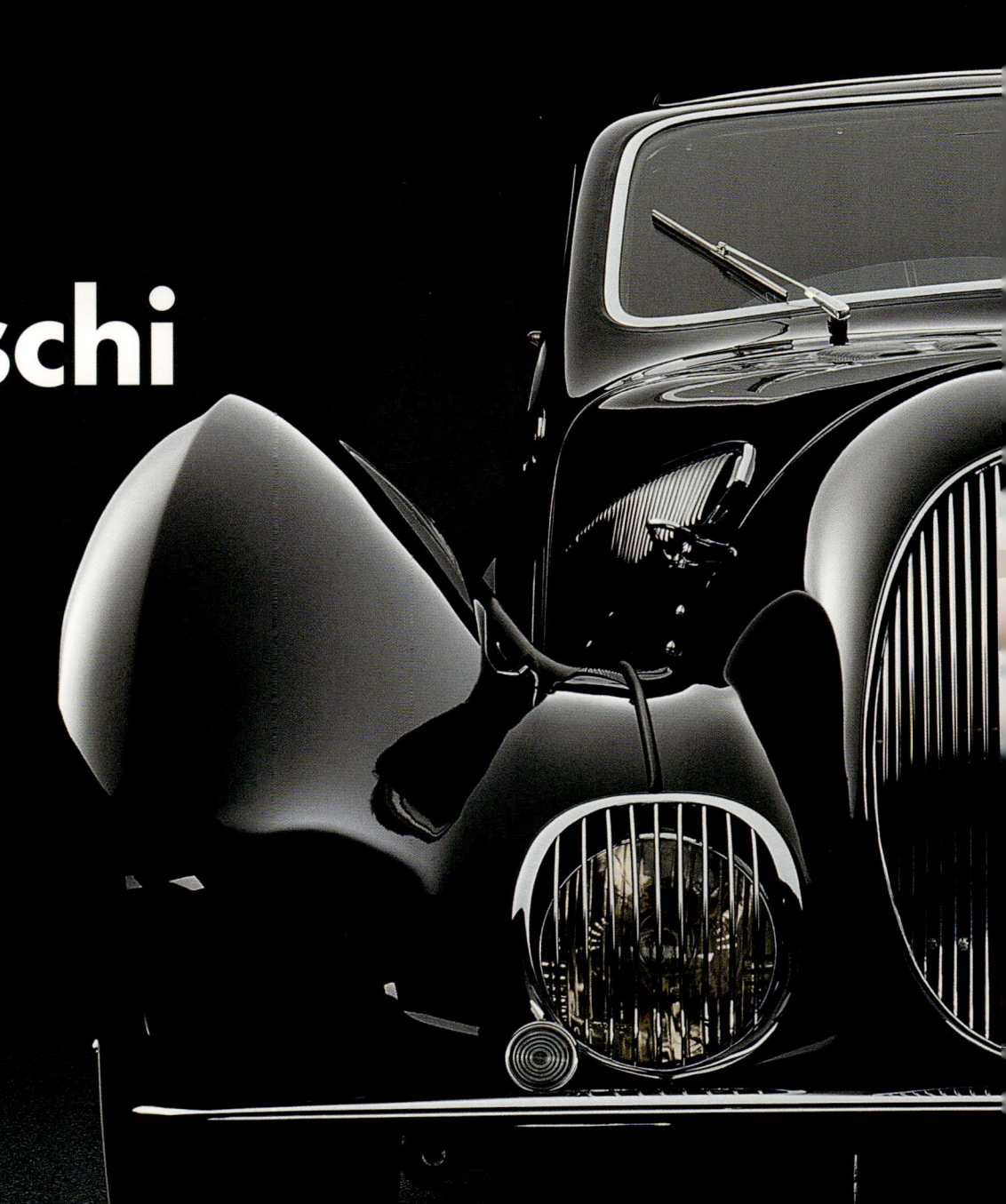

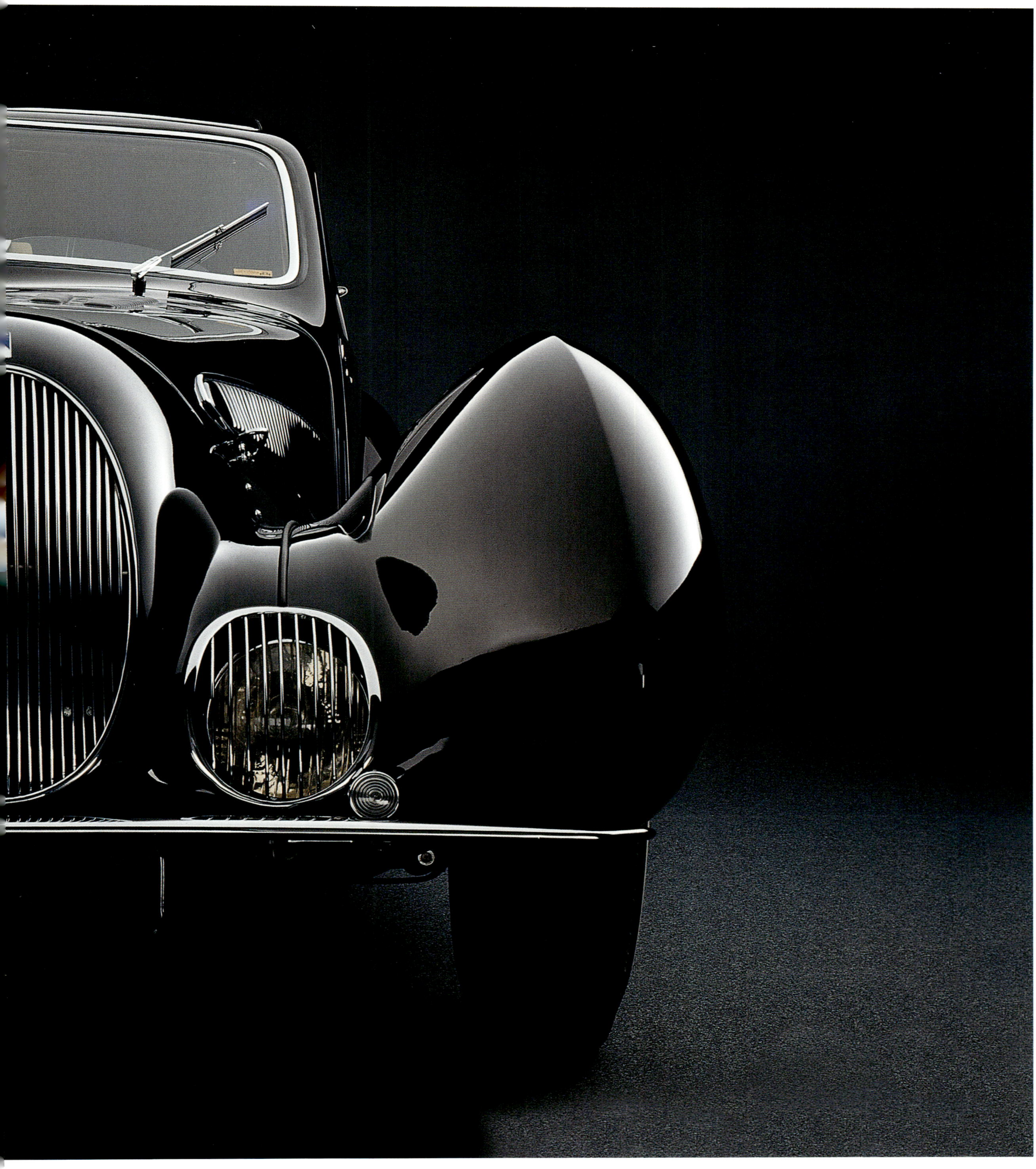

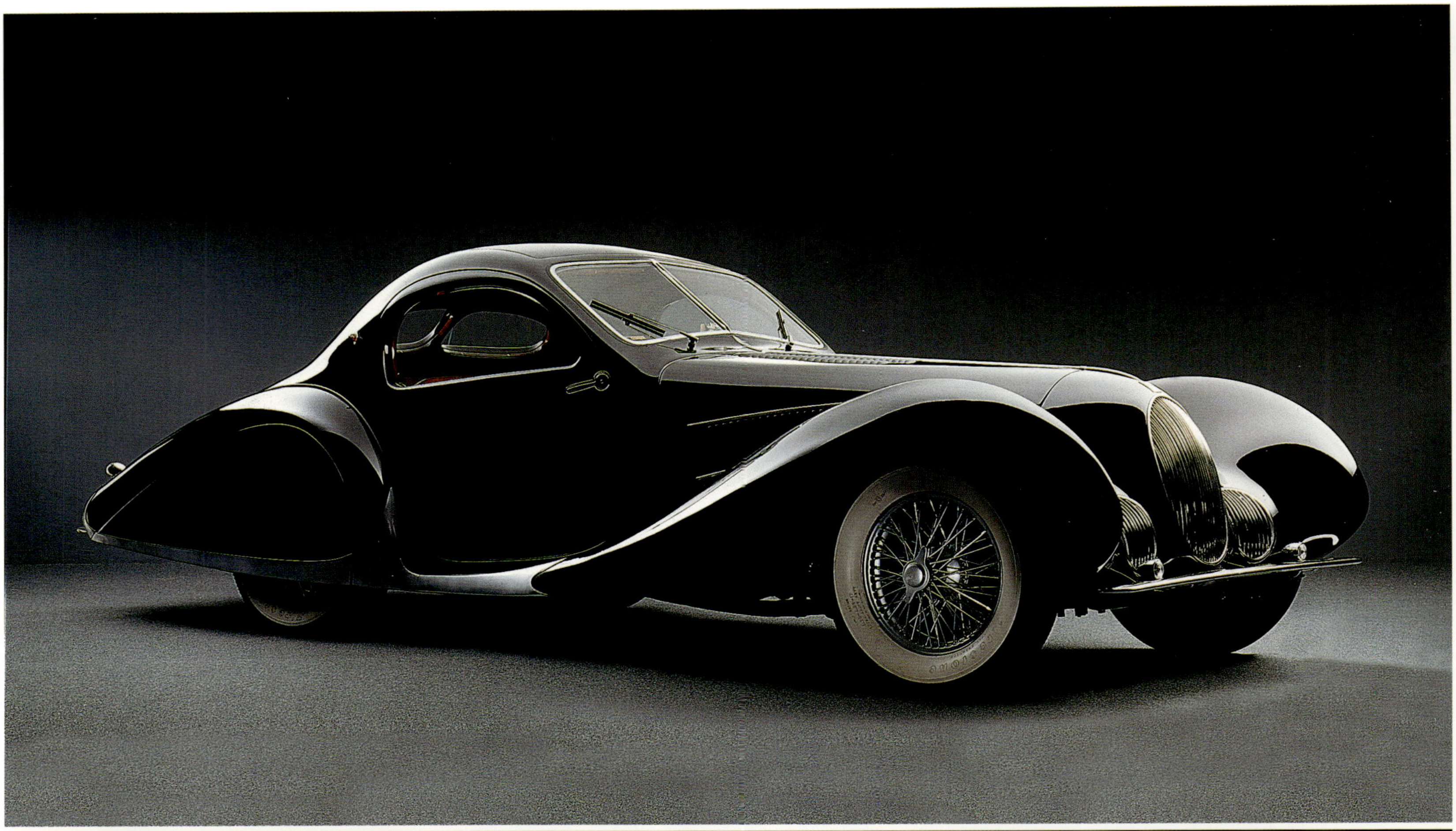

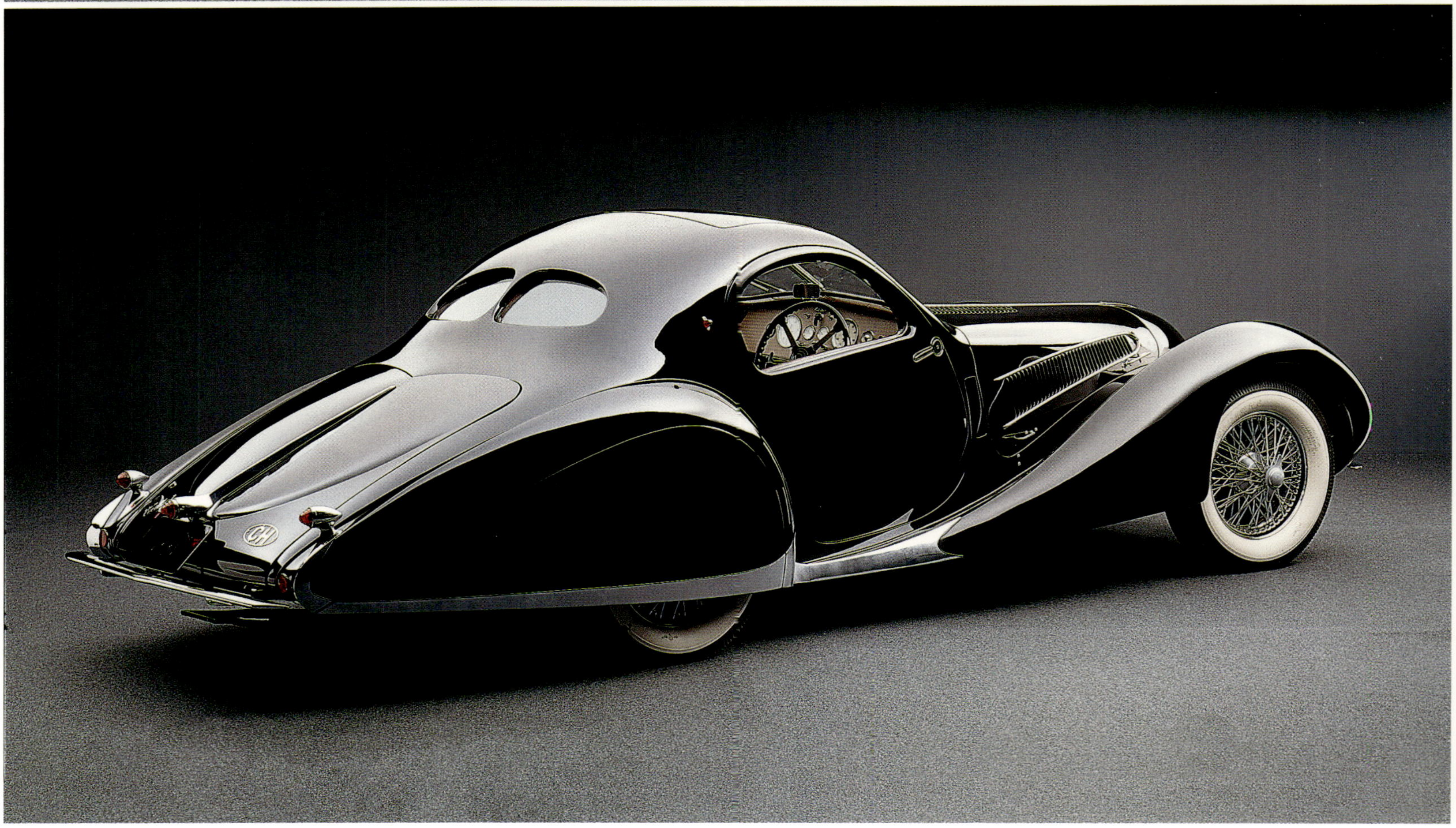

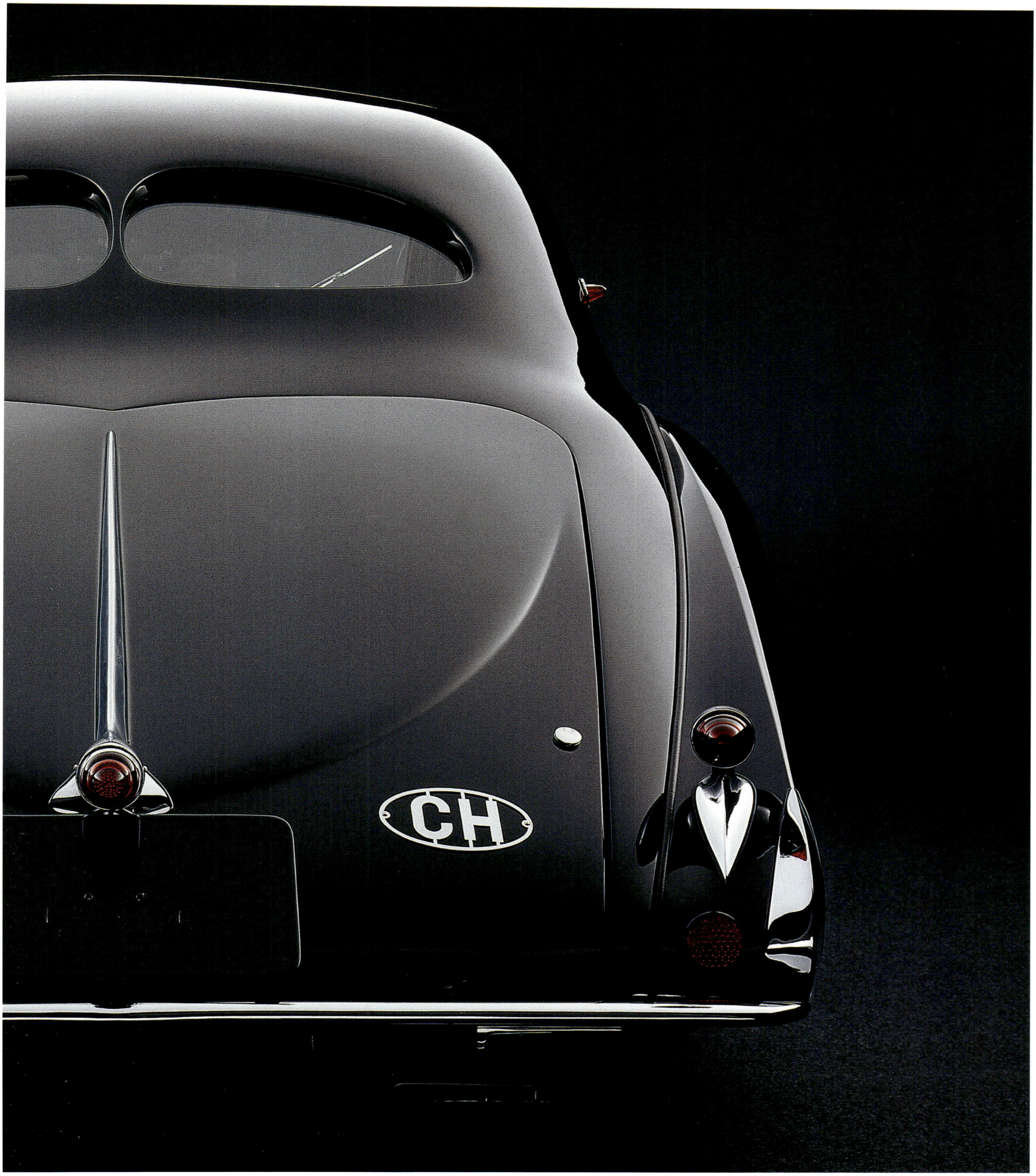
CH

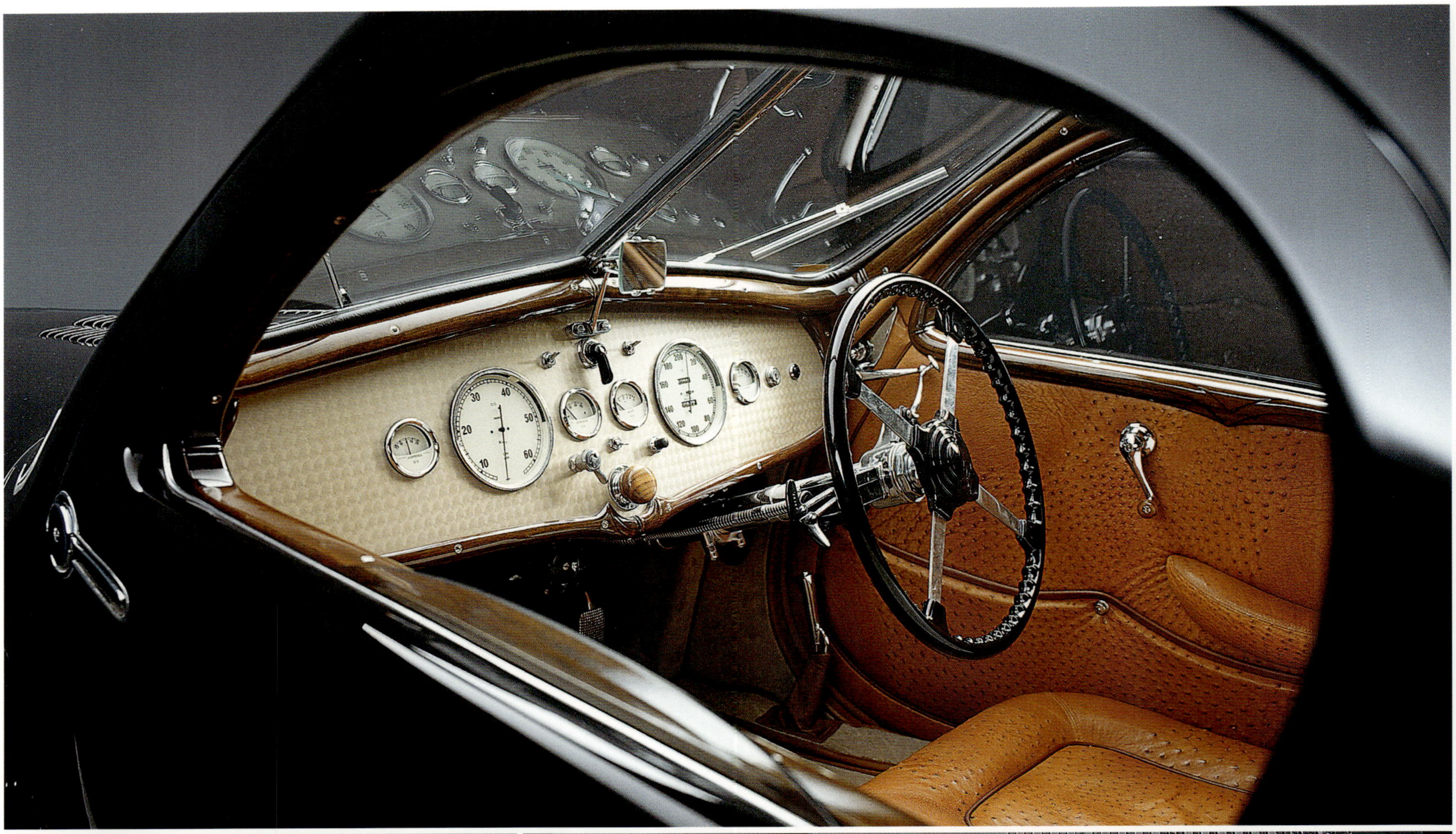

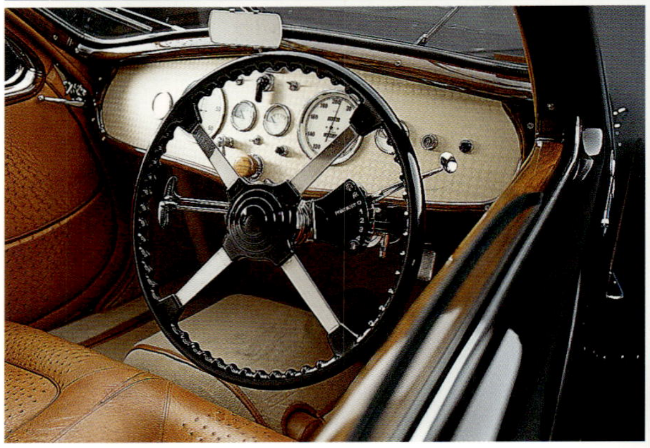

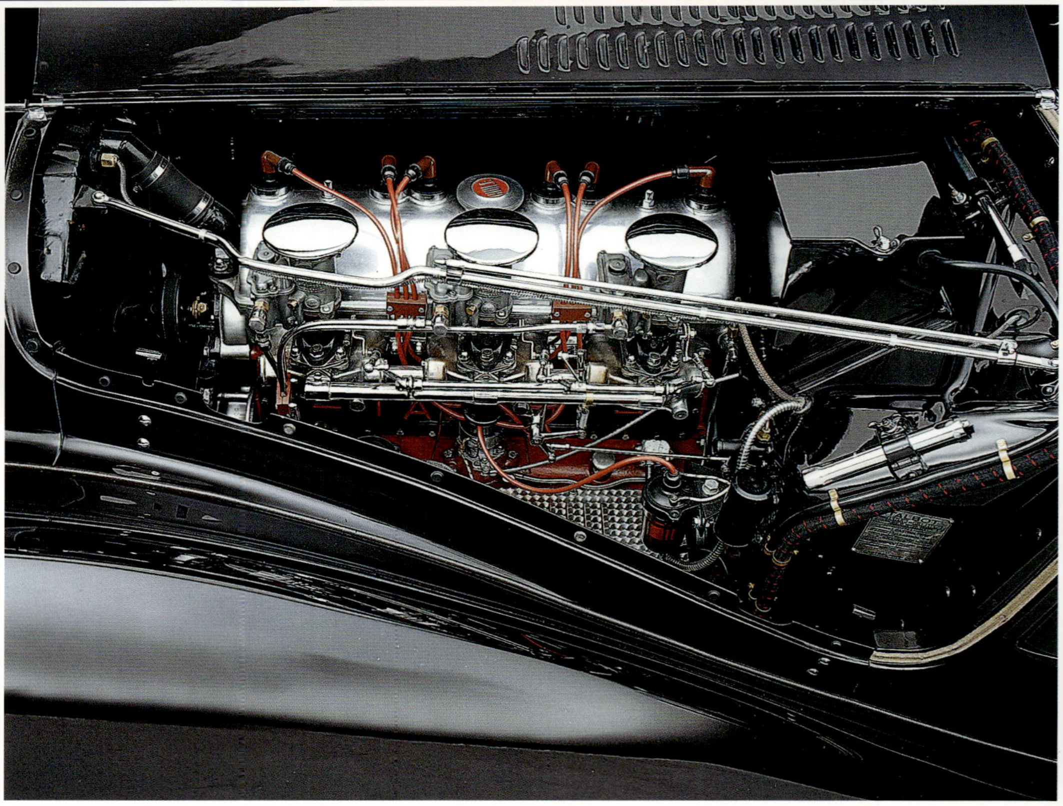

Figoni & Falaschi developed several designs for the Talbot Lago Super Sport chassis, which had a six-cylinder engine with a four-liter capacity. This faux cabriolet (reference 9221) was nicknamed the "Jeancart," after its first owner, differentiating it from the so-called New York model, which was launched in New York. As seen here, the side windows are not oval but bean shaped, and the trunk marks a break with the passenger compartment.

All versions of this car are customarily called "teardrops," an unofficial but apt term. Ten of the Lago SS faux cabriolets produced by Figoni & Falaschi are New York models and four have the Jeancart design.

At the Paris Salon of 1936, the venerable Talbot firm announced the launch of a new high-performance machine, known at first as the Lago Special Grand Sport. It was the prelude to a masterpiece nicknamed the "teardrop."

The Lago Special Grand Sport was soon renamed the Lago Super Sport, and the project began to take shape. The Lago SS was based on a racing car chassis, but for civilian life it needed more sophisticated attire, which Figoni & Falaschi concocted for it. The first version, shown at the Paris Salon of 1937, appeared in the guise of a roadster whose sporting origins could still be detected in its rudimentary lines.

At the New York Auto Show later that year Talbot showed a more urbane Lago SS, the first model in an extraordinary line of aerodynamic coupes. With their curves tapering to a fine point, they became known to posterity as "teardrops." The theme had several variations. Figoni & Falaschi developed a design in the same vein as the New York car. Named the "Jeancart," after its first owner, it differed from the New York iteration in that it had a break under the rear window and its side windows were bean shaped instead of egg shaped.

A major contributor to French bodywork, Figoni & Falaschi designed daringly fluent effects and an abundance of ornamentation. The firm's flamboyant style wavered between classicism and the baroque, between faux modernism and real panache. At a time when a generation of German engineers was taking a scientific, aerodynamic approach to auto bodies, the French school remained intuitive, allusive, and concerned primarily with aesthetics. Notwithstanding a sometimes simplistic futurism and a demonstrative sensuality, the company, based in Boulogne-Billancourt, produced designs that were seductive for their bounteousness.

Of the fifteen or so "teardrop" models, there are four versions of the Jeancart similar to the one that was awarded Best of Show at the Bagatelle concours in 1992.

158
Gabriel Voisin
Voisin Aérosport
1937

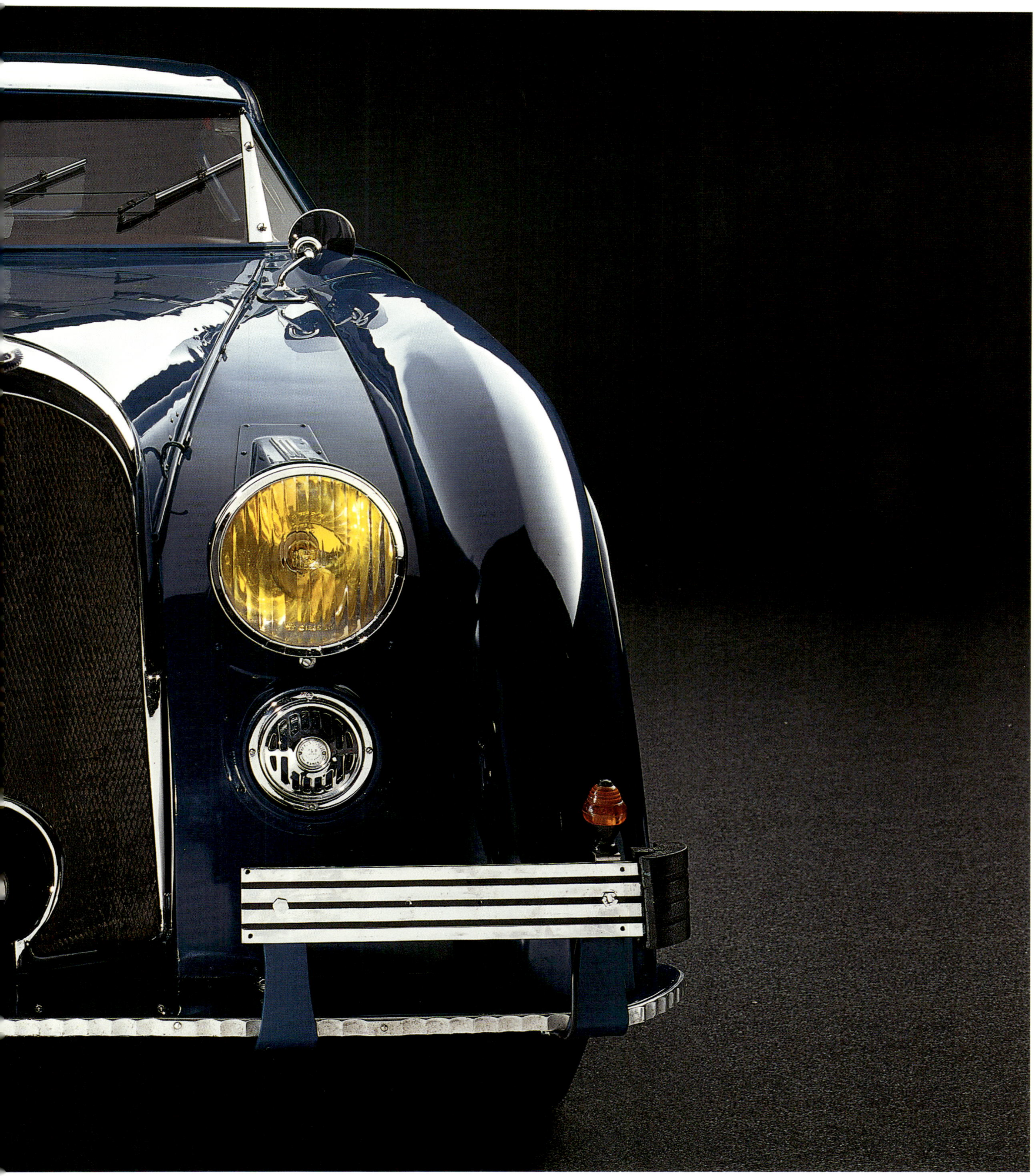

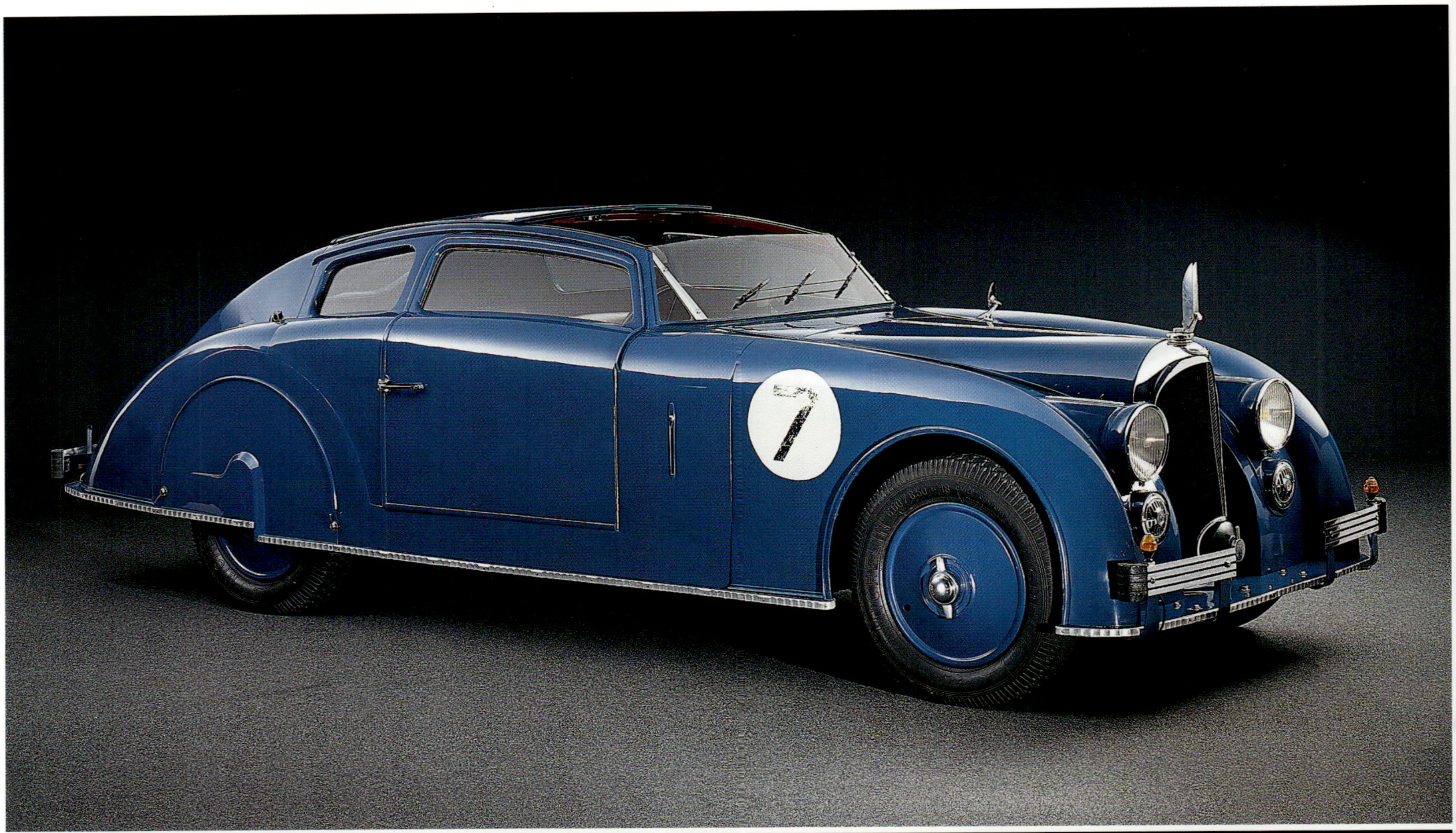

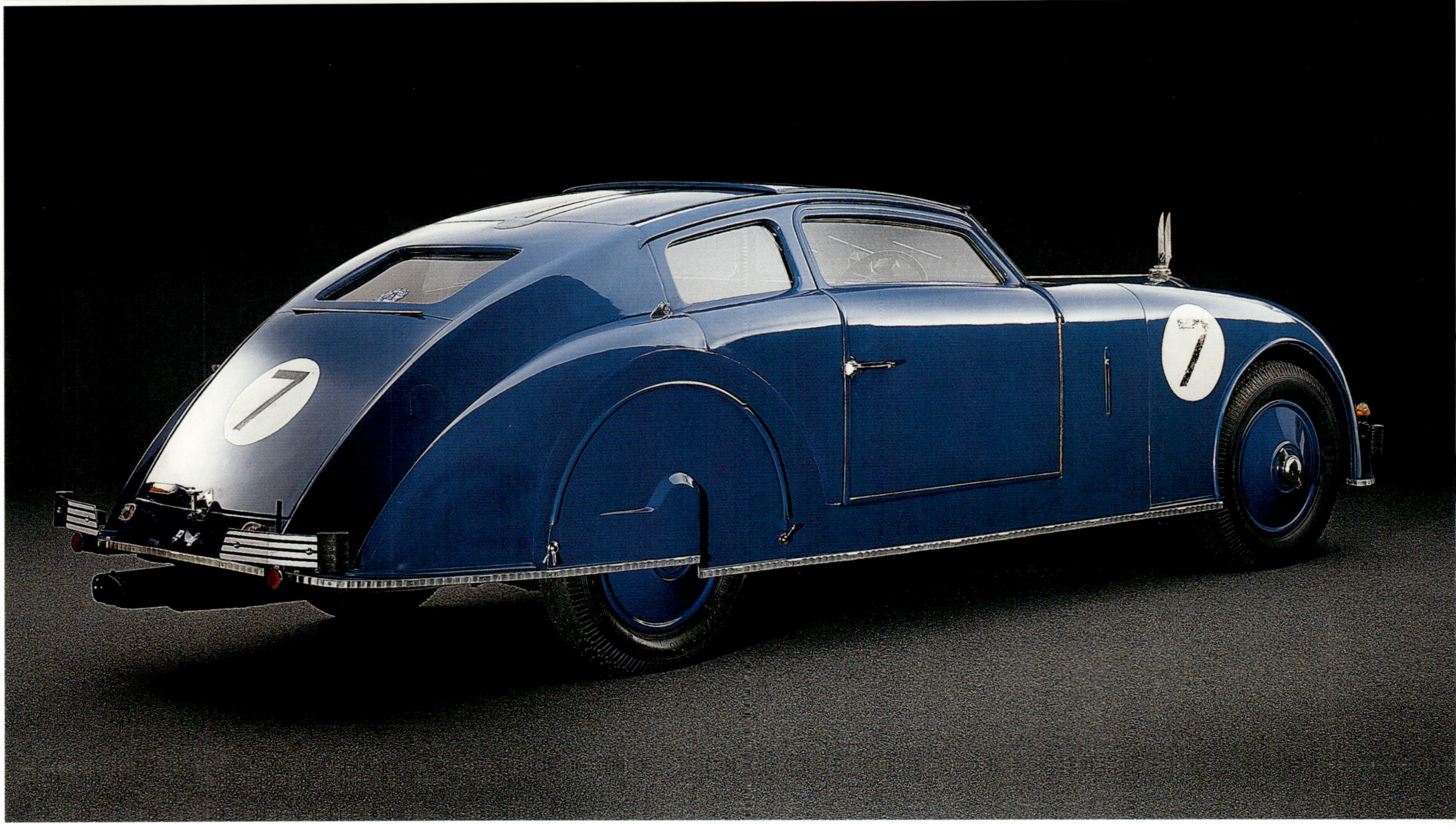

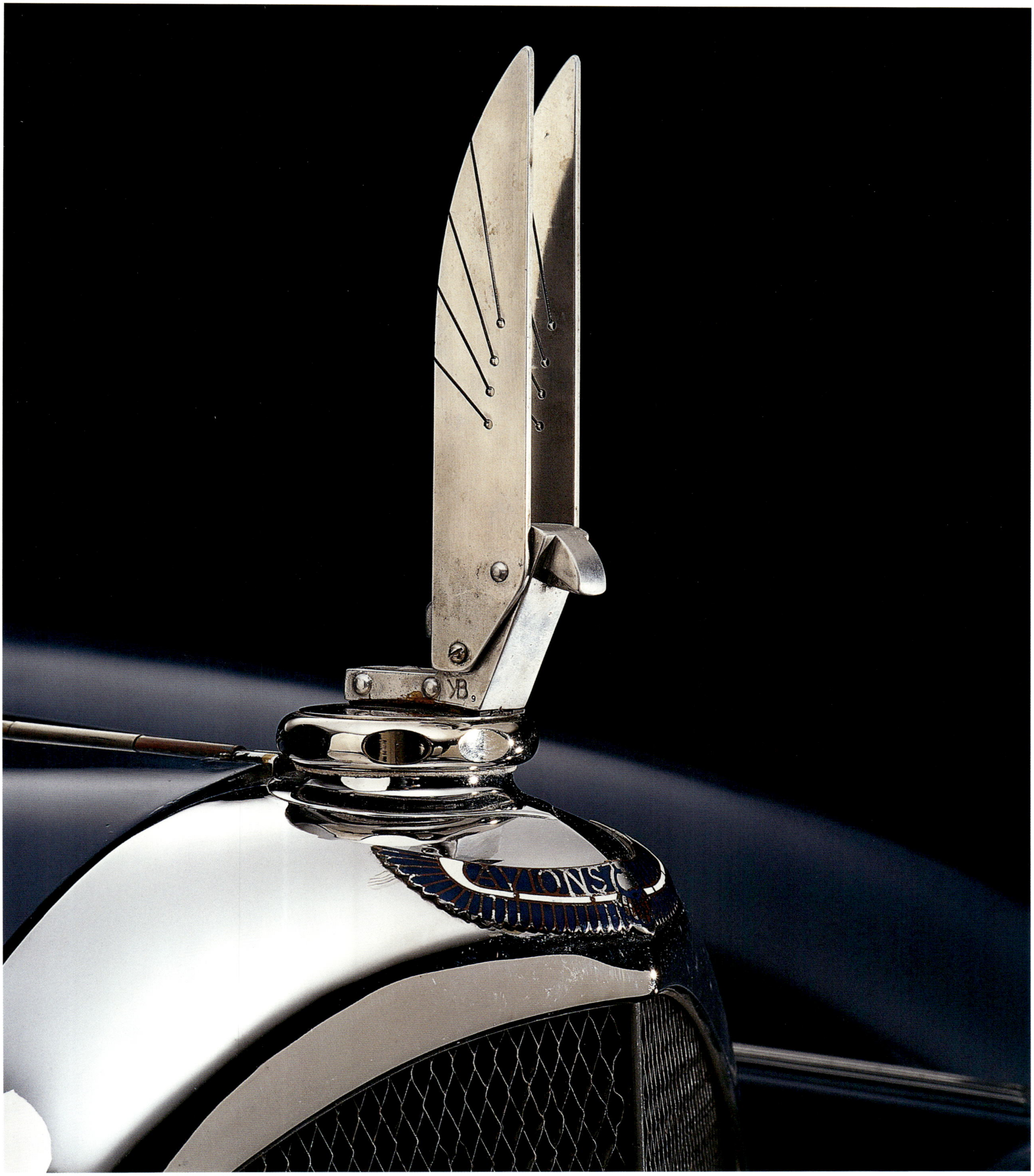
AVIONS

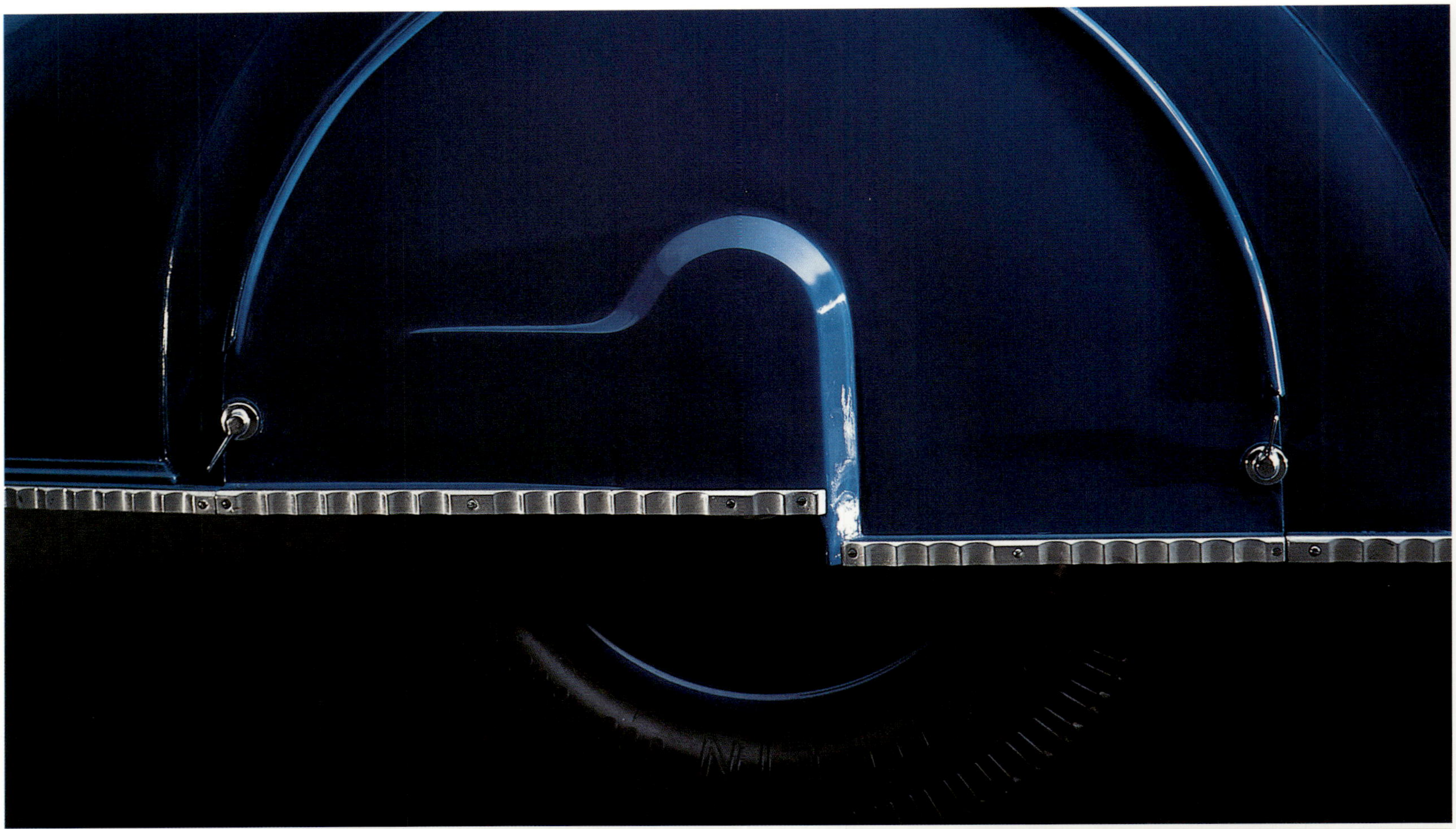

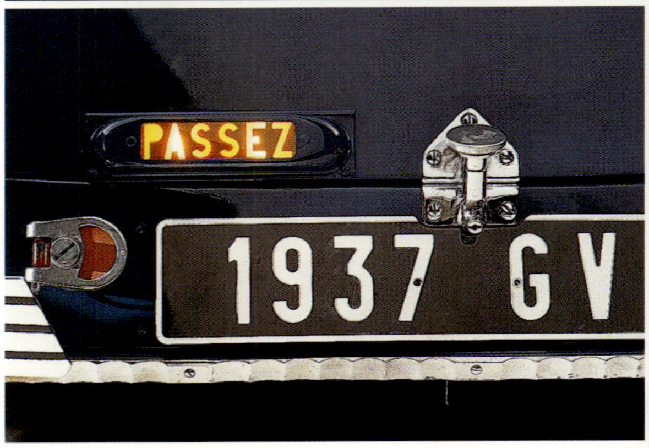
PASSEZ
1937 GV

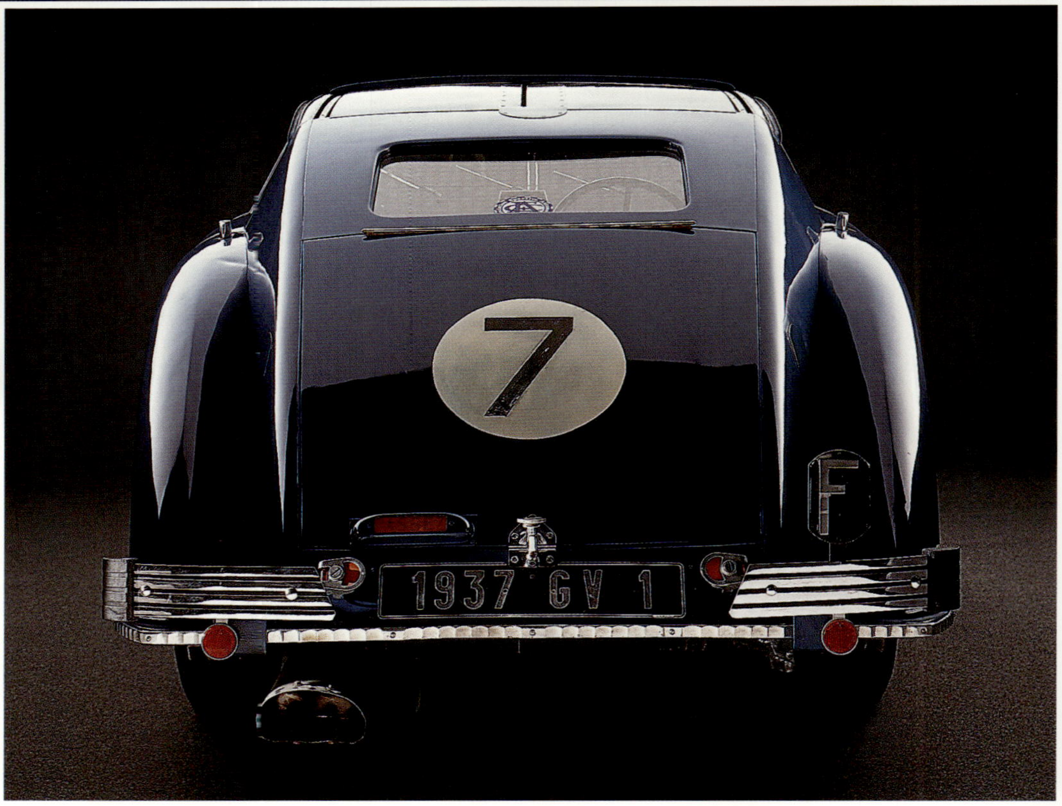
7
F
1937 GV 1

The Aérosport was one of Gabriel Voisin's undisputed masterpieces and one of his last. A pioneer in aviation, Voisin produced the aircraft that achieved the first closed-circuit flight in 1907. He then became involved in wartime industrial production. After the armistice, Voisin left aviation for the automotive world. His cars were as nonconformist as he was. Their bodywork was typically light, unadorned, functional, and streamlined.

Of all the aircraft manufacturers who shifted to car production, Gabriel Voisin was the most provocative and inventive. He made the best use of his aviation experience with a combination of sophistication and innovation. As he put it, "Twenty years in aviation enabled me to integrate aerodynamics into my forms."

Gabriel Voisin ranks among the most brilliant and controversial of manufacturers. His Aérosport—ahead of its time, futuristic, provocative—was among the last of his subversive creations.

Gabriel Voisin was never where he might be expected to be. He was late to jump on the streamlining trend, which other French auto-body makers started adopting in 1933. His cars, known as "Avions Voisin" (Voisin Airplanes) retained their stiff lines for a long time. The firm's financial health was too fragile to risk innovation, but Gabriel Voisin never lost his taste for provocation.

Even while bouncing between bankruptcy and revival, Voisin managed some brilliant achievements with his loyal designer André Noël-Noël, who brought Voisin's fantasies to life. The innovative Aérosport coupe is a major landmark in the history of French bodywork. The first version impressed the visitors at the Paris Salon of 1936 and marked the apotheosis of Voisin's career in the automobile industry.

Gabriel Voisin had dreamed up a revolutionary product. Its bodywork is completely enveloping, integrating the fenders. The sides are high and absolutely smooth, covering the rear wheels. The overall profile is strictly rectilinear, without the slightest contour, forming what was known as a "pontoon" line.

In a vocabulary specific to Voisin, the car seems like a section of an imaginary plane; the arc of the roof line suggests the contours of a cockpit, while the main surfaces simulate a fuselage. The angled windshield optimizes visibility.

The Aérosport evolved slightly in the course of its short career. For its second appearance at the Paris Salon, the line of the front fenders was altered. This was the version shown at the Bagatelle concours—a rare opportunity to see this model, because its production ceased in spring 1937, after only fourteen cars had been made. At that point Gabriel Voisin handed his company over to Paul-Louis Weiller.

164
Touring
Alfa Romeo 8C 2900 Spider 1937

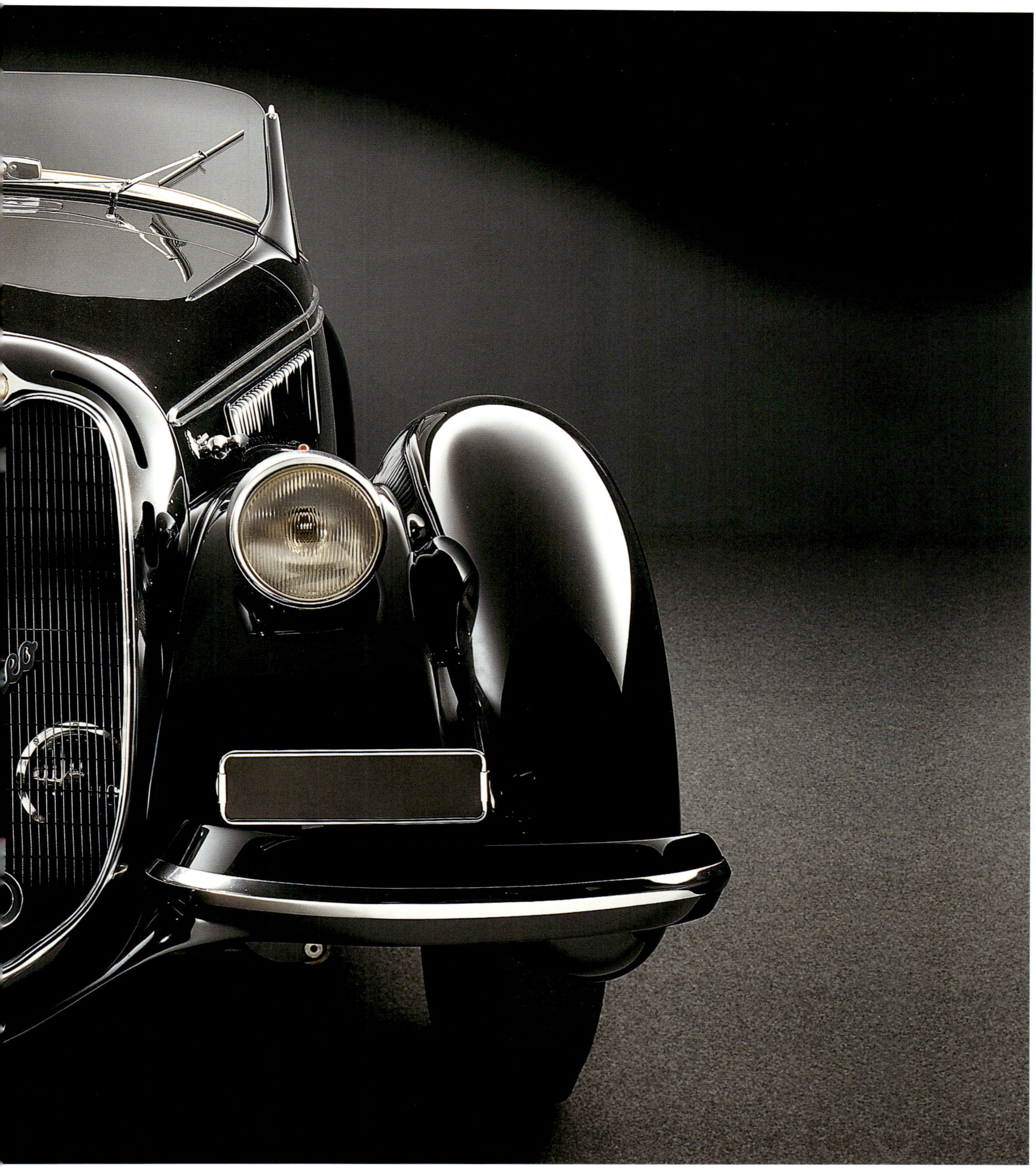

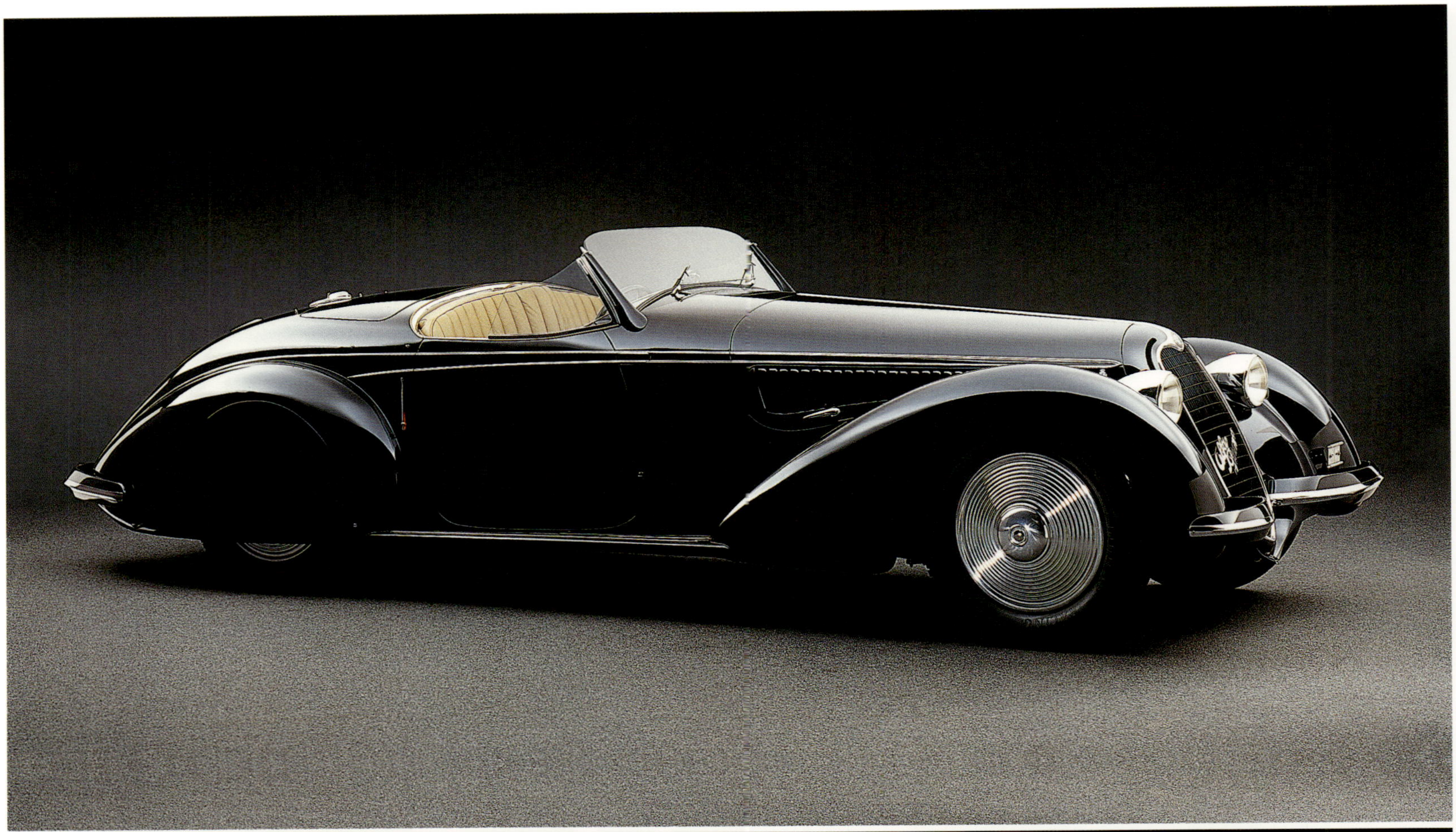

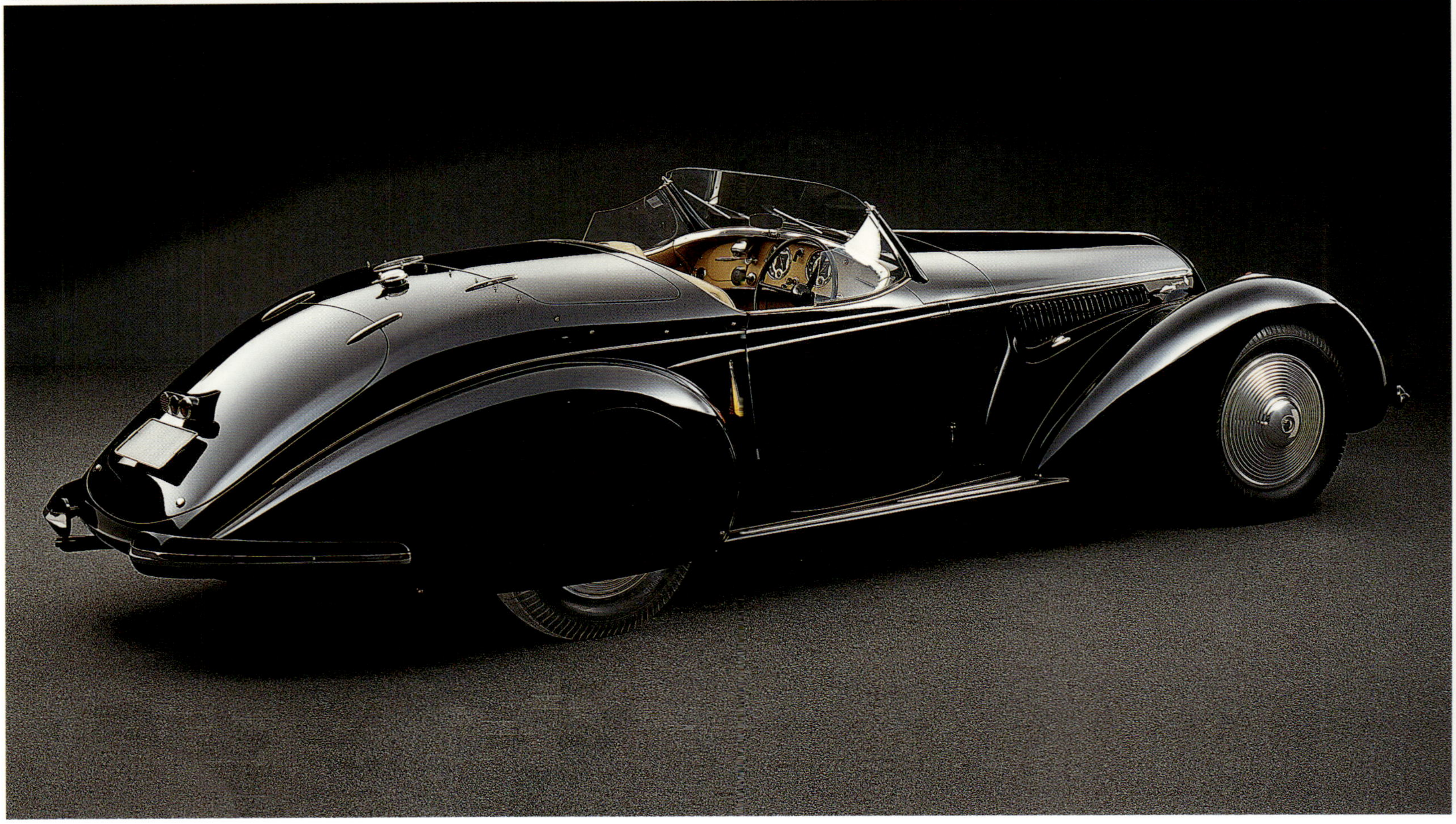

Before the Second World War Touring was without doubt one of the most creative Italian auto-body makers, aesthetically and technically. The company was founded in 1926 by Felice Bianchi Anderloni. Its sporty image relied on a close collaboration with Alfa Romeo.

This model, which won an award at Bagatelle, is one of the five Spiders built on an Alfa Romeo 8C 1900 chassis. It is based on the Superleggera framework, a fine tubular trellis to which aluminum panels are fixed, significantly lightening the body at a time when most were still made with wood.

At the height of its artistic powers, Touring created several series of infinitely desirable automobiles based on Alfa Romeo technology more commonly associated with the thrills of racing.

Throughout the Alfa Romeo 8C 2900's career, luxury blended with sportiness. Although its name appeared on brochures as early as September 1934, its storied life did not really begin until a year later, when the first version of this beautiful series was shown at the Paris Salon.

Under the glass roof of the Grand Palais, amid a sumptuous decor by Pierre Granet, visitors saw a pretty Spider meant for the road, designed and realized in the context of the factory. Some months later the 8C 2900 showed a different face, with three of them entered in the Mille Miglia race. It now had a sportier, less graceful appearance, with simplifed bodywork similar to that of the Grand Prix cars affectionately known as "botticellas" (little barrels). Its racing debut was sensational. The three cars involved won the trifecta at the 1936 Mille Miglia.

Now Alfa Romeo sought to create a version of the 8C 2900 more suitable for touring. This time the company entrusted the bodywork to Touring, which was located nearby in the Milan suburbs. Touring unveiled its first model at the Paris Salon in 1937. It was superb—and only the beginning of a range of sumptuous cars. Three weeks later the Spider arrived in Milan on a shortened wheelbase. The following year Touring showed the same Spider transposed to a lengthened chassis. These three Touring models formed a trilogy that have enjoyed lasting fame.

One of the luxurious short-chassis Spiders was awarded Best of Show at the Bagatelle concours in 1996. This celebrated car was built in 1937. Today it is California-based collector John Mozart who listens to the delicate music of its eight-cylinder engine.

168 Henri Chapron Delage D8-120 Cabriolet 1938

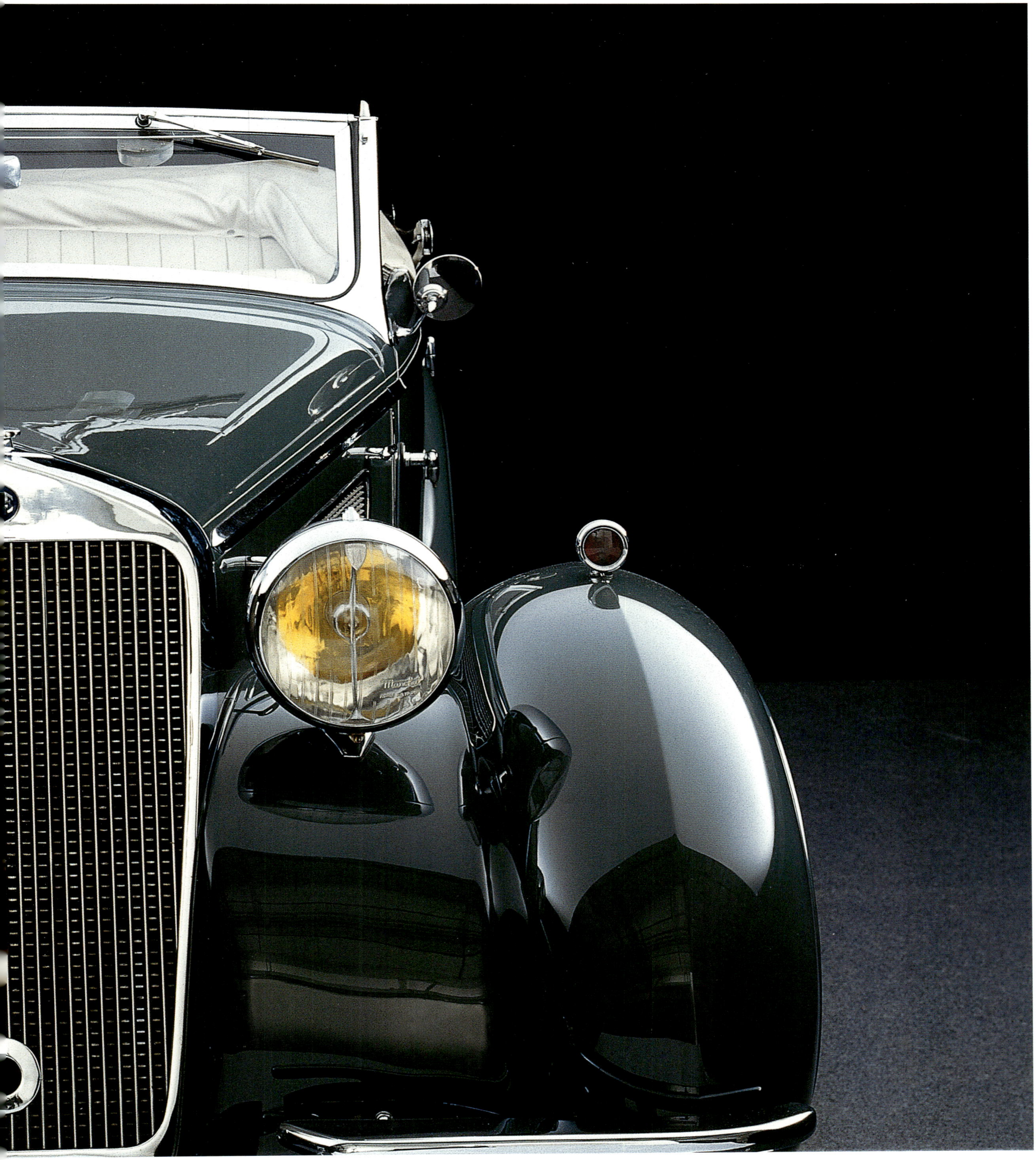

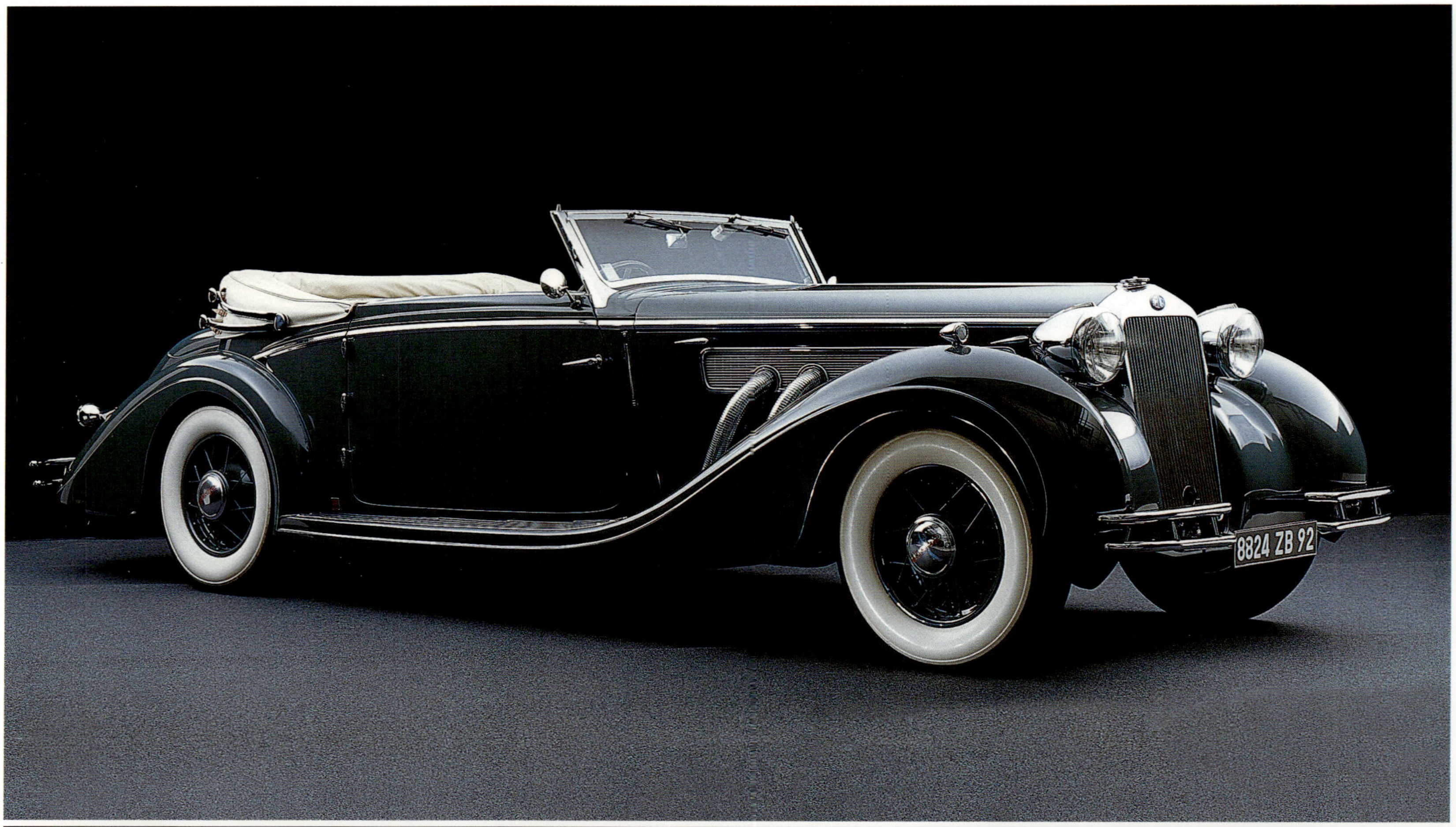
8824 ZB 92

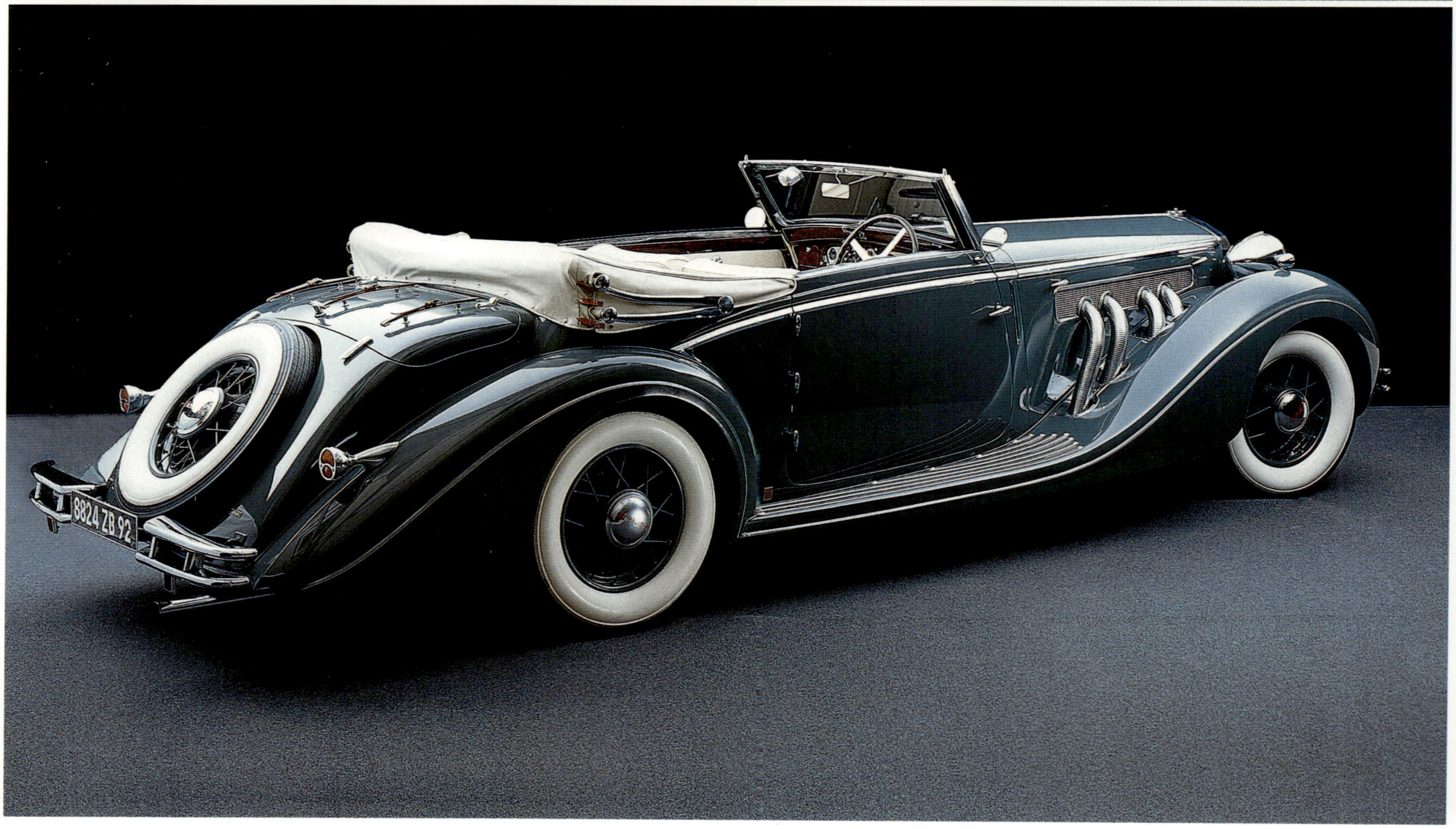
8824 ZB 92

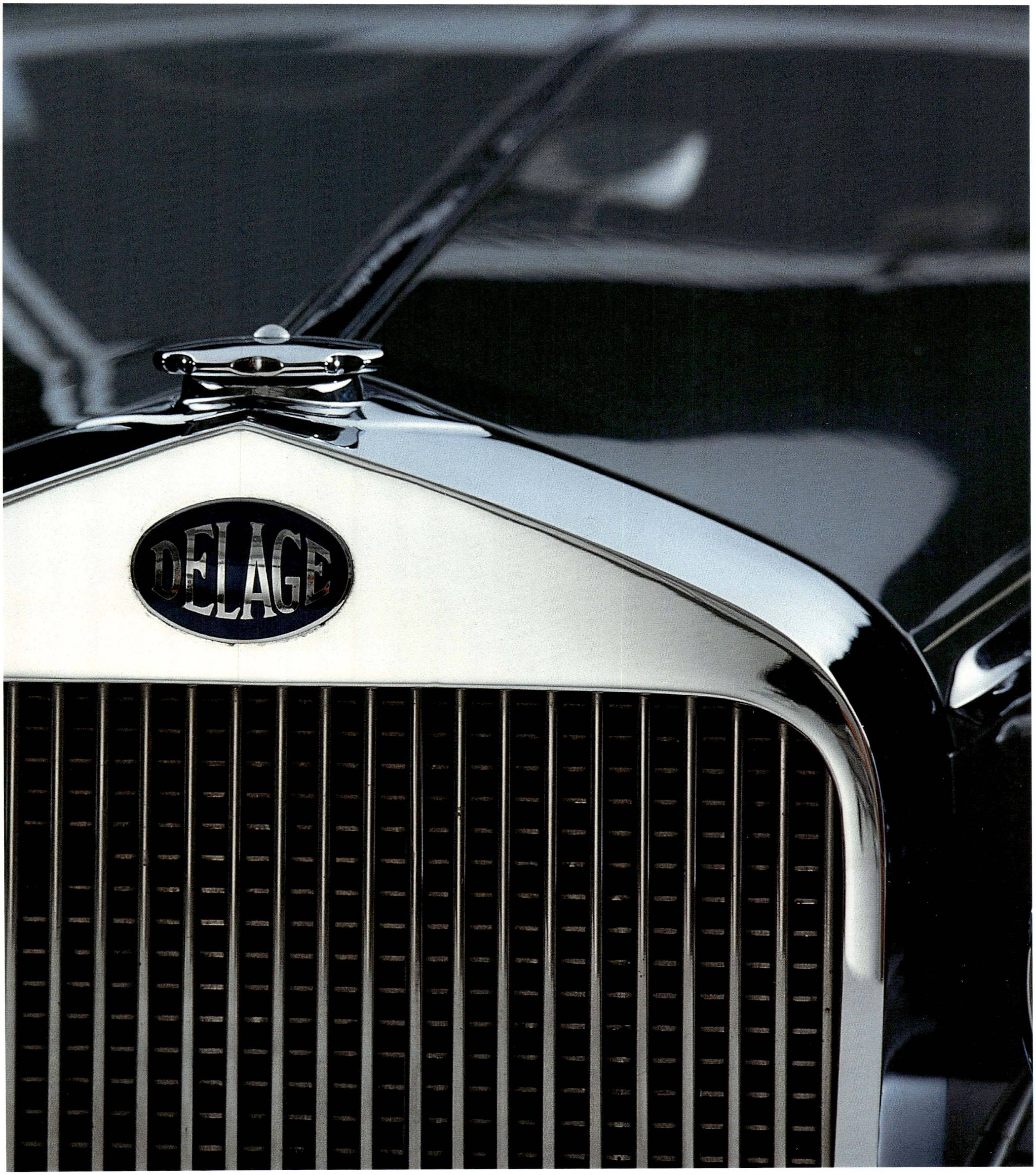
DELAGE

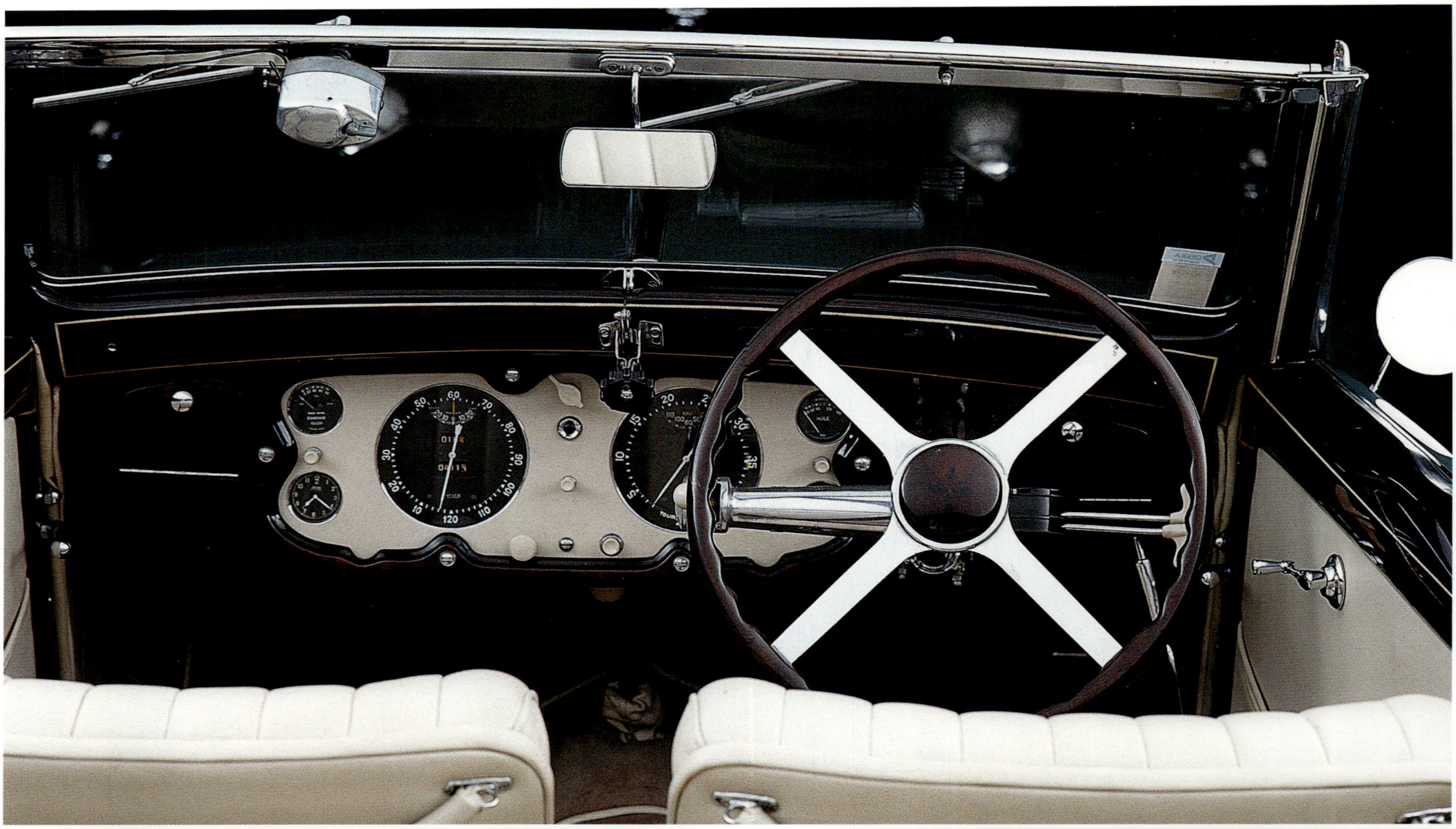

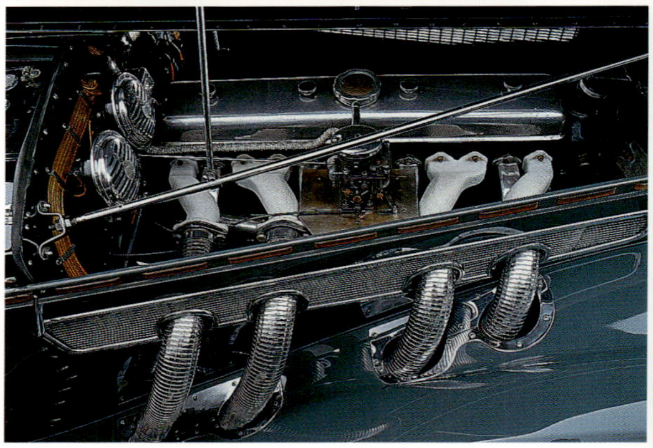

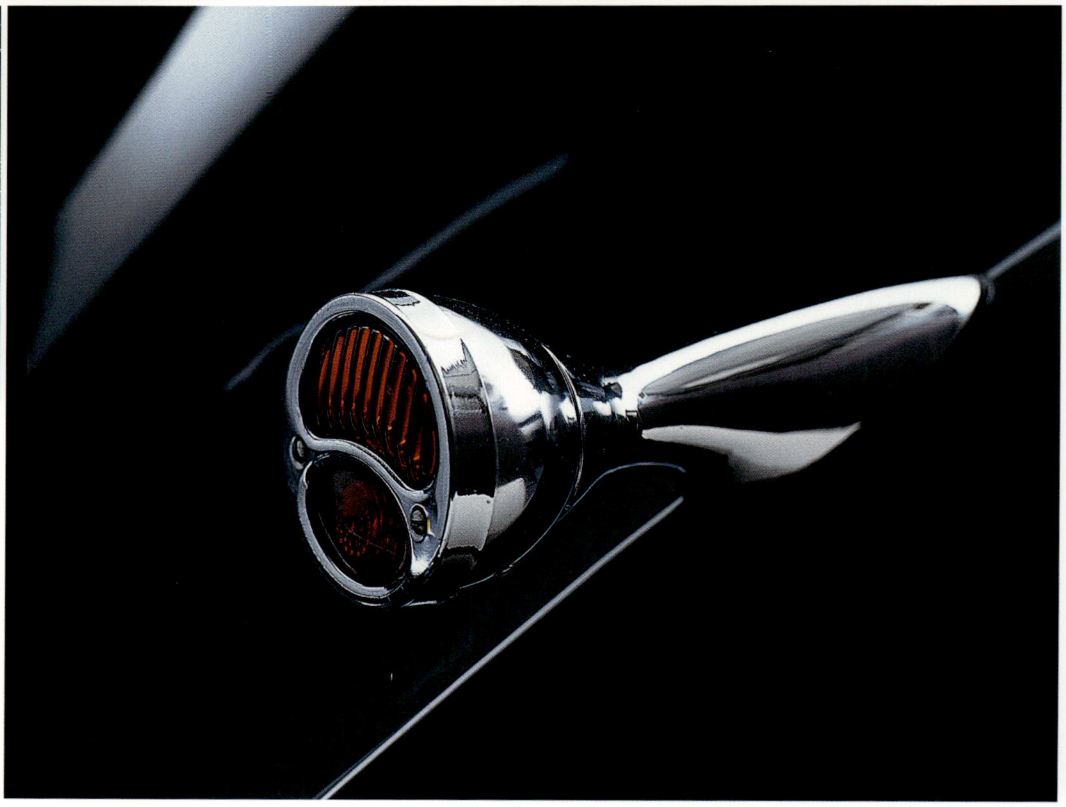

Henri Chapron's reputation relied first and foremost on his long and close collaboration with Delahaye. Henri Chapron also had a special partnership with Delage as a result of the mid-1930s merger of Delage and Delahaye. The companies worked together from the early 1930s until the 1950s and the end of automobiles' great prestige brands.

The same designs were used on Delage's and Delahaye's mechanical bases. For example, copies of this Delage convertible can be seen on the Delahaye 135 chassis. The more ambitious machinery of the Delage D8-120, propelled by a long, straight-8 engine, allowed for a more slender design.

Henri Chapron is the most highly respected representative of the neoclassicism in French automobiles that blossomed in the late 1930s. An elegant illustration of his work is the Delage D8-120 convertible.

Henri Chapron was never a fantasist. Since his workshops first opened, in Neuilly in 1919 and in Levallois-Perret in 1923, Henri Chapron made his reputation by producing well-made cars that were discreetly elegant and never ostentatious.

His name is still associated with a certain type of French good taste. He was never carried away by excesses of streamlining, ornamentation, or faux Americanism. He himself was a rather reserved, even austere character, but he did not reject the idea of luxury. In the early 1930s he tended to prefer the chassis found at LaSalle, Rolls-Royce, and especially Delage, which for a while was his exclusive partner.

Louis Delâge's eminently serious approach to manufacturing was perfectly suited to Henri Chapron's sober, distinguished, restrained style and contributed magnificently to its success. Henri Chapron mastered proportions and handled decoration with discretion; sometimes his products showed a British-style rigor. His success in Britain was therefore no accident, and he eagerly participated in the London Motor Show.

Classic lines and perfect balance did not rule out a few stylistic signatures. The motif underscoring the bodywork's profile, designed as always with care, played with the calligraphic swoops of the chrome strip running along the side panels.

With the large-bodied Delage D8-120, Henri Chapron illustrated his generous yet sleek style without resorting to decorative artifices of any kind. The version shown here was exhibited at the 1992 concours organized by *Automobiles Classiques* and Louis Vuitton.

174
Saoutchik
Delahaye 135 MS 1948

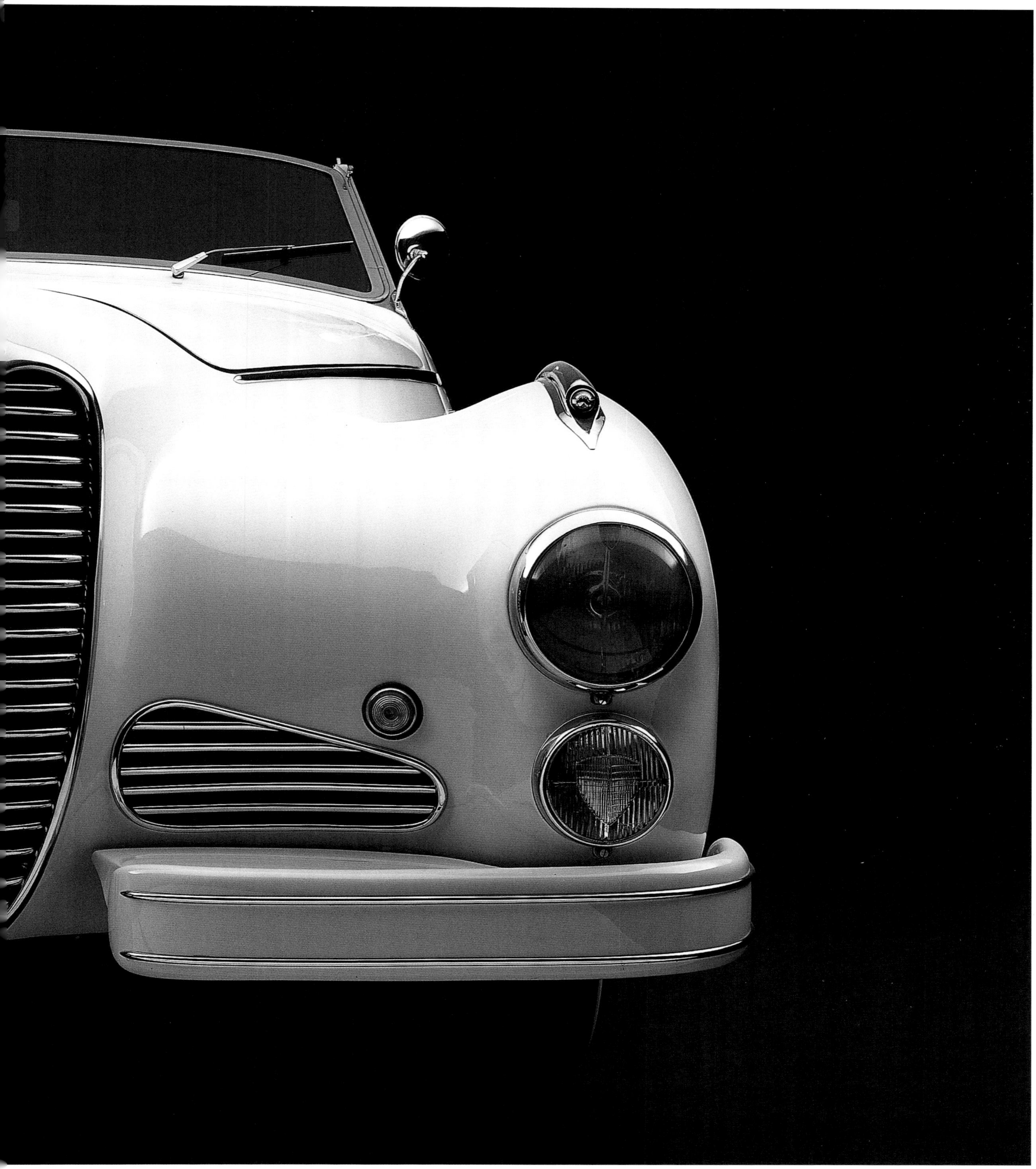

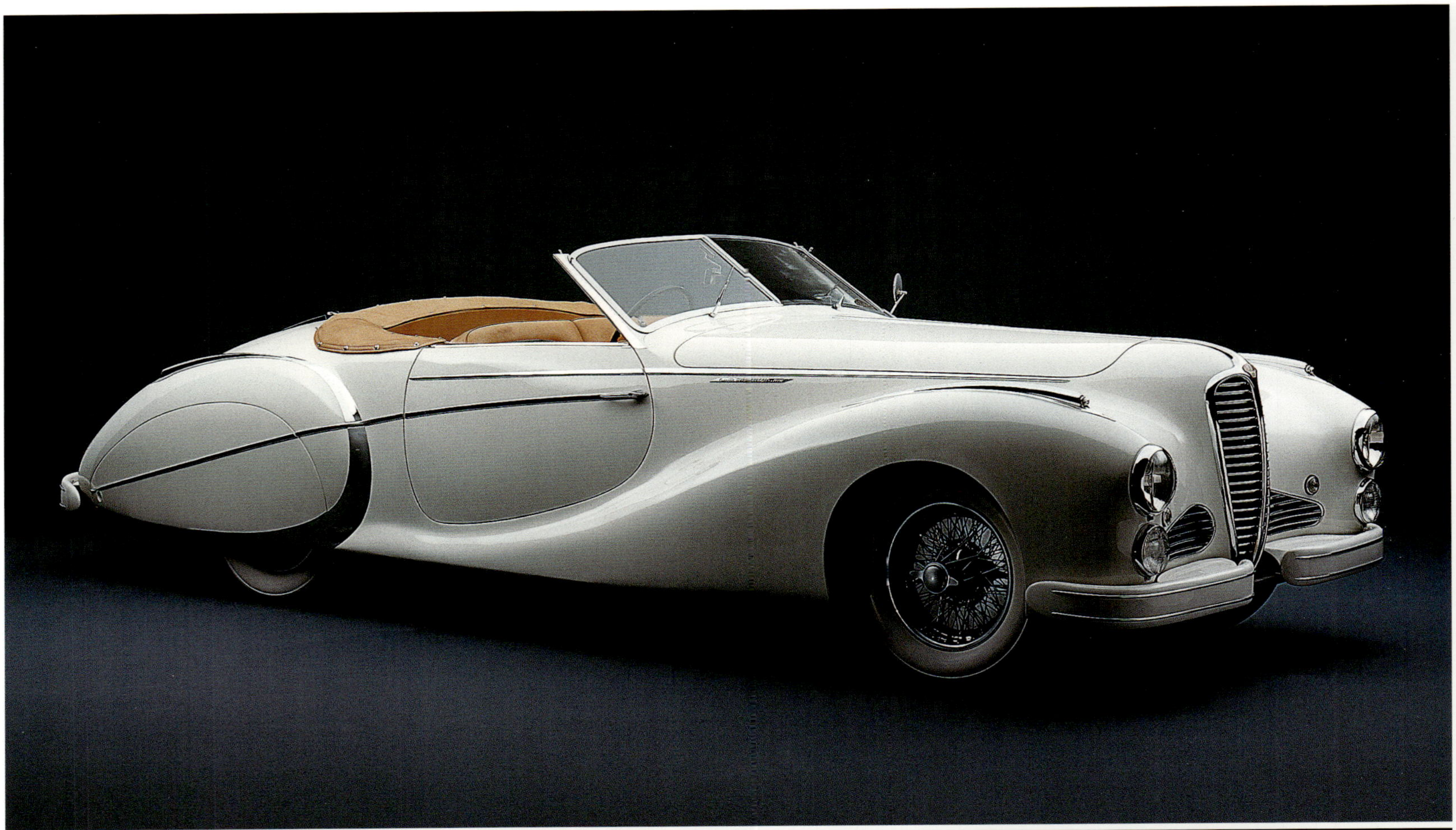

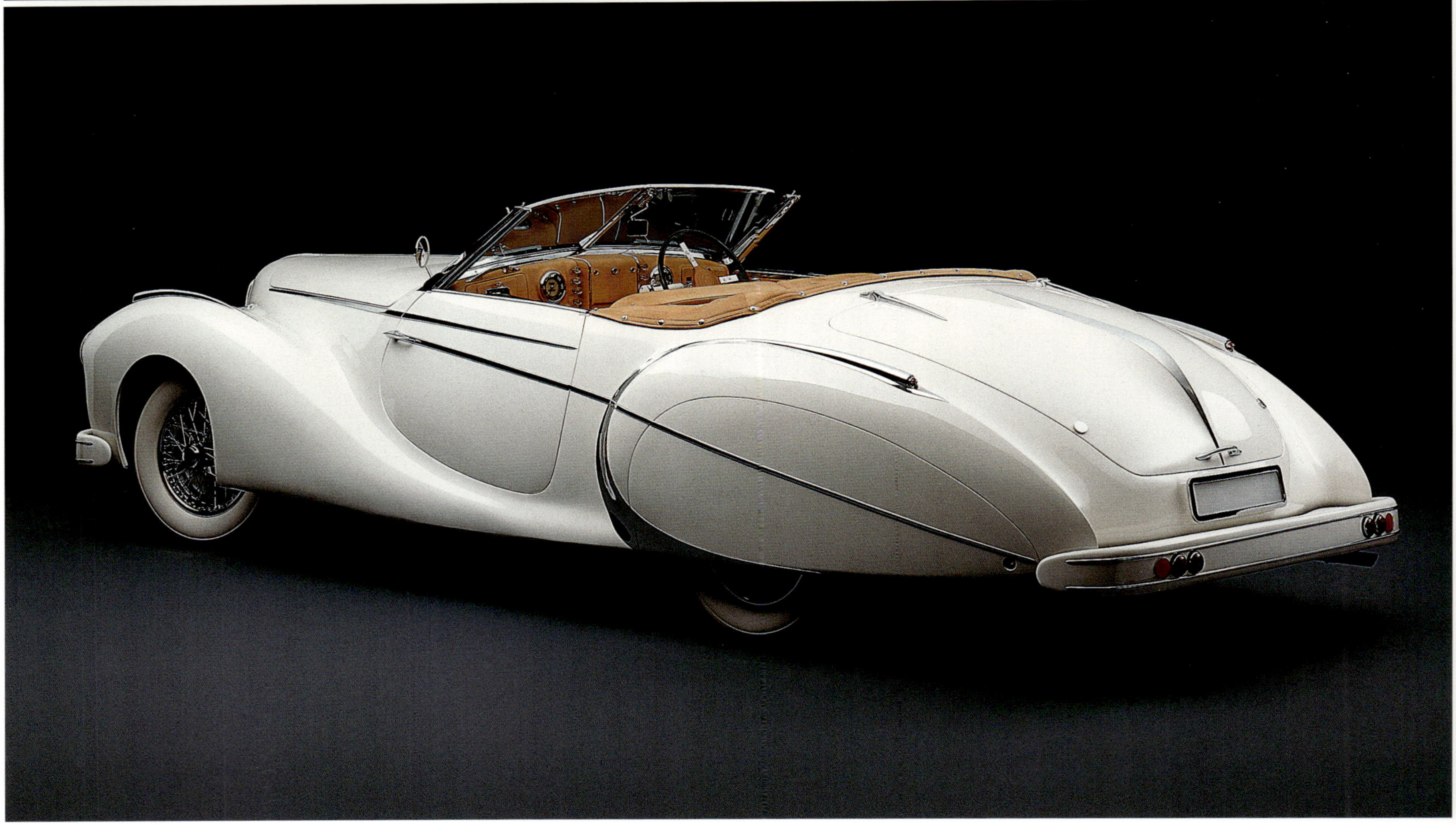

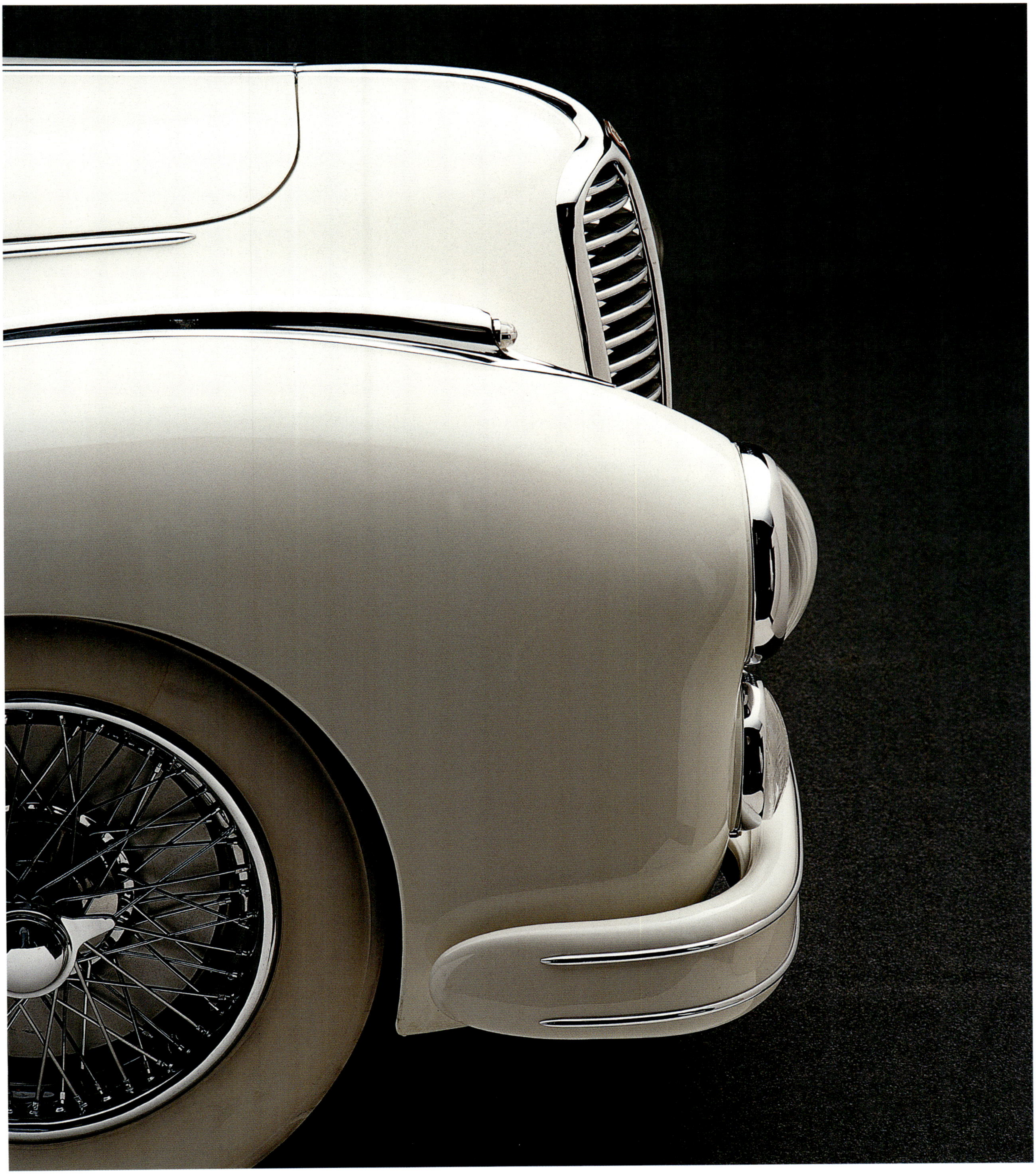

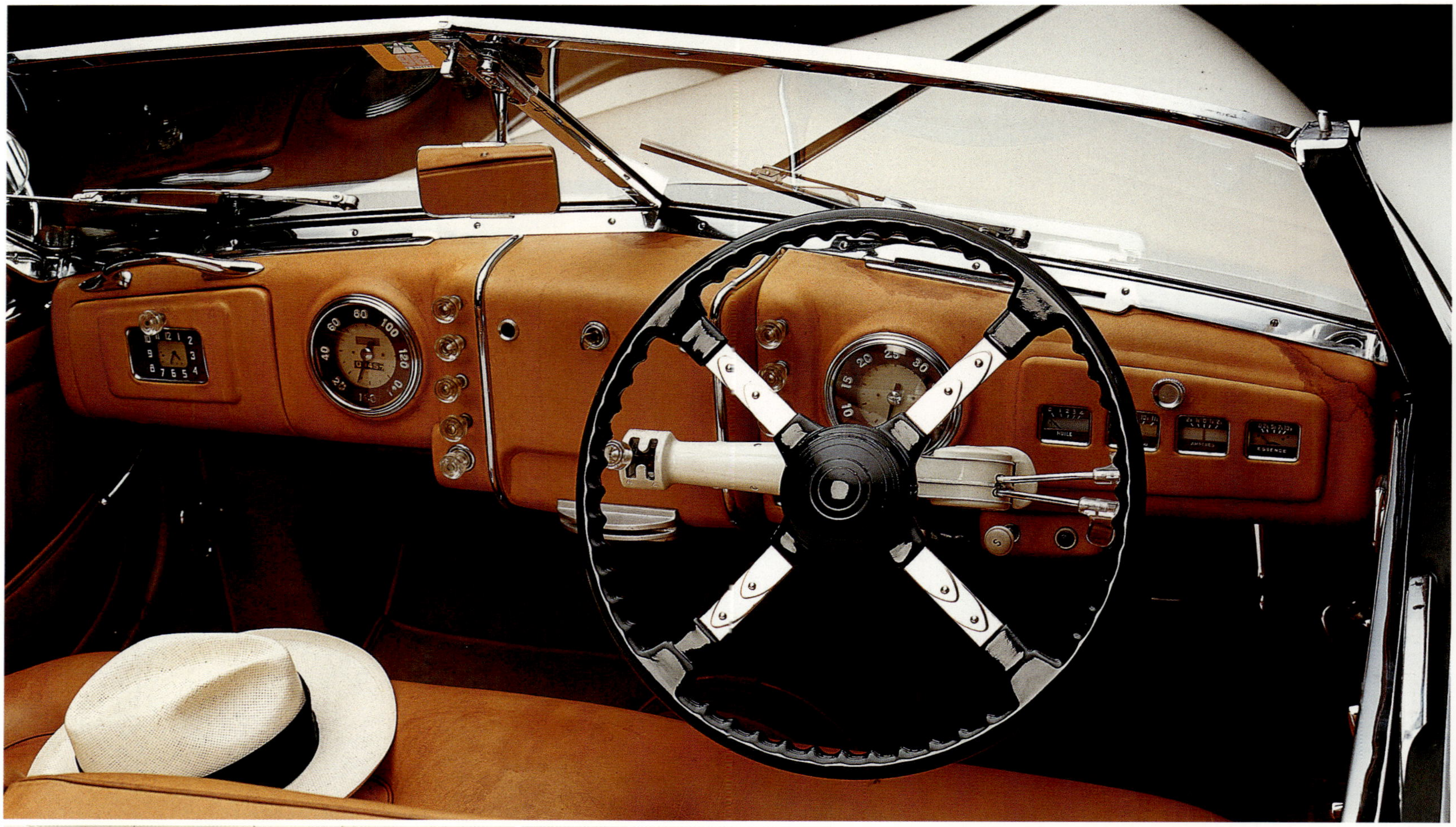

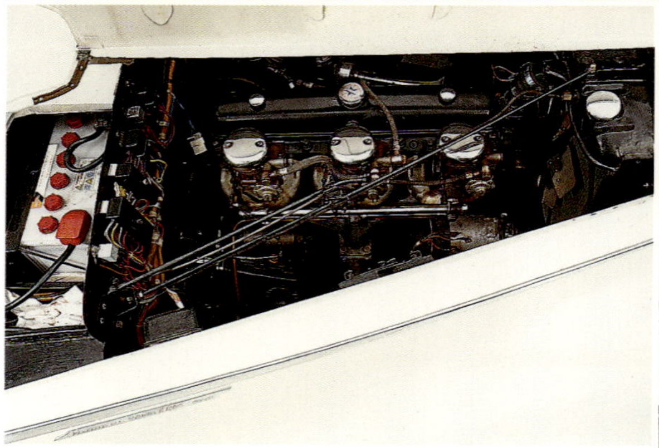

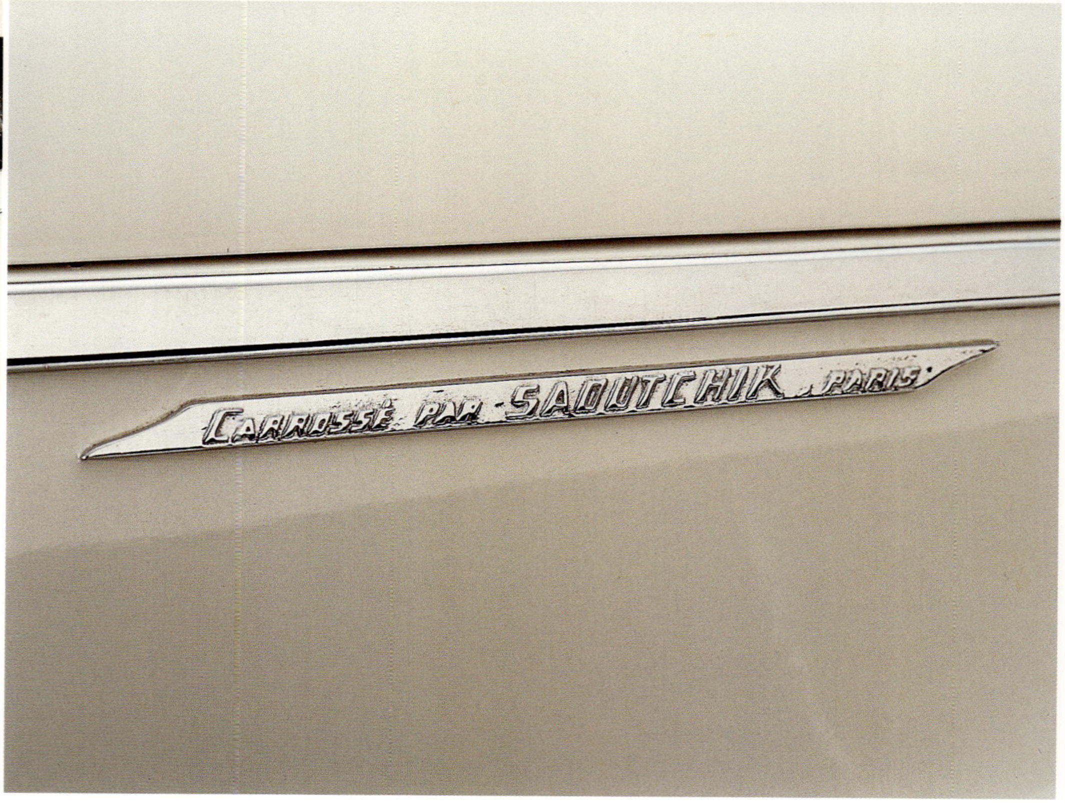
CARROSSÉ PAR SAOUTCHIK PARIS

Applied Arts

The great French auto-body makers began dying out after the Second World War. Unable to adapt to new economic circumstances, they continued clinging to traditional fabrication methods rather than follow the Italian-led evolution of style. Moreover, all the prestigious automakers ceased production of luxury cars: Bugatti in 1952, Delage in 1953, Hotchkiss and Delahaye in 1954, Salmson in 1956, and Talbot in 1960. Without their exceptional chassis to work on, the bodywork firms disappeared one by one.

Saoutchik's last creations were weighed down by heavy swirls of chrome and steel, a sort of desperate flamboyance.

The model 135 was a milestone in the history of Delahaye. There were many versions, but it reached its apotheosis just after the Second World War in the flamboyant creations of Saoutchik.

The model 135 completely changed Delahaye's fortunes. With it Delahaye joined the elite of the French automobile industry, taking a place alongside Bugatti, Delage, and Talbot.

The Delahaye 135 had an extra panache that allowed for its development as a sports car. It was one of the most versatile cars in history, capable of winning the Monte Carlo Rally and dominating the Le Mans Twenty-Four Hour Race as well as shining at various concours d'elegance. Even after the Second World War, ten years after its creation, the 135 was the foundation of the Delahaye catalogue. Sooner or later all the French auto-body makers lent their talents to the machine: Henri Chapron, Guilloré, Figoni & Falaschi, Antem, Dubos, Letourneur & Marchand, Saoutchik. It was the last of these that dreamed up the most stunning designs.

Jacques Saoutchik was based in Neuilly-sur-Seine but of Ukrainian origin, and he gave free rein to his Slavic soulfulness and exuberance. A refined man who cared about luxury and respected tradition, he injected his sense of sophistication under heavy swirls of chrome and steel. Saoutchik was perhaps the most immoderate participant in the postwar feast of extravagance and ornamentation in bodywork. His designs were extremely elaborate, with exaggerated volumes and an overabundance of decoration, but they exude a sort of touching, desperate flamboyance.

Even as the Italians were moving toward a cleaner, lighter style, French auto-body makers seemed to indulge in self-parody. Saoutchik was the undisputed master of the baroque movement, but his style was synonymous with panache. He was responsible for several memorable creations based on the Delahaye 135 M chassis, notably the convertible shown by a Swiss collector at the 1991 Bagatelle concours.

180
Facel-Métallon Bentley Mark VI 1951

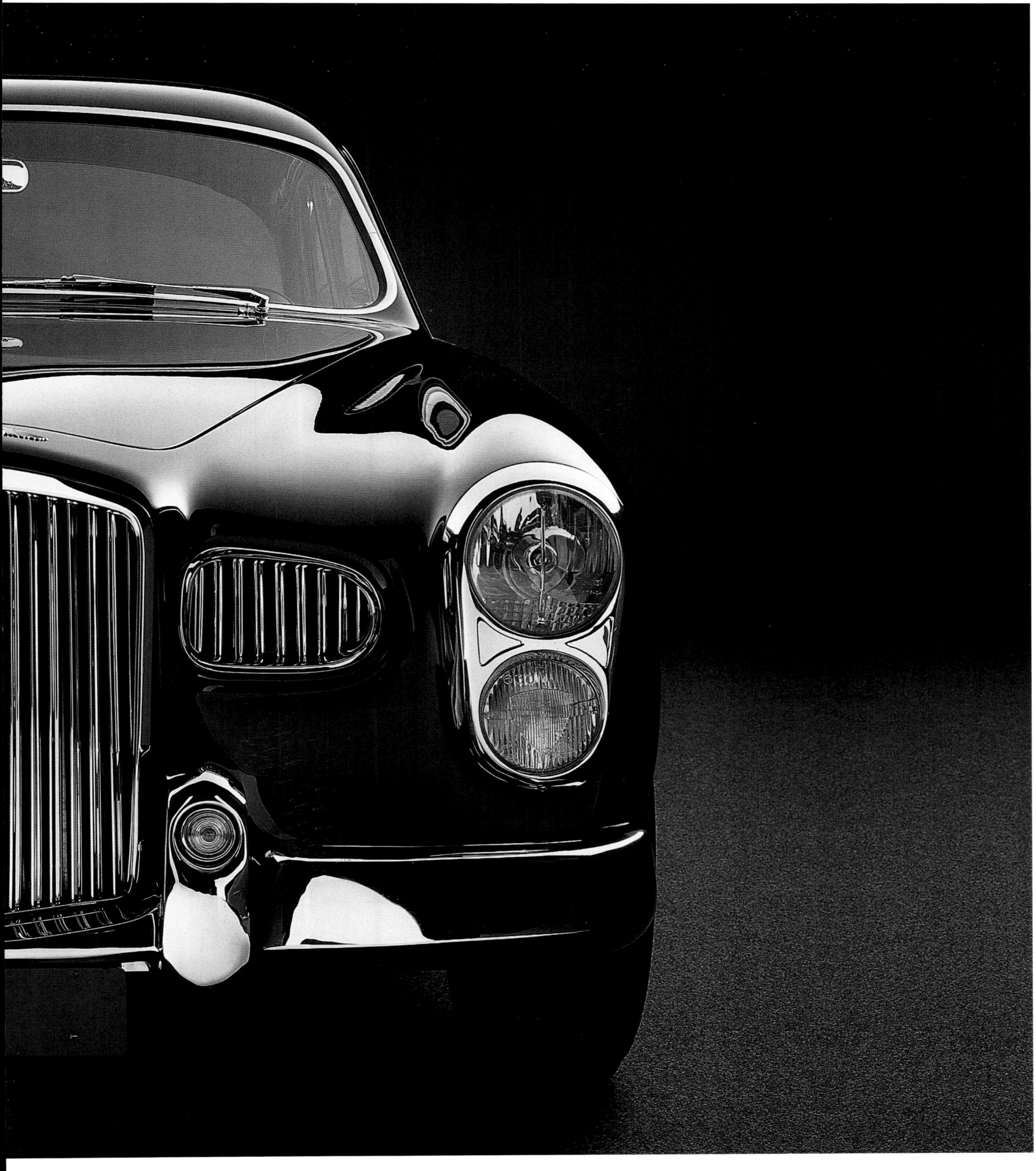

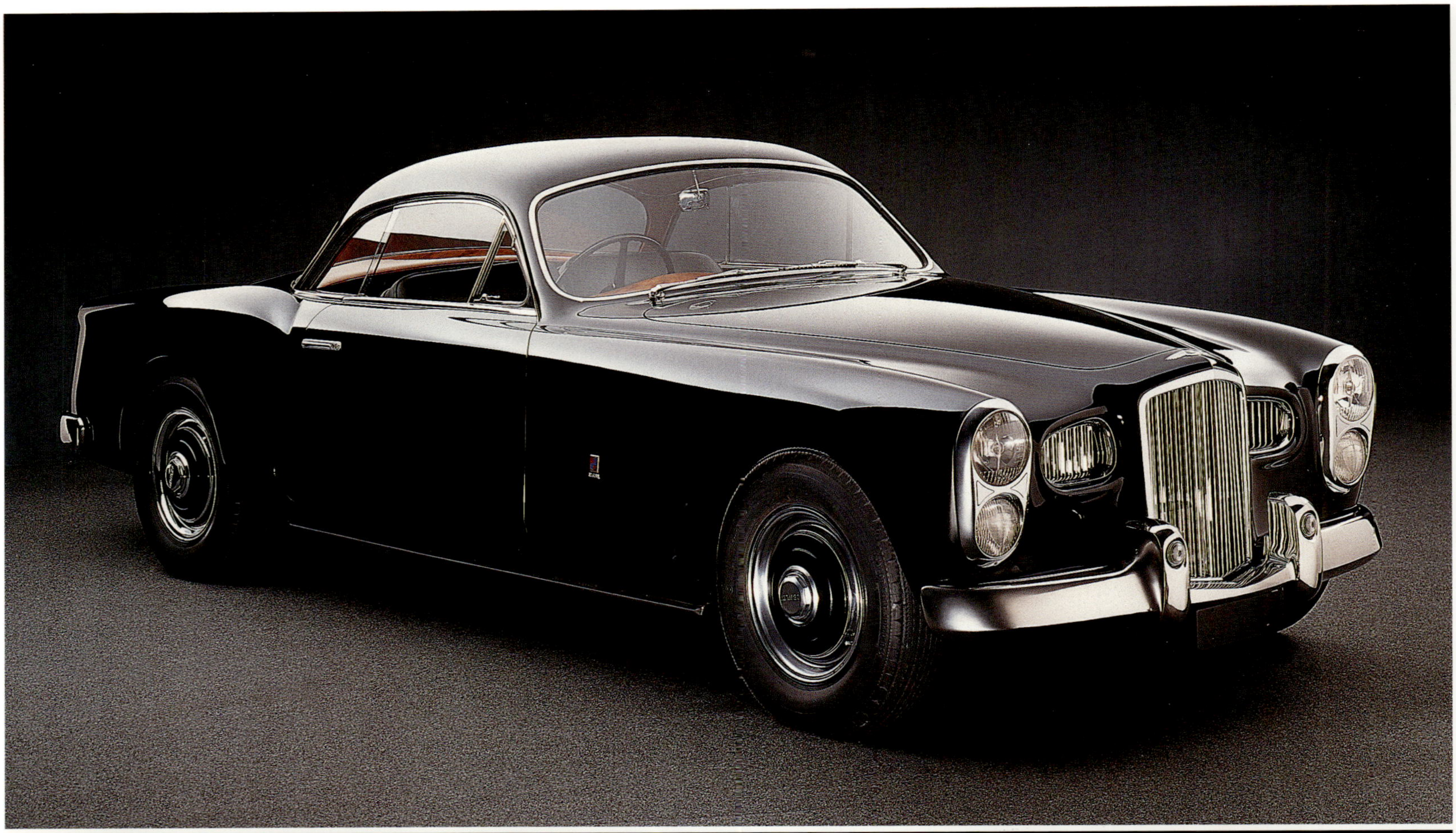

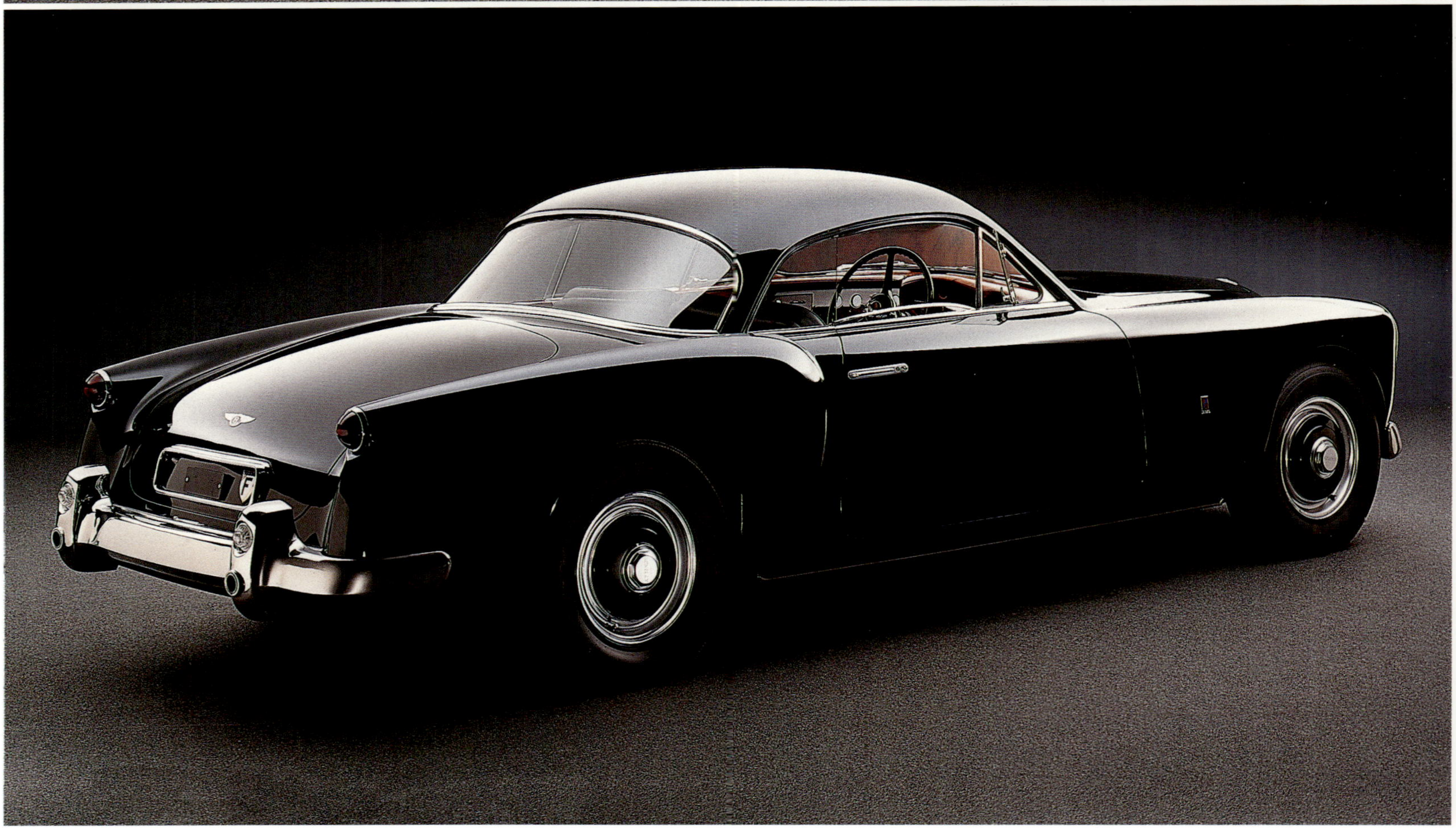

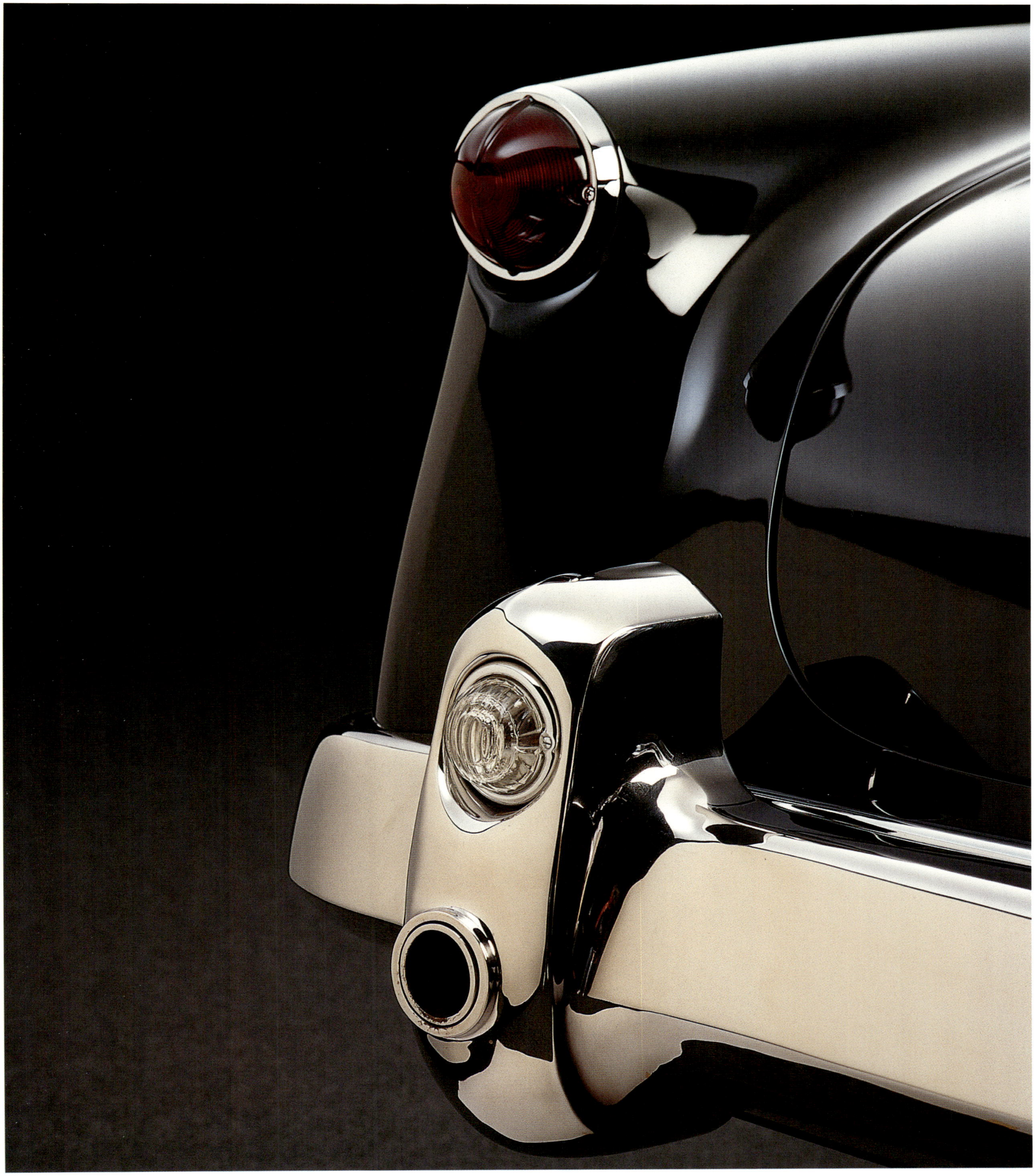

FACEL PARIS

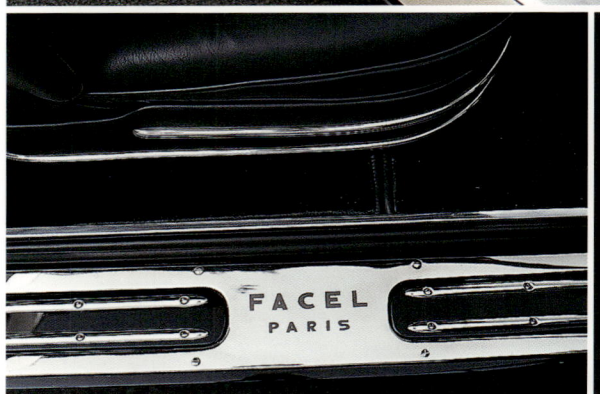

An act of lèse-majesté! This Bentley was designed not by a British firm but by a French one, Facel-Métallon, a commercial auto-body maker run by Jean Daninos before the launch of Facel-Véga. The sleek lines of the Bentley Special foreshadowed those of the Facel-Véga cars—luxury automobiles that Daninos intended to revive the art of French bodywork. This Bentley's Latin style was a departure from the stiff, often outmoded forms most British companies designed at the time.

The Bentley's front end simultaneously referenced the Bentley brand's formality and presaged the Facel-Véga FVS, which came out three years later.

Even as the most prestigious French automakers were slowly dying out, a new star suddenly shone in the firmament of the French automobile industry. This forward-looking Bentley was a harbinger of the Facel-Véga.

Jean Daninos, brother of the novelist Pierre Daninos, inscribed his name in the history of the French automobile industry as author of the Facel-Véga, though his prior achievements, less well known, were equally brilliant.

Jean Daninos began in the bodywork department at Citroën in 1928. In December 1939 he founded FACEL, an acronym for Forges et Ateliers de Construction d'Eure-et-Loir (Ironworks and Construction Workshops of Eure-et-Loir), in Dreux. A merger with Métallon in August 1945 resulted in the Facel-Métallon Company. Following the Second World War the business responded to large automakers' demand for subcontractors to manufacture their bodywork. Facel-Métallon went on to produce auto bodies for firms such as Panhard, Delahaye, Ford, and Simca. For the last two, however, Facel-Métallon offered another aspect of its expertise and designed the bodywork itself.

Jean Daninos demonstrated his talent by designing several special auto bodies for Bentley. These were initially manufactured by Pinin Farina in Italy but were then produced entirely by Facel-Métallon. At the 1951 Paris Salon visitors admired a Bentley Mark VI designed and manufactured by Facel-Métallon.

The style harmoniously fused Latin taste and a bit of American influence. With its tight, sleek lines, the Bentley bore an indisputable resemblance to the Ford Comet, which appeared at the same Salon, and the Simca 9 Sport, which came out the following year. It also clearly foreshadowed Jean Daninos's Facel-Véga FVS, which would be presented in July 1954: The front of the Bentley already conveyed the FVS's personality, with its vertical radiator grill flanked by two horizontal air inlets and two double headlights set in a casing.

186
Pinin
Farina
Maserati
Sport
2000
1954

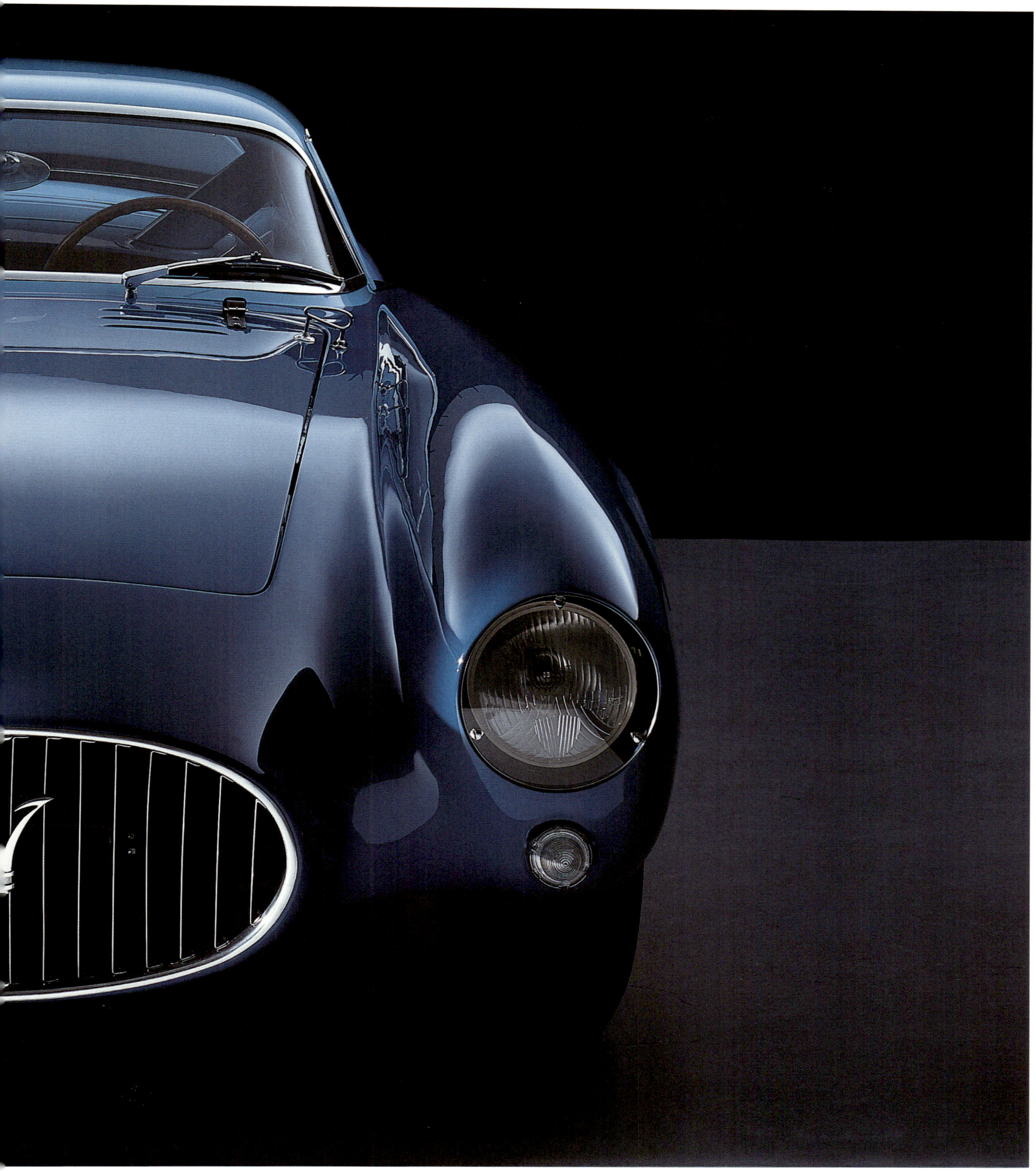

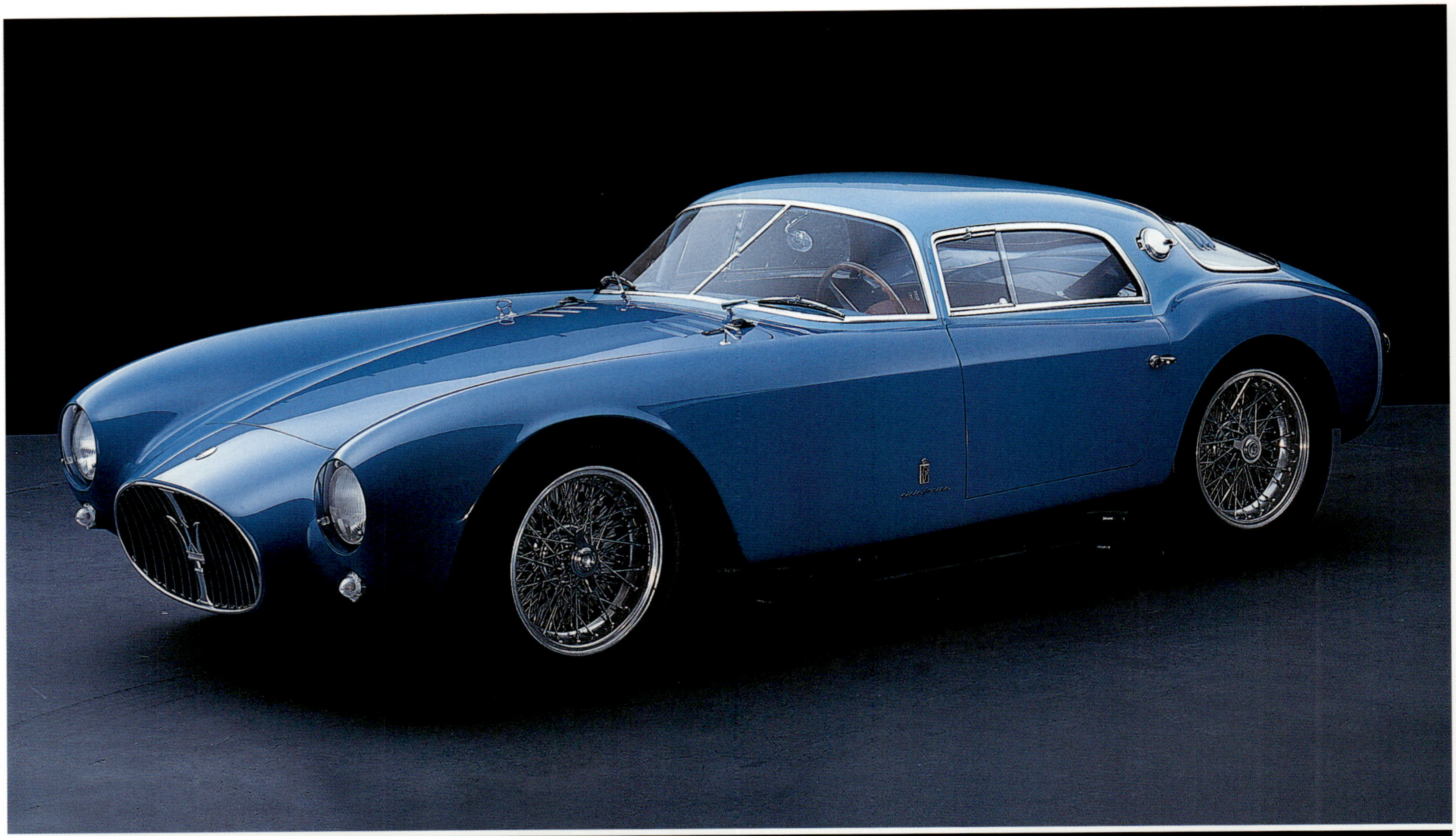

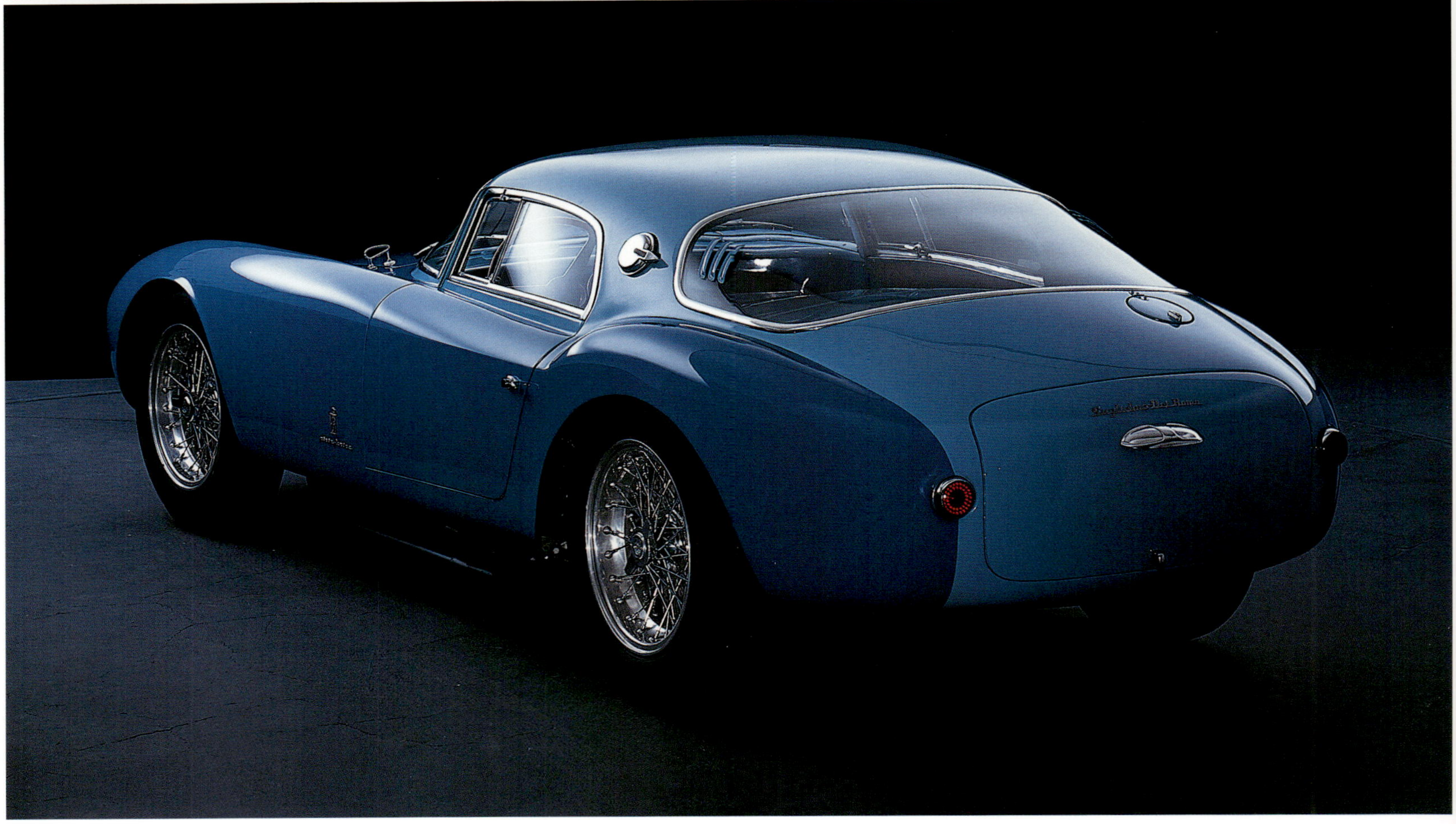

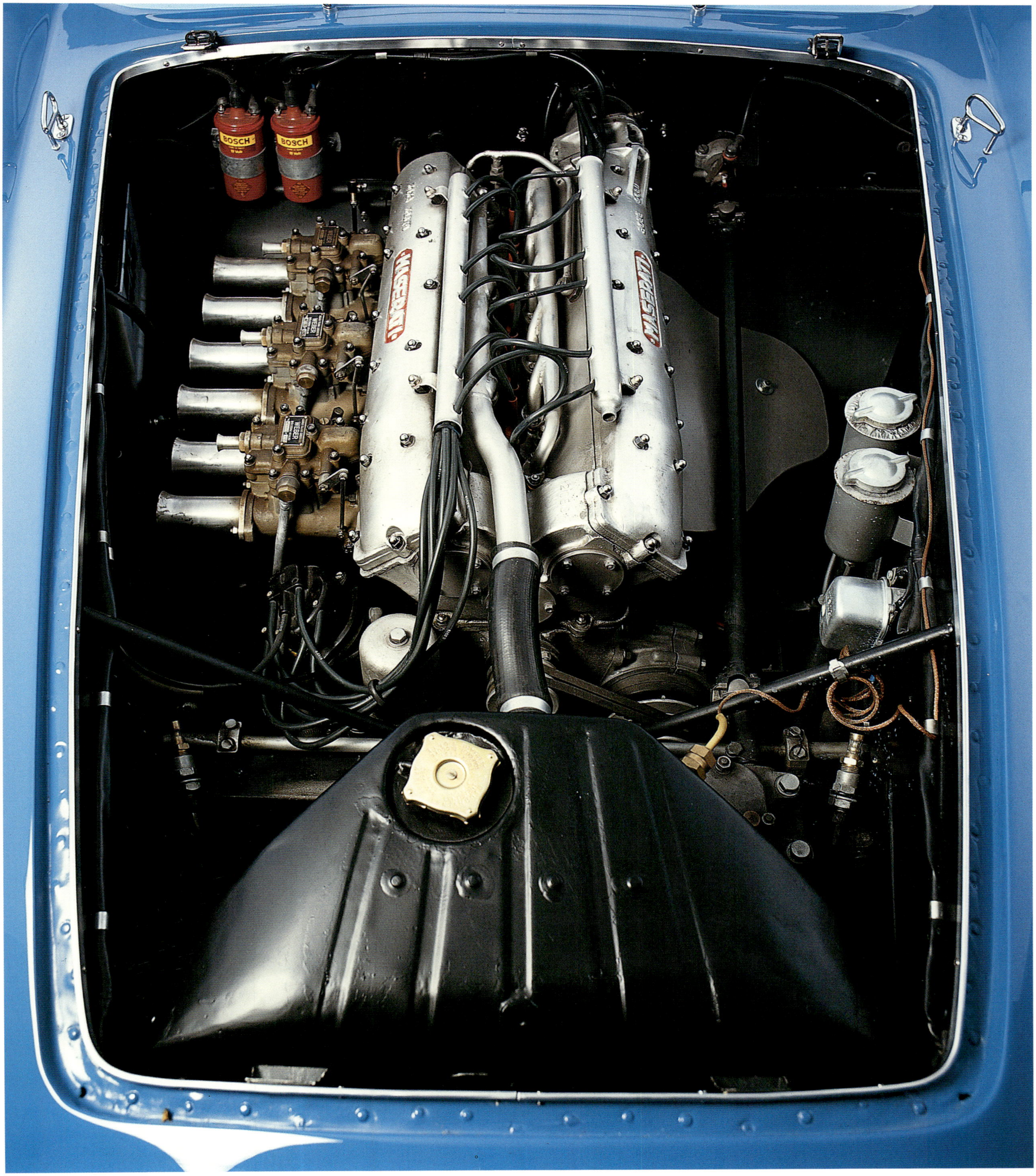
BOSCH
BOSCH
MASERATI
MASERATI
WEBER

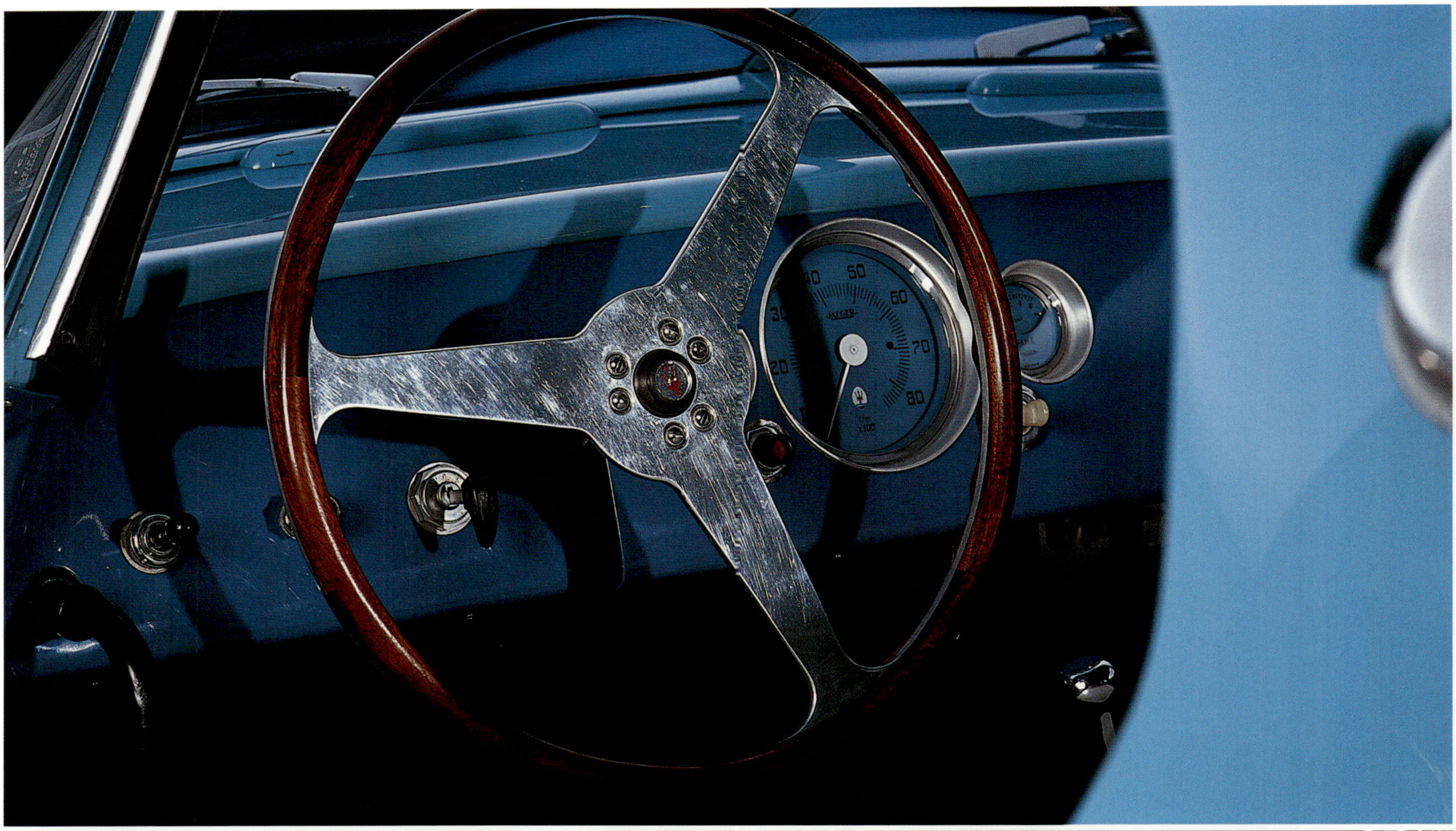
20 30 40 50 60 70 80

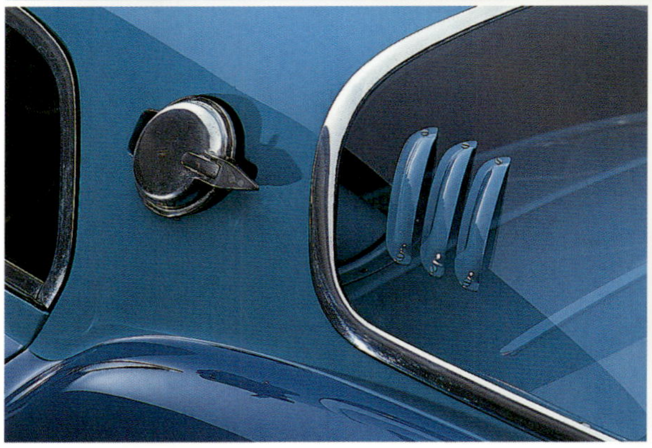

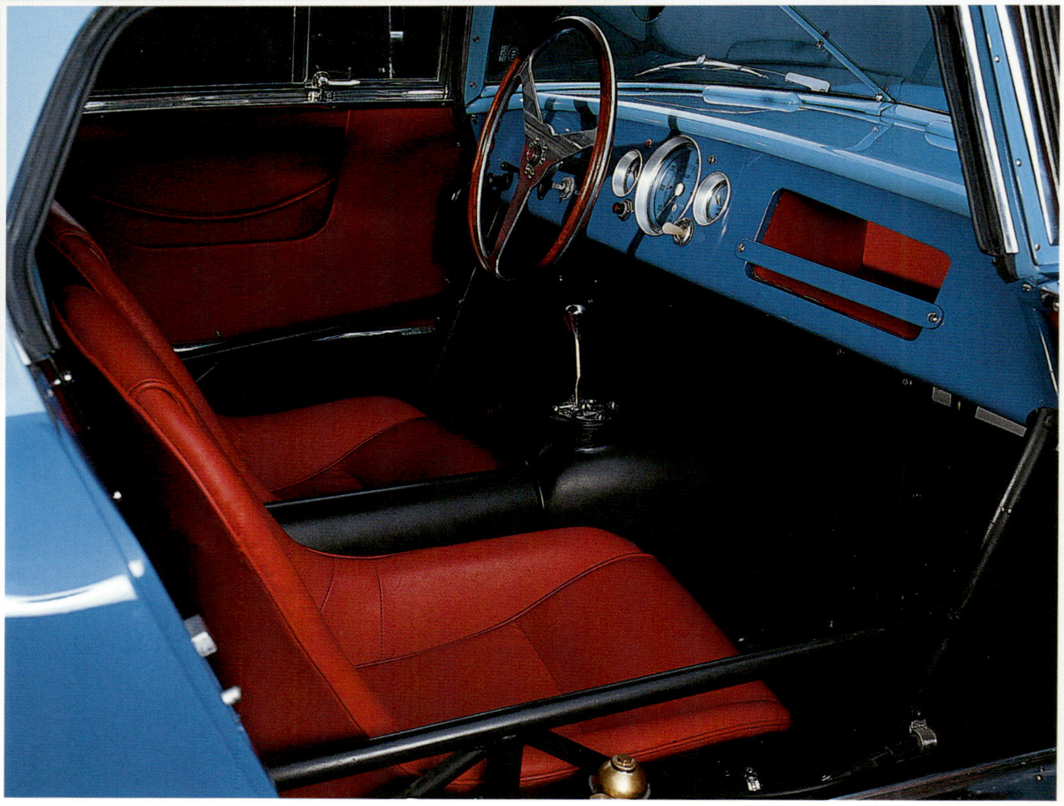

Applied Arts

Founded in 1930 by Battista Farina, Pinin Farina (written as one word from 1961 on) was one of the most highly reputed auto-body makers in operation in the 1950s.

The firm began a regular and fruitful collaboration with Ferrari in 1952 and a few years later with Peugeot, but much more rarely worked on Maserati chassis. Pinin Farina's Maserati creations include this 2000 berlinetta, one of four cars developed for the Type A6G CS, which was intended for racng but was transformed into a Gran Turismo vehicle. After a meticulous restoration, this car (chassis no. 2057) was repainted in the two colors it had sported at the 1954 Turin auto show.

It can be difficult to resist turning a marvelous racing car into a Gran Turismo car. Pinin Farina yielded to this temptation and created a berlinetta based on the Maserati Sport 2000.

A racing car makes an ideal basis for a Gran Tourismo car, or so goes the conventional wisdom. That was the rationale that tempted Pinin Farina to convert the Maserati Sport 2000 barchetta (Type A6 GCS) into a more general-purpose car. The short wheelbase, large wheels, and long hood containing a straight-6 engine made it seem like a logical, attractive choice. It just took the talent of Pinin Farina and its designer, Aldo Brovarone, to turn the dream into reality.

Aldo Brovarone began working for the Turin-based firm in 1953, when he was twenty-seven. Transforming a Maserati barchetta into a berlinetta was one of his first assignments. The young designer embarked on an exceptional work, exaggerating the proportions of the car, coming up with a very small cockpit, and pressing it onto a body whose tight, simple lines nestled between fenders as muscular as the haunches and shoulders of a big cat. The front was superb, with its oval radiator grill looking like a hungry mouth. Skimming over the asphalt, the greedy muzzle seemed to belong to a Formula 1 machine.

Although it was a great success aesthetically, this closed body adaptation of the Maserati Sport 2000 was not easy to live with; it was as impractical to use as it was sumptuous to look at. In fact, two of the four berlinettas built by Pinin Farina underwent major alterations to make life on board easier. Among the changes was a return to an open body, a style that was definitely more Spartan but better ventilated.

The car shown here, which was exhibited at the 1954 Turin auto show, was one of the two berlinettas that had been rebodied. However, the original bodywork of this extremely rare piece had such artistic appeal that owner Franco Lombardi decided to restore its original form and two shades of blue, which is how it was shown at the 1999 Bagatelle concours.

192
Bertone
Alfa Romeo
2000
Sportiva
1954

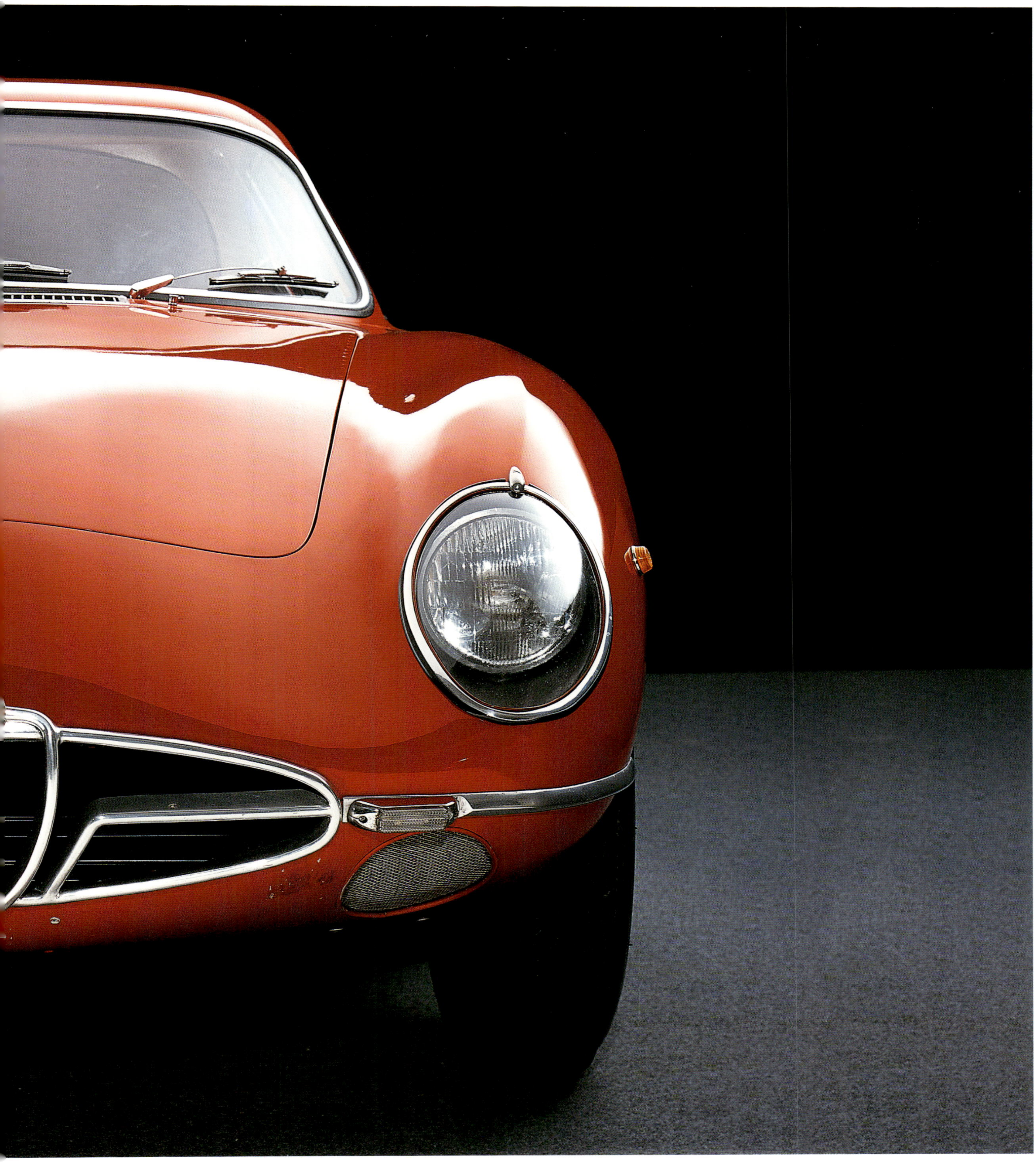

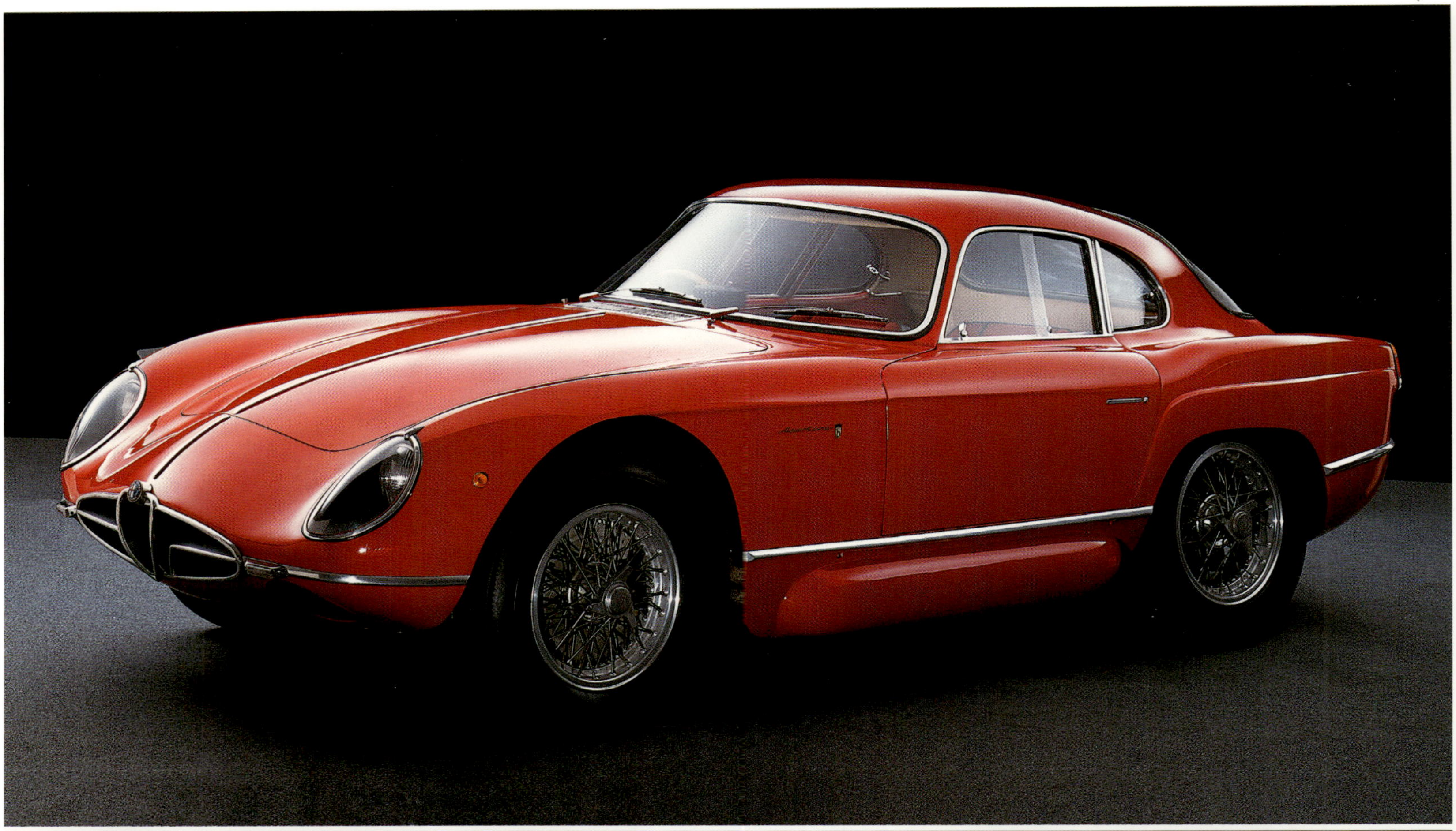

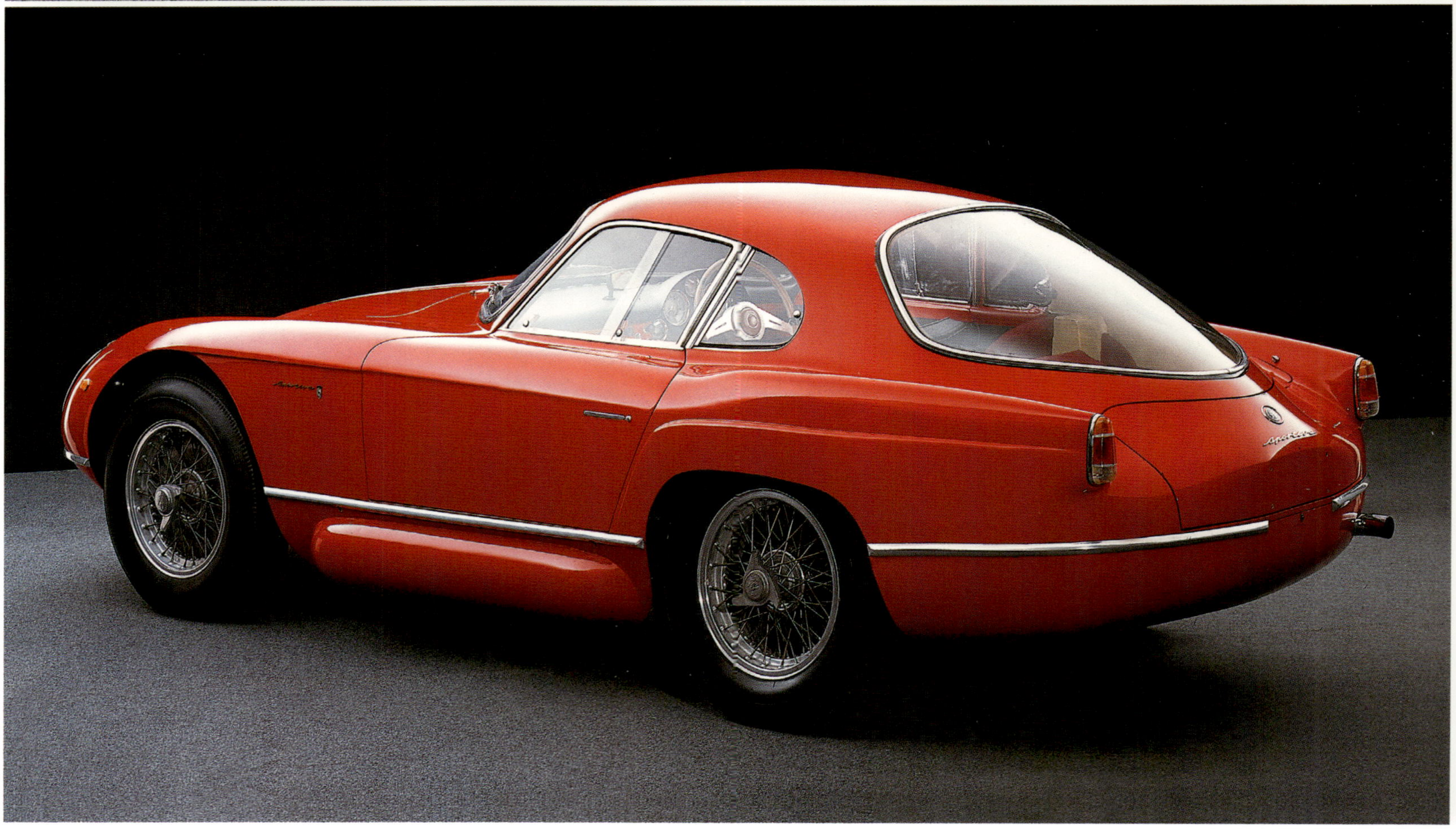

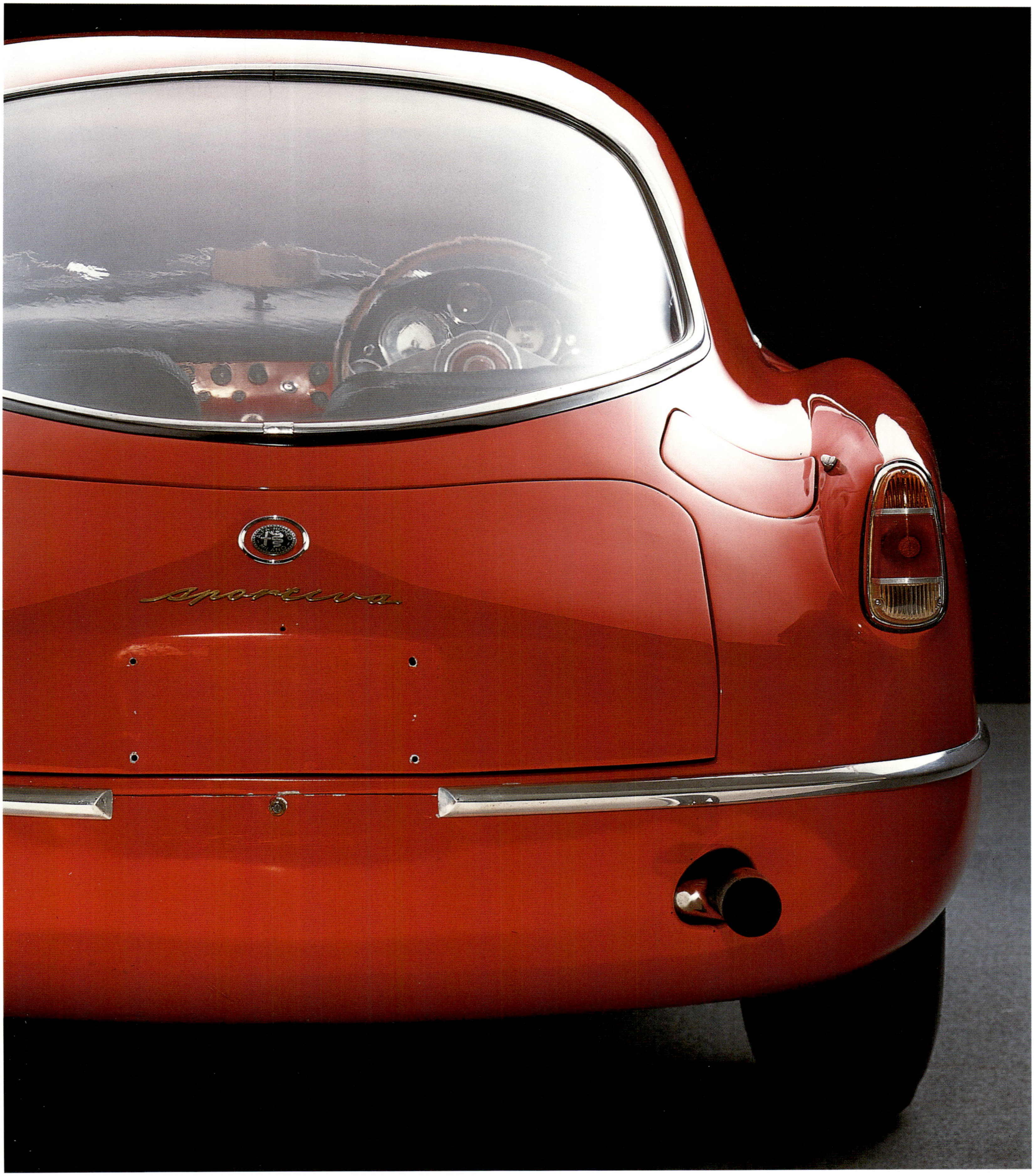
Sportiva

Alfa Romeo
OLIO
WEBER

ALFA ROMEO
MILANO
sportiva

BENZINA
TEMP ACQUA

In 1954 Bertone produced several prototypes for Alfa Romeo: a sports car and two berlinettas, one of which, shown here, has been preserved by a private collector. These cars were intended to transpose the sporty qualities of Alfa Romeo racing cars to a Gran Turismo model and were built on cutting-edge machinery. With the name Sportiva, they were propelled by a fine four-cylinder engine.

In the end Alfa Romeo found these slender, superb cars too costly for mass production. The Milanese firm opted instead for a more affordable model, the Giulietta Sprint. Though more modest, it retained the Sportiva's style, created by designer Franco Scaglione.

A superb rough draft for the Alfa Romeo Giulietta Sprint, the Sportiva reveals the mastery and the brio of designer Franco Scaglione, one of those who left a lasting imprint on the style of Bertone bodywork.

After the Second World War Nuccio Bertone gradually took over the business his father had founded in 1912, when the company built its first auto body for an SPA chassis. Nuccio Bertone gave his brand a different feel by working with new types of chassis, moving out of the craft sector, and assuming a more commercial dimension. Faced with intensifying competition, the Italian auto-body makers called on a new generation of designers with a deeply individual style: Francesco Martinengo at Pinin Farina, Federico Formenti at Touring, Mario Savonuzzi at Ghia, and Franco Scaglione at Bertone.

With Scaglione Bertone entered new phases of creativity and production. A secretive, mysterious figure, Franco Scaglione was one of the major designers of the 1950s. The Turin-based Bertone had been characterized by conservative styles until the early 1950s, but Scaglione infused it with a more radical, original look. The designs were disconcerting, avant-garde, lyrical, and streamlined. At the same time Bertone expanded its manufacturing business with subcontracting work for automakers.

The Alfa Romeo Sportiva, which was unveiled at the Turin auto show in April 1954, was a magnificent berlinetta that would inspire the Giulietta Sprint. Its lines were supple, strong, and feline. The front of the car was typical of the make, with its central nose cone and streamlined headlights. The passenger compartment was well lit by wraparound windows.

Alfa Romeo produced three 2000 Sportivas, one sports model and two berlinettas. One of the berlinettas, which the manufacturer stored at Arese, was displayed at Bagatelle; the other, shown here, belongs to a Swiss collector.

198 Scaglietti Ferrari 375 MM 1956

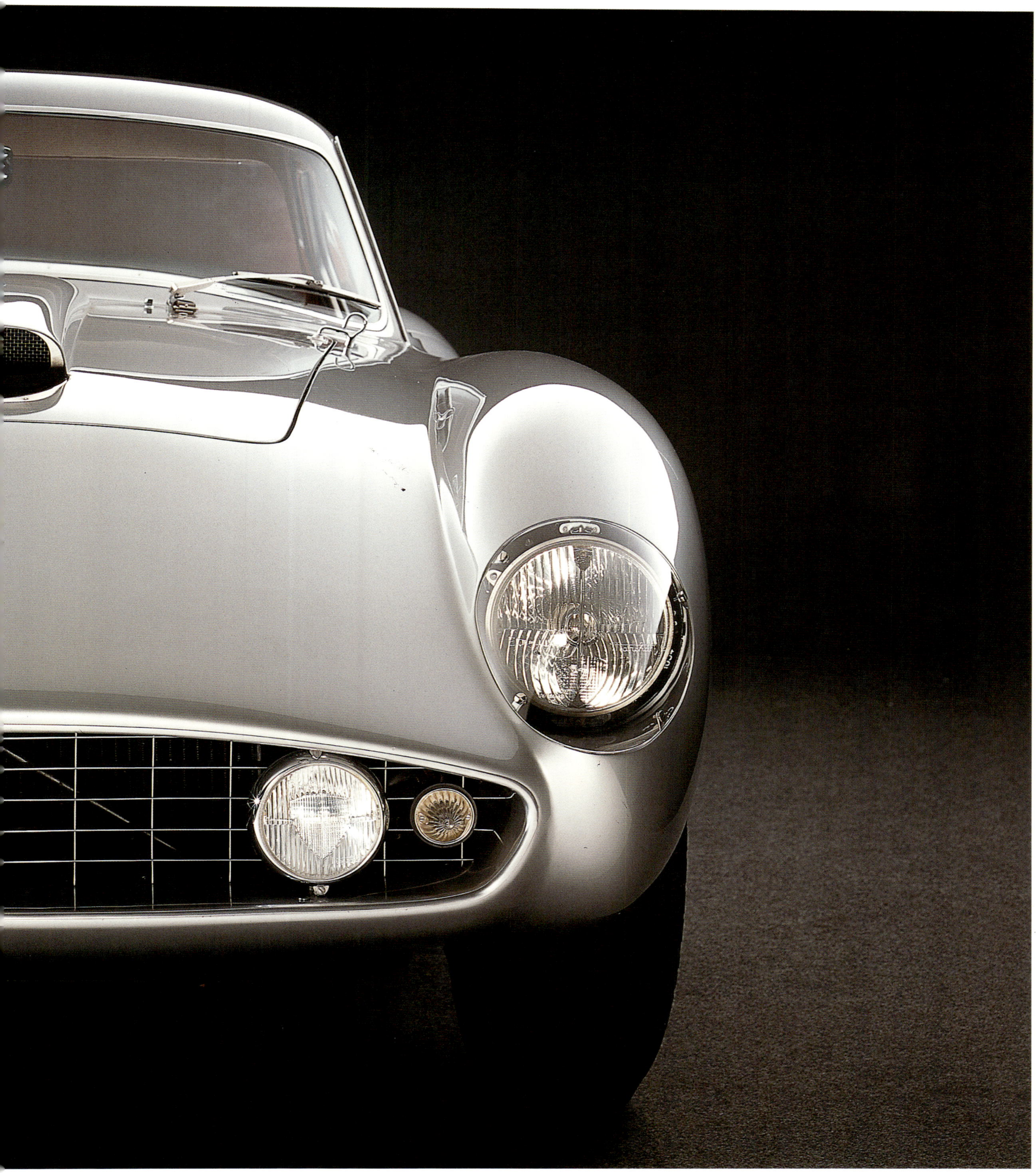

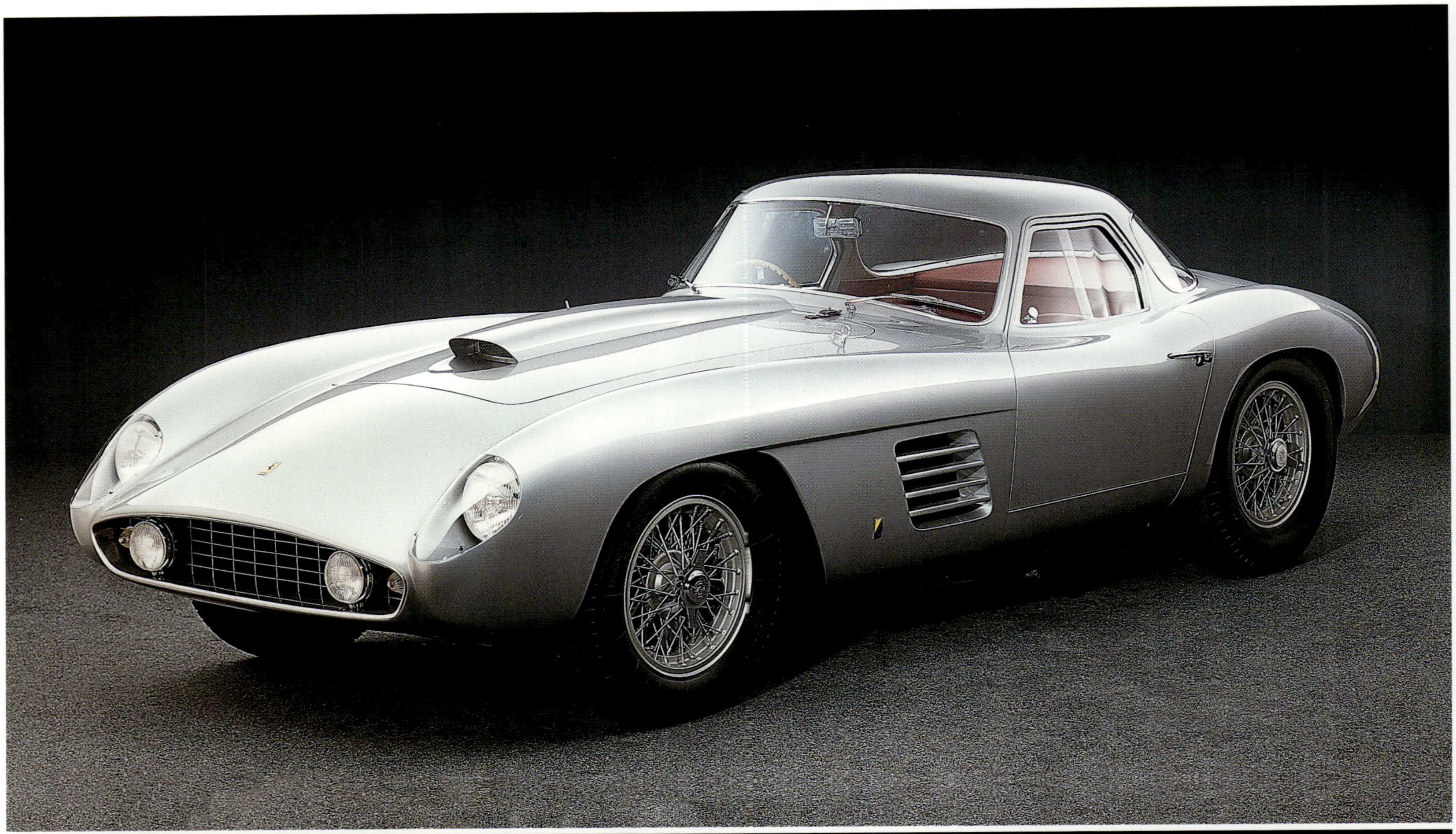

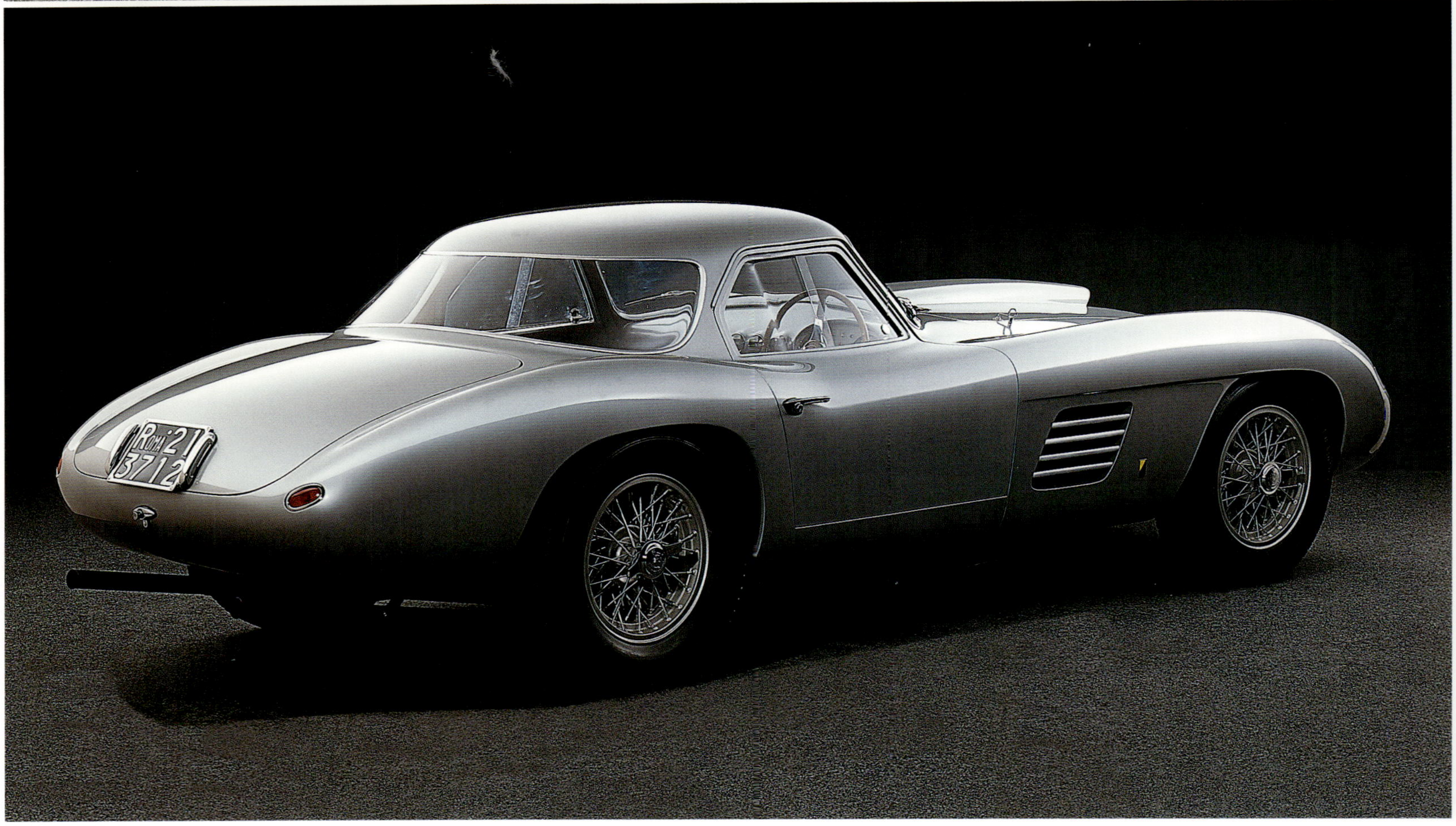
ROMA 21
3712

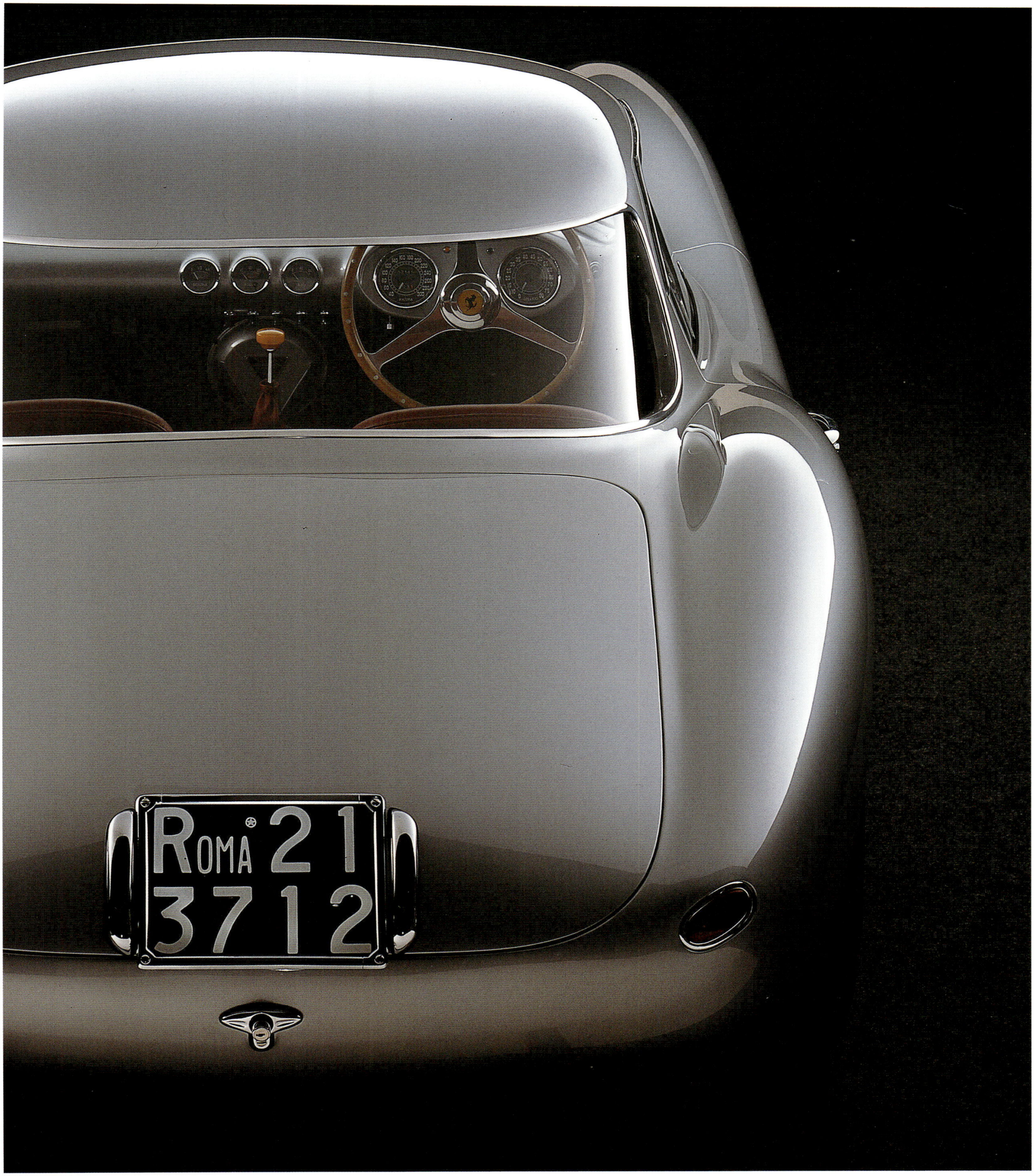
ROMA 21
3712

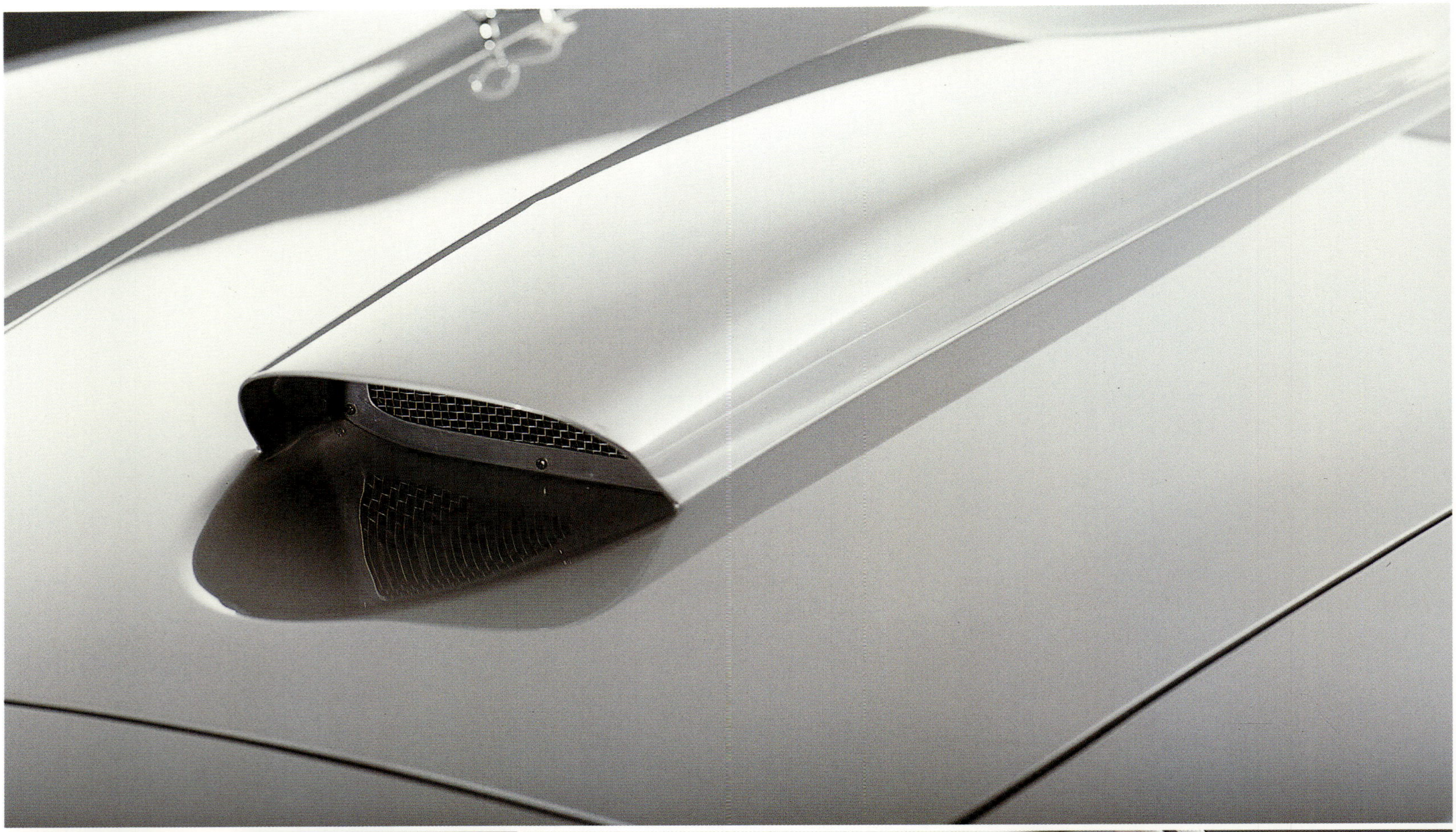

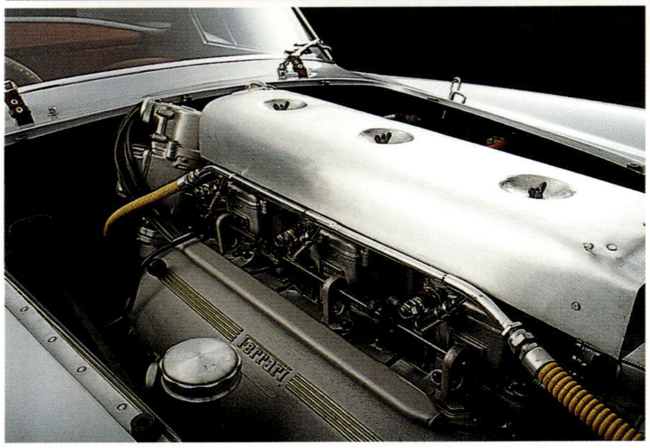
Ferrari

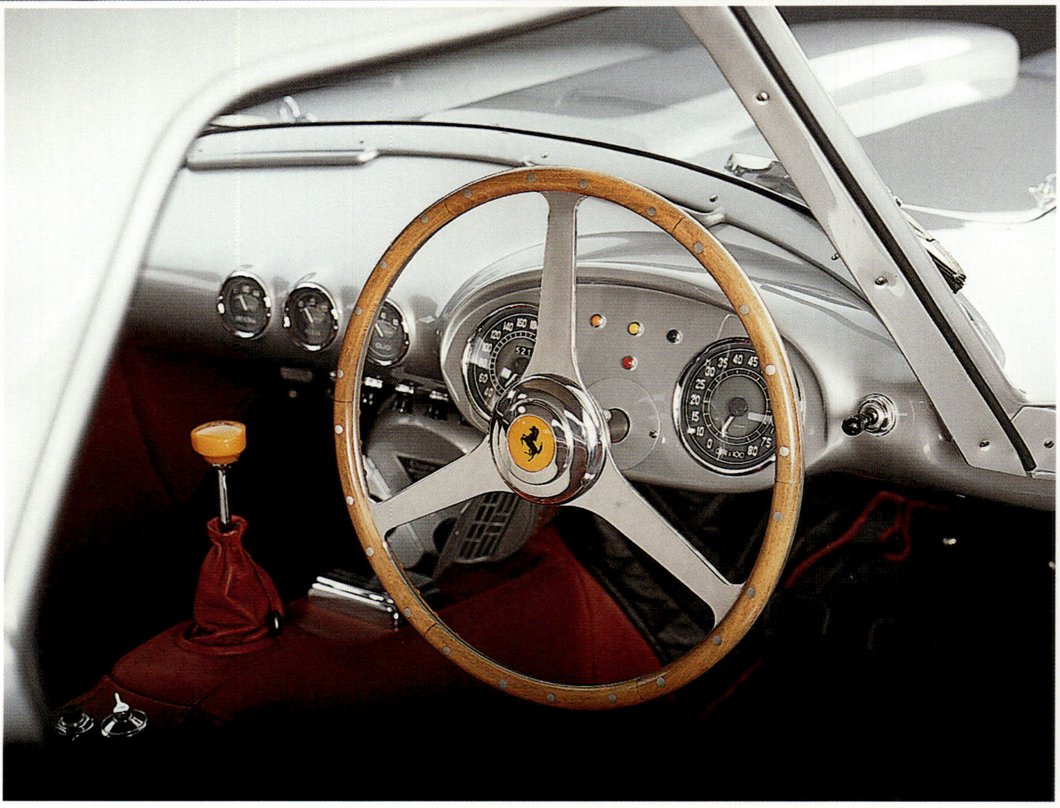

In the mid-1950s Scaglietti and Pinin Farina shared the privilege of producing bodywork for Ferrari racing cars. But while Pinin Farina also handled road cars, Scaglietti limited its activity to racing cars—with one exception: this berlinetta built on an eminently sporty chassis.

Sergio Scaglietti designed and developed this car for a Ferrari 375 MM Spider (chassis no. 0402/MM) the director Roberto Rossellini had acquired in 1954. After several months Rossellini decided to give it a more general-purpose outline and hired Scaglietti for the job. He delivered this version with closed bodywork to Rossellini in January 1956.

A great lover of sports cars, Roberto Rossellini commissioned Scaglietti to create a unique body for a Ferrari chassis.

In 1954 Ferrari was competing in the World Championship for Makes with its thundering 375 MMs. That same year *Voyage to Italy* was released, starring George Sanders and Ingrid Bergman. The movie was written and directed by Roberto Rossellini. Bergman and Rossellini had met in 1949; the following year they collaborated on the film *Stromboli* and married.

Roberto Rossellini's love life, cinematic work, and automobiles were always intertwined. He was passionate about driving. In 1952 he competed in the Mille Miglia at the wheel of a Ferrari 250 MM with bodywork by Vignale. In 1954 the director of *Rome, Open City* presented Ingrid Bergman with a specially commissioned berlinetta, which was shown at the Paris Salon the same year. The car, built by Pinin Farina on a 375 Mille Miglia chassis (0456/AM), also took part in the Bagatelle concours in 1991.

An insatiable enthusiast, Rossellini bought another 375 MM soon afterward, the Spider Competizione (0402/AM). In late 1955 he commissioned Scaglietti to create new and unique bodywork for that racing car, in the form of a berlinetta. The tubular chassis and fierce mechanics were retained, but its lines were completely new. Sergio Scaglietti was not a designer, but he was a brilliant sheet-metal worker; he had produced bodywork for numerous Ferrari racing cars. With intuitive know-how, he created an aggressive design that was no doubt influenced by its contemporary, the Mercedes 300 SLR, notably in the treatment of the rear of the car.

The 375 MM, purchased by the American collector Jon Shirley, was converted for use in civilian life and eventually became an exhibition car. In 1998 it was shown at both the Bagatelle concours run by *Automobiles Classiques* and Louis Vuitton and the Louis Vuitton Classic at Rockefeller Center in New York City. In June 2007 it was declared Best of Show at the concours d'elegance held in Maranello, Italy, Ferrari's base, to celebrate the company's sixtieth anniversary.

Innovations

5

Innovation in design finds its ultimate expression in concept cars. Some of the most significant advances in contemporary automobiles have been unveiled at concours d'elegance.

5

Whether known as concept cars or prototypes, "dream cars" or special bodywork, such machines are the very embodiment of designers' dreams. The terminology varies from era to era and country to country but, whatever they're called, these creations always press forward, advancing the thinking behind automaking and design.

Some concept cars are truly unique avant-garde designs, while others are precursors of models that someday will be mass produced. Developed by the car manufacturers themselves or by independent designers, concept cars exemplify creativity, innovation, and dynamism. They are like glimpses of the future.

Concept cars are essentially declarations of intent. They are by nature over-the-top and, as one-of-a-kind products, doomed to obsolescence. Sometimes opportunistically, sometimes with foresight, they express the tremendous responsiveness of the automobile industry to contemporary needs and desires. Thus considerable long-term research may go into progressively eliminating any negative aspects of a car, optimizing safety, eradicating pollution, and taming technology to create a healthier relationship between man and machine. Such dreams for the future convey great optimism.

The birth of a concept car is always extraordinary and exalting. By its nature—and thanks to the brilliance of its manufacture and purpose, its permitted excesses and skillfully judged limitations—the concept car is totally atypical, superlative in many ways. It doesn't have to apologize for deliberately pushing the boundaries that normally constrain commercial products. Unlike them, the concept car is not inhibited by technical, commercial, or economic contingencies. It is not held back by the shackles of legislation or feasibility. It does not risk censure and poor sales by overstepping the unpredictable limits of public acceptance.

The concept car is thus a free agent, representing an exchange of friendly services between the creator who provokes and the spectator who reacts, just as one would before a work of art but with a different ulterior motive. The concept car flirts with utopianism, but its escapism and excess are carefully controlled. It is not gratuitous. It is an act of faith.

208
Bertone
Nivola
1990

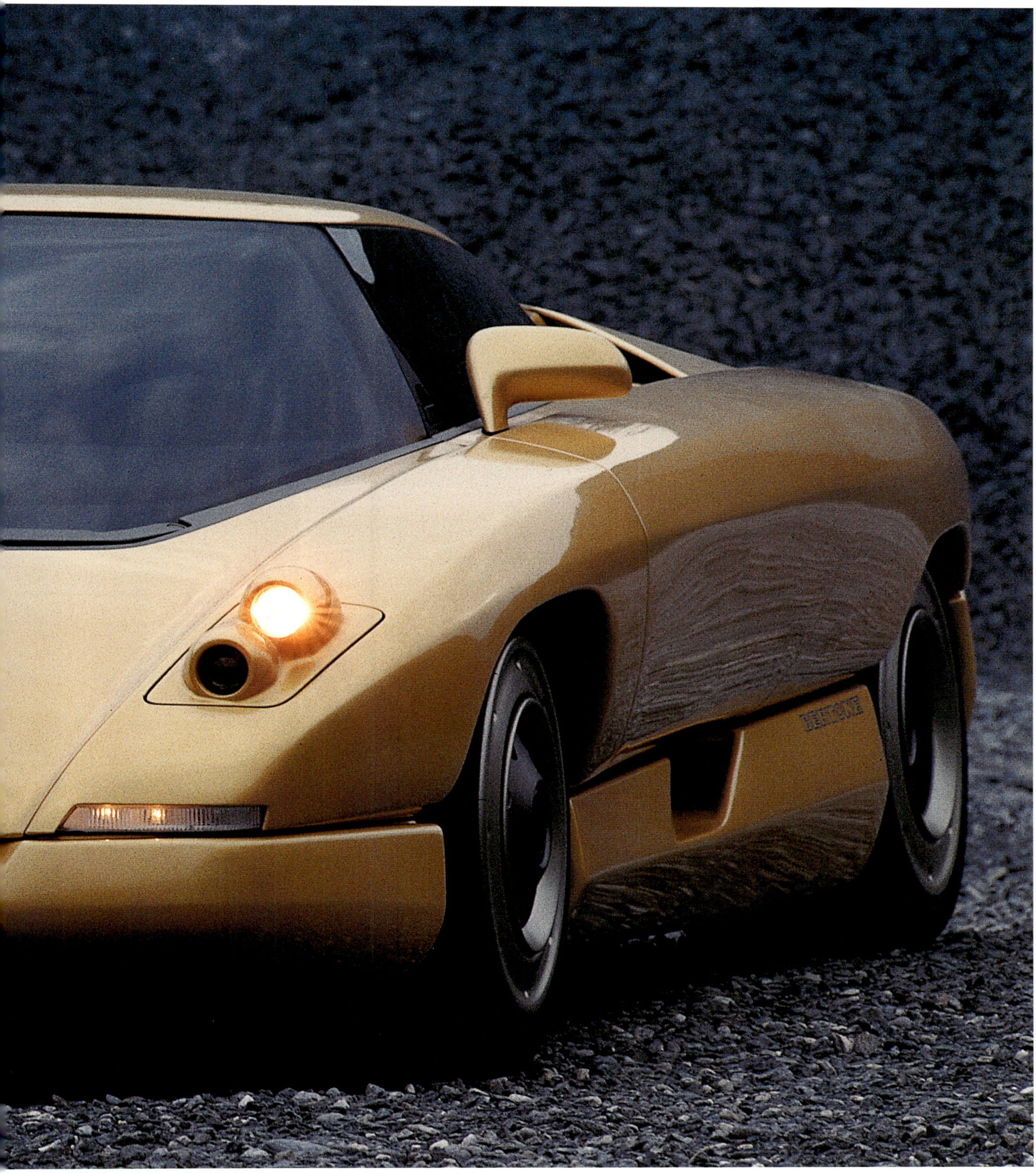

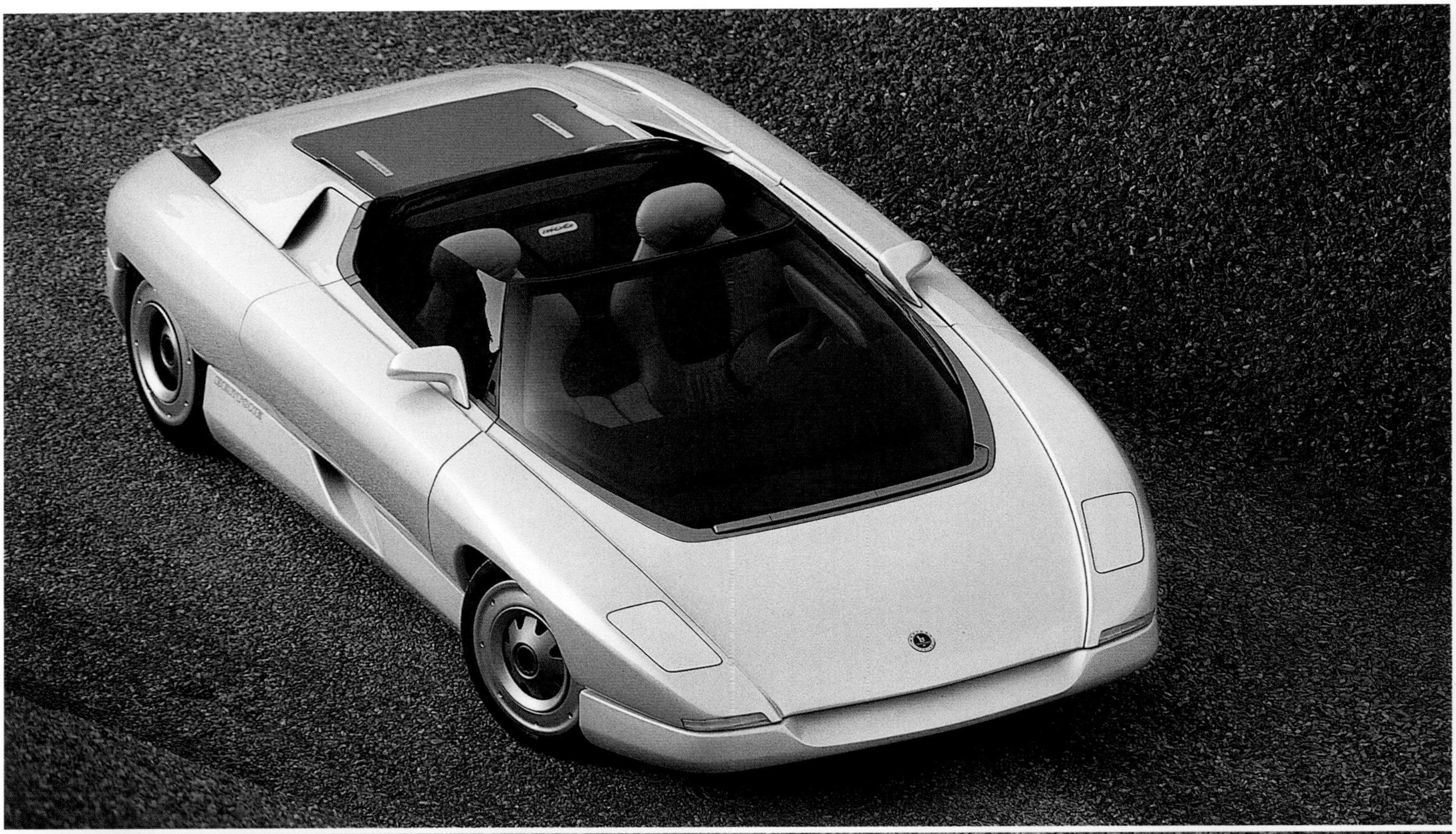

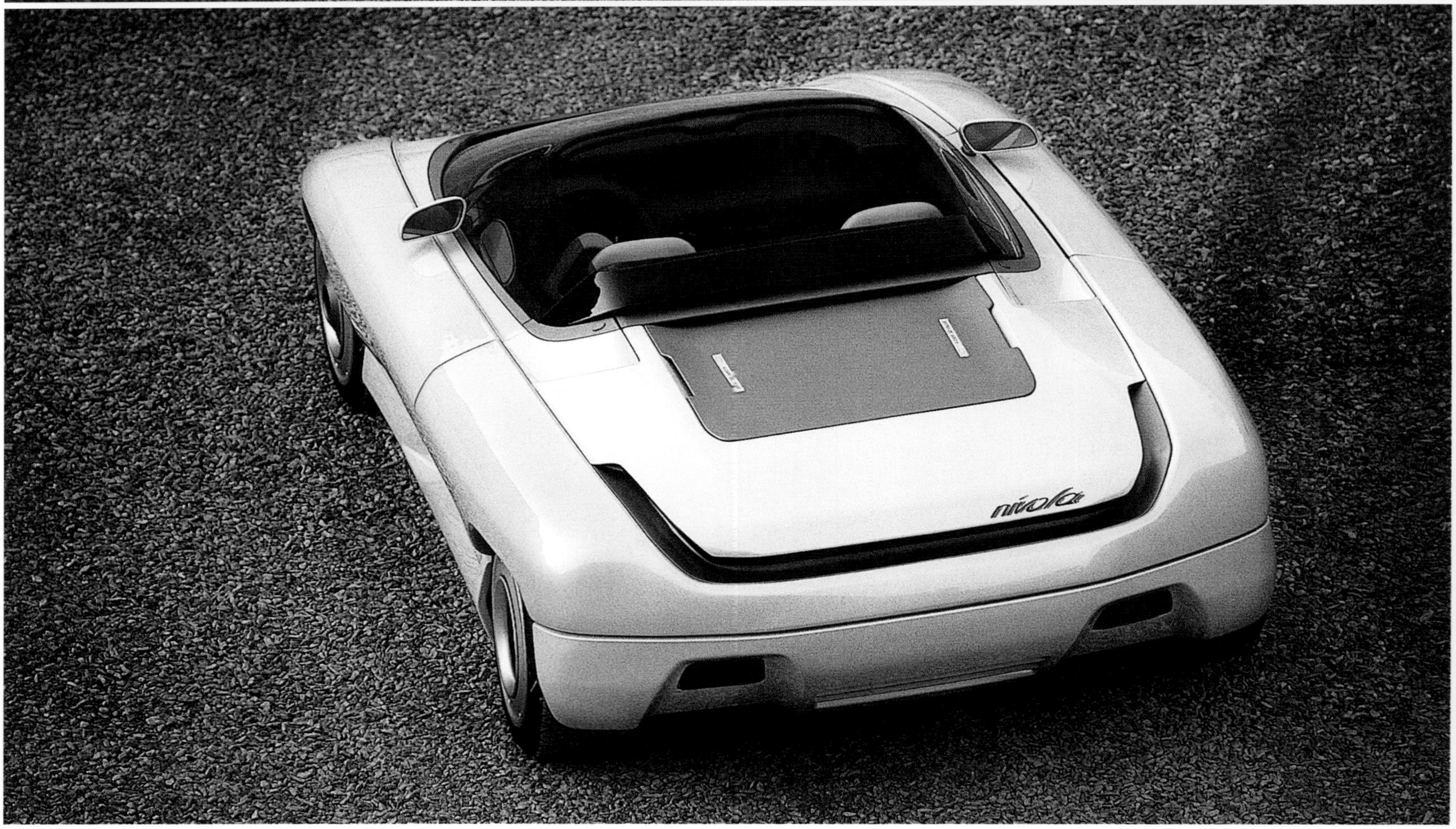
nivola

Beginning in 1953 and continuing to this day, a series of prototypes has been developed on the theme of the mythical Corvette, the most popular of American sports cars. In contrast to the standard model, with the engine at the front and rear-wheel drive, most of these concept cars have a central engine. Such is the case for this Nivola, which Marc Deschamps designed for Bertone.

Building innovative bodywork on existing chassis, essentially sublimating the machinery to their designs, auto-body makers seek to win collaborative contracts with car manufacturers. That was how Bertone created an idealized image of the Chevrolet Corvette at the beginning of the 1990s.

Among Nuccio Bertone's great gifts when he was running his family business was his ability to discover new talent. He was one of those bosses with a genius for surrounding themselves with exceptional colleagues. In 1979 he appointed Marc Deschamps as head of his design studio: a reserved, self-effacing man with an unusual artistic streak. The French designer came from the Renault Design Center, where he had created the Renault 5 Turbo. At Bertone he was in the unenviable position of succeeding three leading figures in Italian bodywork: Franco Scaglione, Giorgetto Giugiaro, and Marcello Gandini.

While softening the style of Bertone design, Marc Deschamps maintained his predecessors' spirit by playing with sophisticated details and the structure of the cars' volumes. Like them he favored style over design and aesthetics over function: The interplay of proportions, the amount of light, the surface contours, and the way the different planes connected were more important than the overall concept. Every work was a complex edifice of superimposed masses. He also discovered original solutions for the layout of the cockpit, the systems for opening doors, the dashboard display, and the arrangement of the controls.

The Nivola project, unveiled at the Geneva International Motor Show in 1990 and shown at Bagatelle six months later, is exemplary in these regards. It is a spider powered by a central engine borrowed from the Chevrolet Corvette ZR-1. But the Nivola's style makes no reference to the American purebred whose machinery it uses. The treatment of volumes is unusual and complex but harmonious.

The Nivola was one of Marc Deschamps's last creations for Bertone before Luciano d'Ambrosio took over from him in 1992.

212 Chrysler 300 1991

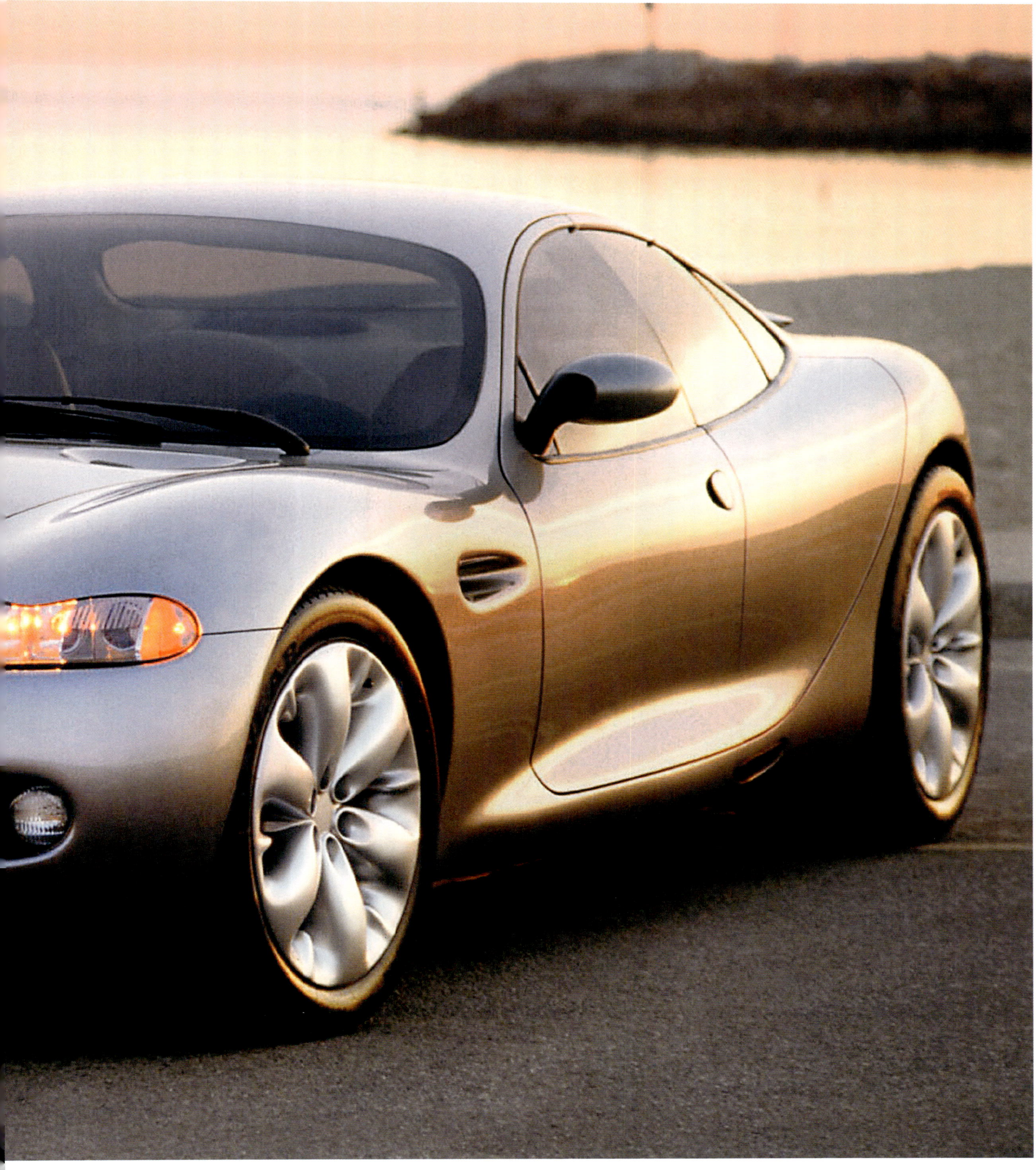

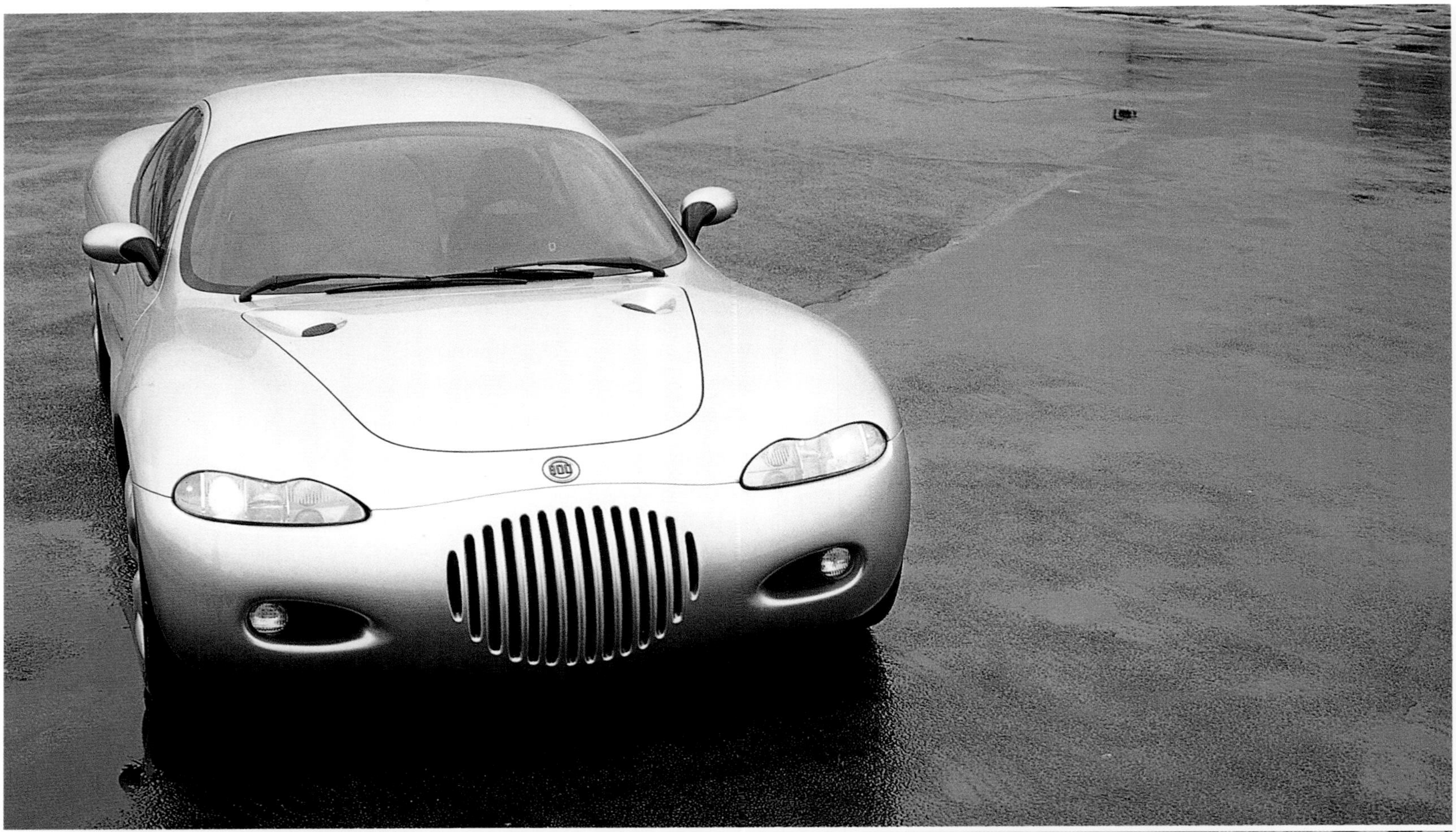

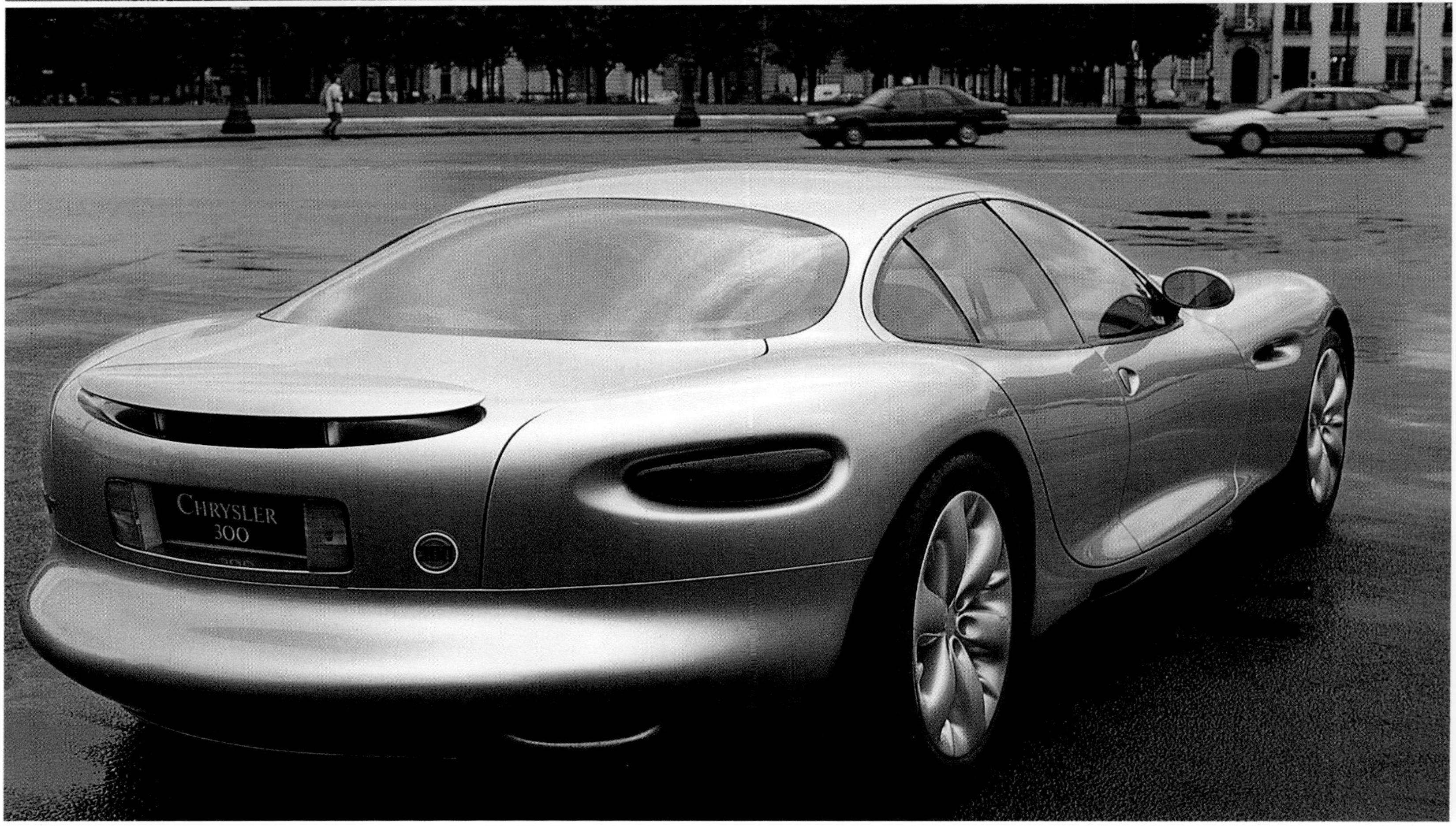
CHRYSLER
300

In the early 1990s Chrysler tried to breathe life into its styling by reflecting on its past. The Chrysler 300 was an idealized projection of what might have become of the 300 series, which was launched in 1955. While adhering to its predecessor's spirit, the new 300 took the form of a high-performance touring car. Its long, voluptuous curves and exaggerated proportions, pushed to the point of caricature by the long hood, are reminiscent of the sports cars of the 1960s. It is propelled by an eight-liter, ten-cylinder engine. The project was developed in the Chrysler Pacifica studio, a California branch of the firm.

Postmodern or neoclassical style was a major design trend in the late twentieth century. Chrysler welcomed the use of this nostalgic design vocabulary to reference some of the legendary cars in its own history.

The postmodern trend began in the 1980s and became entrenched over the following decade. Many designers seized on this nostalgic aesthetic, searching through memories of historic brands and models for references and recalling the reassuring values of the past with humor, derision, and sometimes subversion. Postmodernism was a reaction against the excesses of modernity. The motorcar, seaching for its roots, took a detour from newness to pay homage to the past.

The Chrysler 300 paid tribute to the most flamboyant era of Chrysler design. It revived the spirit that enlivened Chrysler's 300 series of sporty high-performance touring cars from the mid-1950s.

The 300 concept car, unveiled at Detroit's International Auto Show in January 1991, returned to the exaggerated proportions and design vocabulary of its illustrious ancestors: the extremely long hood containing a monstrous ten-cylinder engine, the aggressive front with its large oval radiator grill, the padded fenders at the front, and the sculpted ones at the rear.

The Chrysler 300 was developed by Neil Wailing in the design studio Chrysler set up in 1983 in Carlsbad, California. Many automakers believed it would be useful to send designers off site, allowing them to take the pulse of the planet, breathe in the air of the times, and get a sense of how fashion was developing.

The Japanese had started this trend of locating branches of their studios far from the corporate headquarters. Realizing they were lagging behind, American automakers rapidly caught up. In the mid-1980s the Big Three—Chrysler, General Motors, and Ford—opened offshoot studios on the Pacific coast, near Los Angeles, which had a far more glamorous aura than the austere city of Detroit.

216 Italdesign Bugatti EB 112 1993

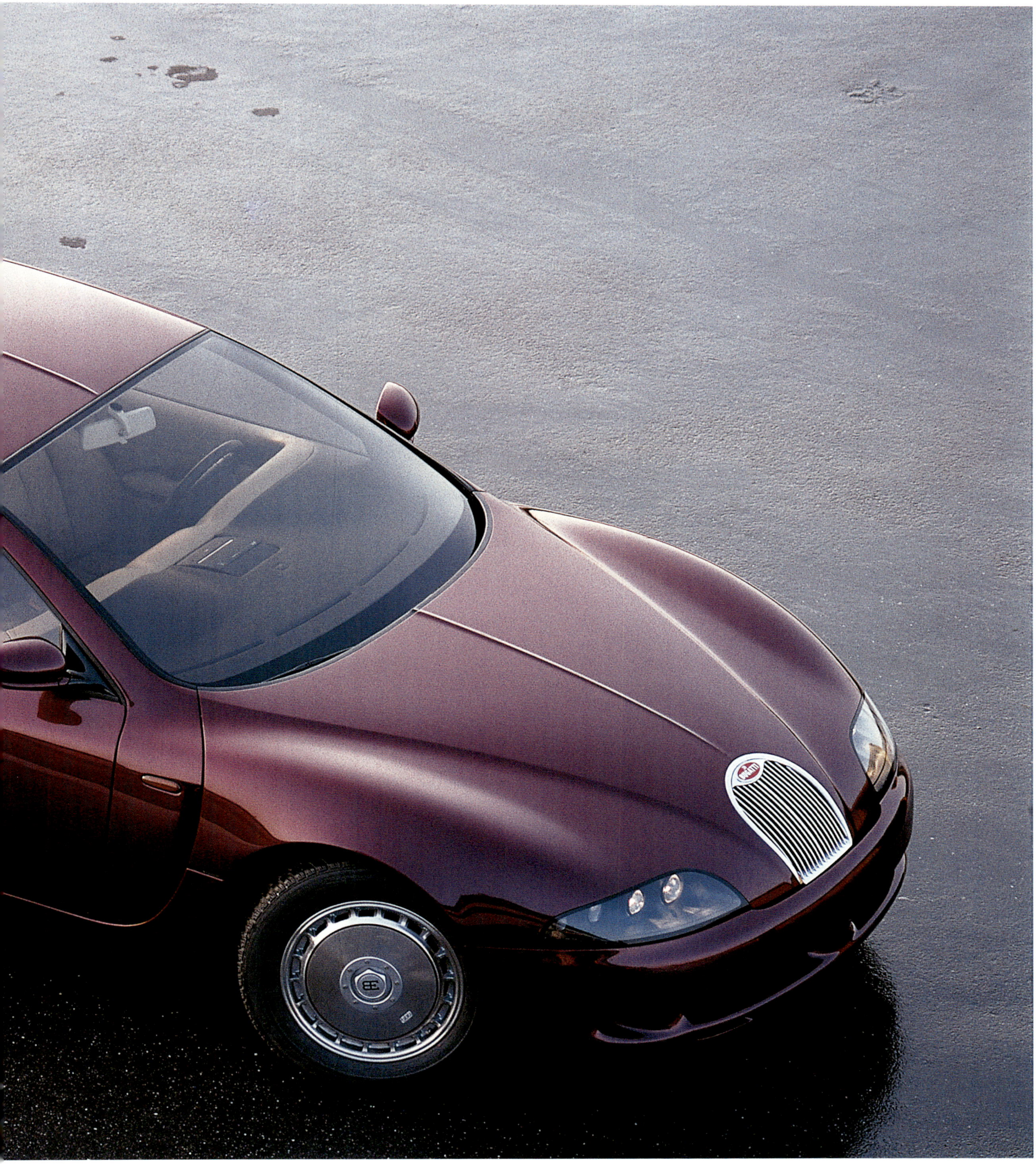

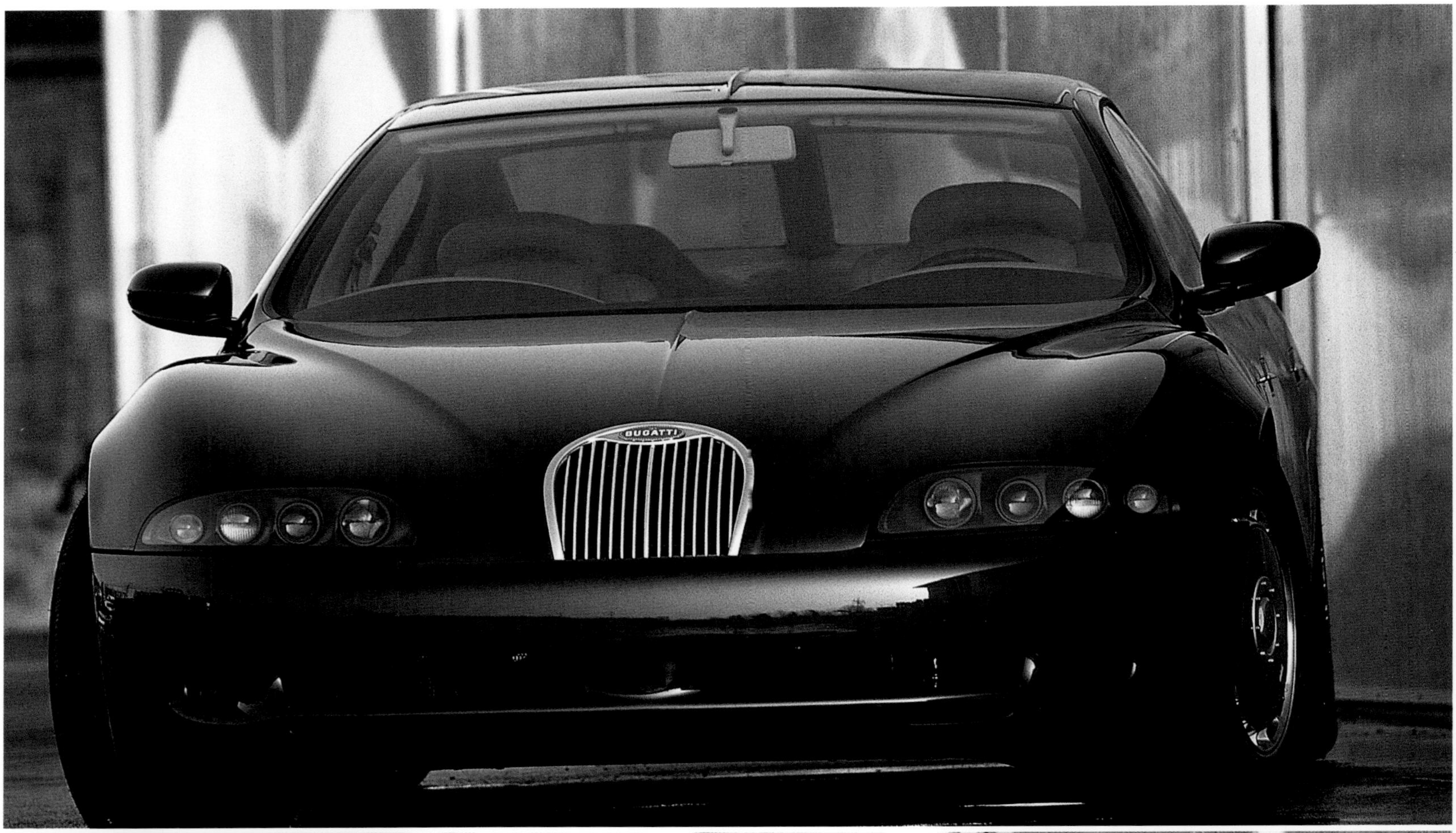

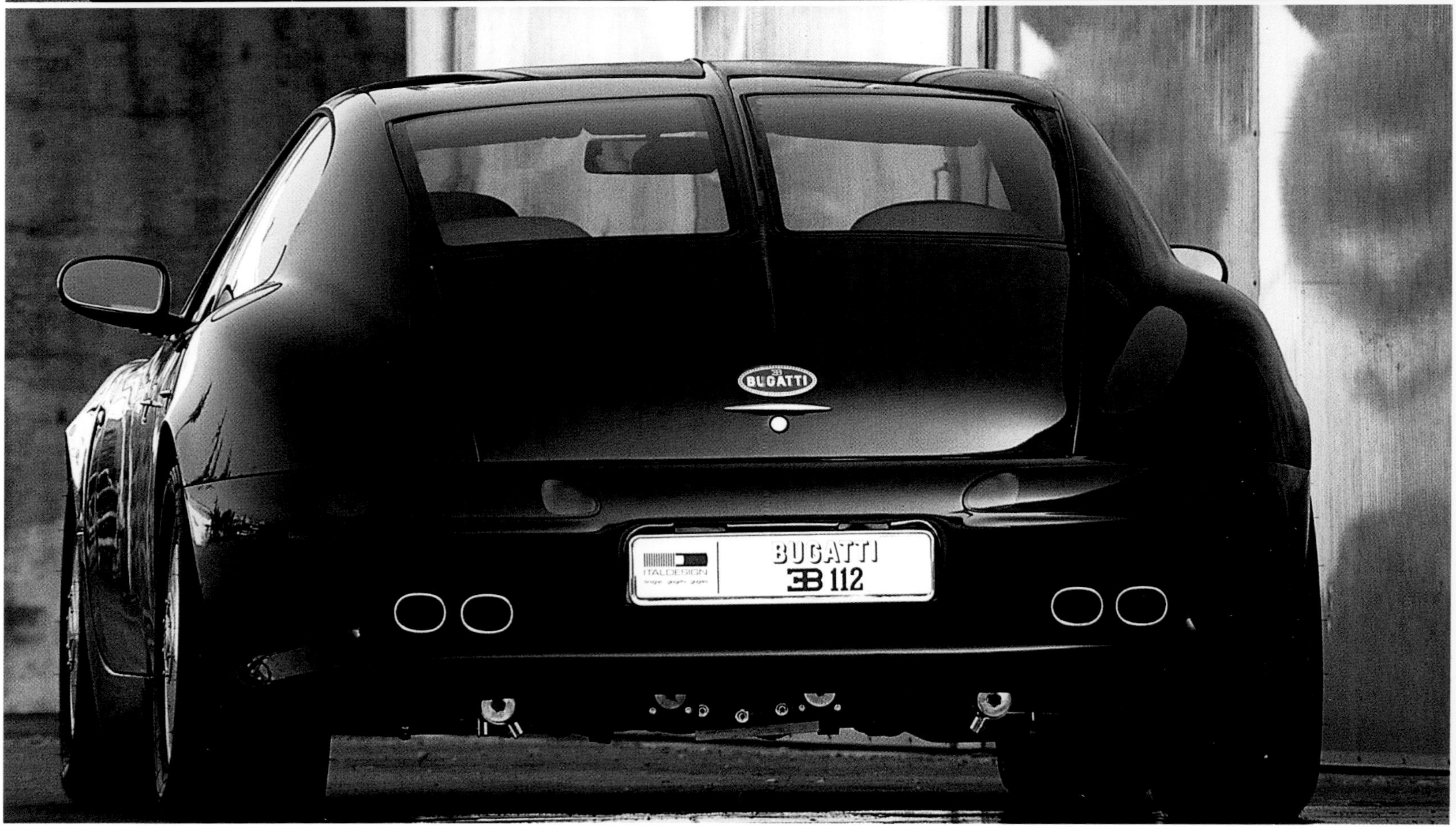
BUGATTI
ITALDESIGN
EB 112

After years of dormancy, Bugatti was revived in 1991 in Italy. The new line began with a Gran Turismo coupe, but soon plans were made to produce a four-door sedan. Italdesign's research led to the prototype Bugatti EB 112. In addition to its completely new bodywork, the EB 112 introduced a new structure, with the engine placed at the front; this was an impressive 655 horsepower V12 with a six-liter capacity. However, bankruptcy caught up with Bugatti Automobili before it had time to carry the project through to production.

Bugatti's revival took place intermittently until the firm began being effectively managed by the Volkswagen group. Even so, the Italian phase of this saga led to some very appealing projects.

Before Volkswagen announced its takeover of Bugatti in 1998, other revivals of the venerable Alsatian brand had been attempted over the years. The company first ceased activity in 1956, after the fleeting and final appearance of a single-seater Bugatti at the Automobile Club de France Grand Prix. It was absorbed by Hispano-Suiza in 1963, then lay dormant as part of the Messier-Hispano-Bugatti group, which was formed in 1977. Ten years later an Italian businessman and a group of investors, seeking to breathe life back into Bugatti, formed a holding company, acquired the brand, and established Bugatti Automobili.

Though this period in Bugatti's history proved tumultuous, it had its high points. Italdesign, run by Giorgetto Giugiaro since its formation in 1968, was much involved in Bugatti's revival in the early 1990s. Italdesign developed a magnificent sedan, the EB 112, but its potential was cut short by Bugatti Automobili's bankruptcy in 1995.

Bugatti Automobili had been extraordinarily ambitious. In September 1990 an ultramodern factory opened at Campogalliano in the Bologna area. A year later the Bugatti EB 110 was ready—a superlative berlinetta. Plans were in place to develop the line further with a high-performance sedan, a comfortable touring car to balance the EB 110's uncompromising character. Work on this new car was handed to Italdesign's Giorgetto Giugiaro and resulted in the EB 112, exhibited in March 1993. The designer had given it an original outline with round, supple contours and some features harking back to the Bugatti heritage, such as a radiator grill suggesting the traditional Bugatti horseshoe and the central spine running the car's full length.

The Bugatti EB 112 never reached the production stage. It was overtaken by the fate of the overambitious Bugatti Automobili, which ceased operations in two years after the EB 112's debut.

220
BMW
Z13
1993

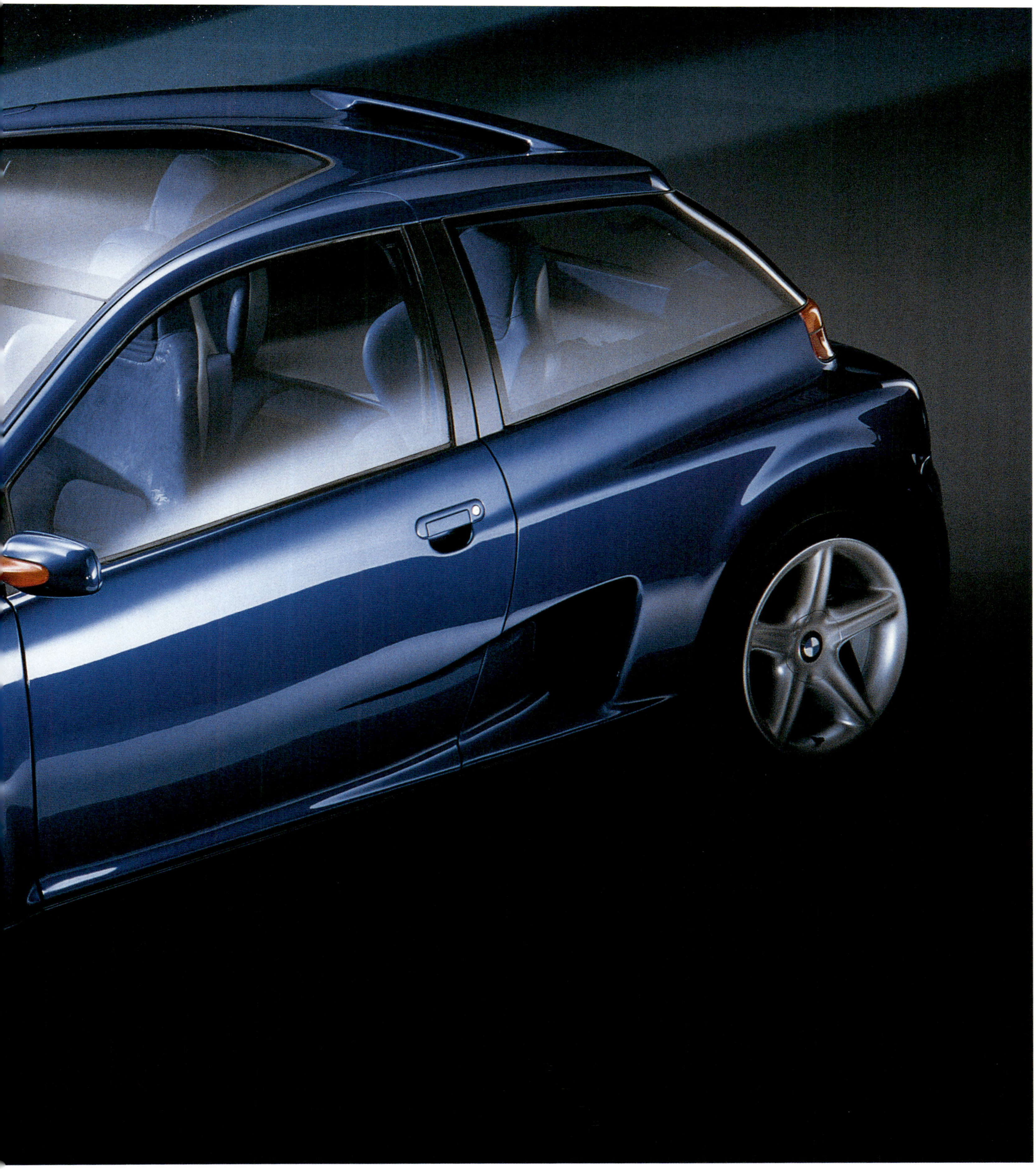

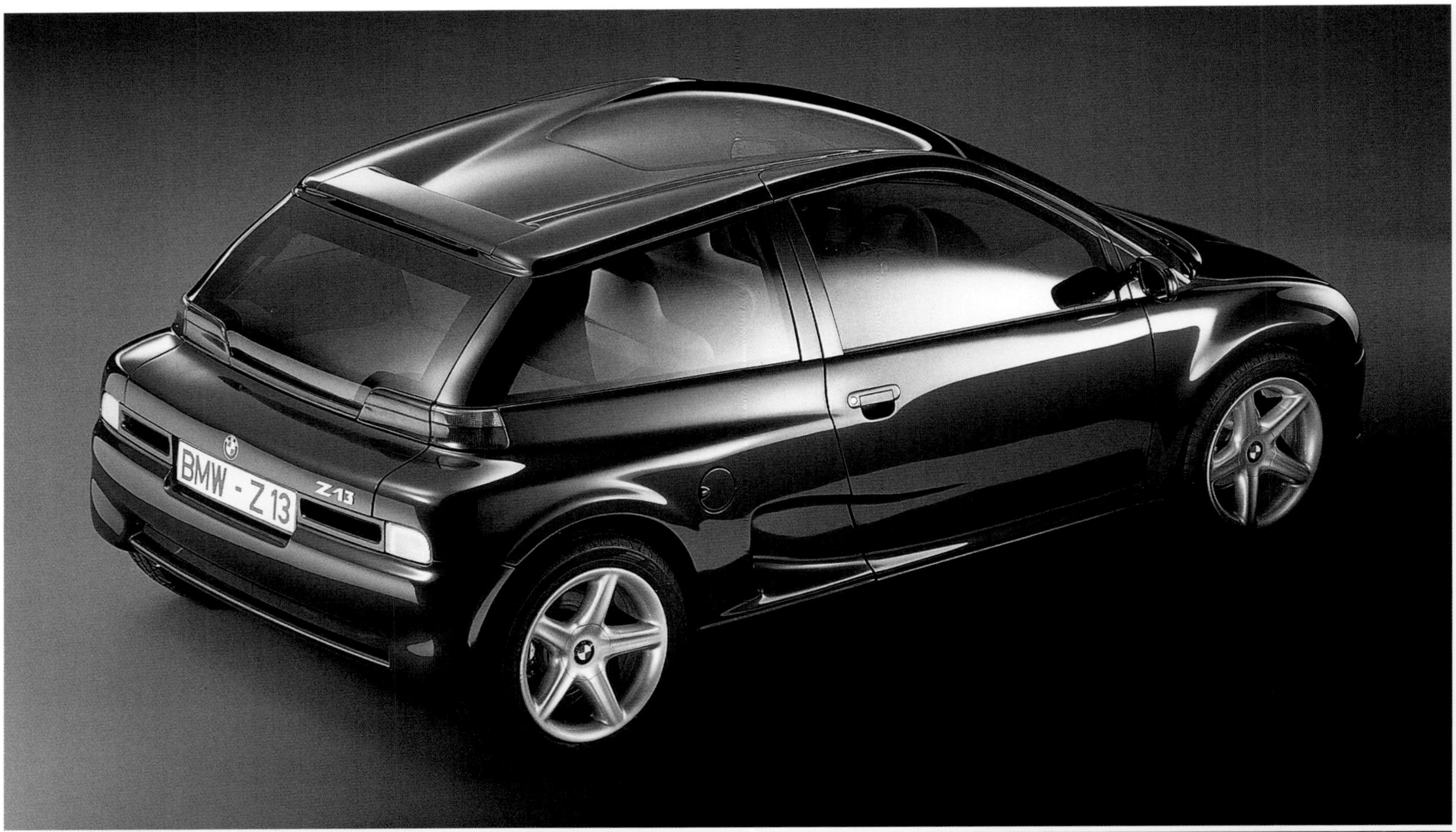
BMW - Z 13
Z13

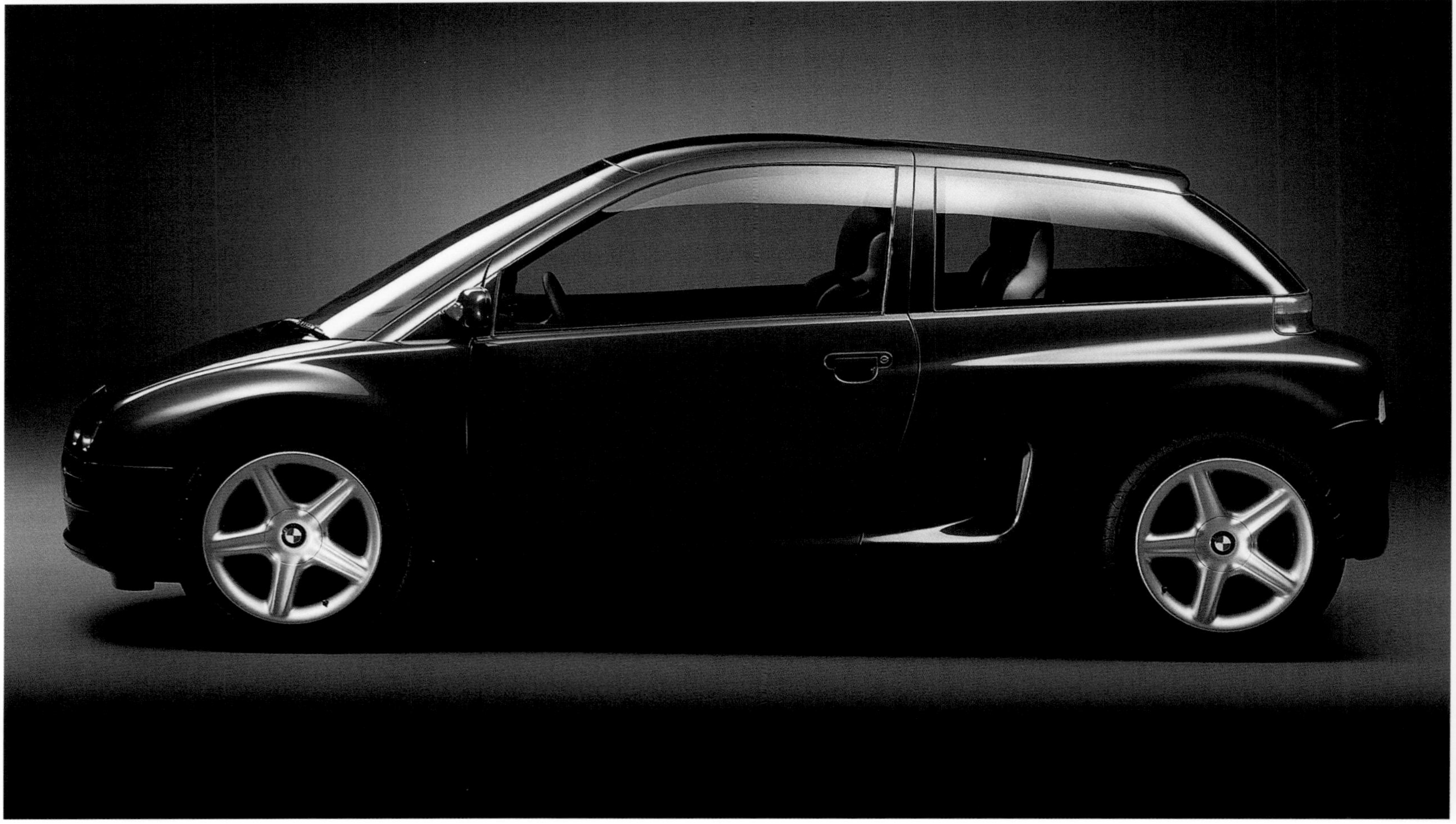

Diversification of products was one of the major developments in the auto industry in the late twentieth century, exemplified by BMW's Z13 project. BMW researched a very compact car driven by a motorcycle engine, the four-cylinder engine of the K1100 RS. An unusual feature was the Z13's three-seat interior: The driver sat in the middle of the front seat, with two passengers in back. With its sharp exterior styling and lively engine, the Z13 was clearly a member of the sporty BMW family.

In the last decade of the twentieth century the BMW brand was infused by a new design strategy initiated by Christopher Bangle. Throughout his career the Ohio-born designer has advocated for deliberately provocative design.

After graduating from the Art Center College of Design in Pasadena, California, Chris Bangle joined Opel, where he initially specialized in interiors. One of his first jobs was designing the ingenious passenger compartment for the Junior concept car (1983). He then joined Fiat, where he designed several archetypal cars, including the Fiat Coupé.

    Everywhere he went Chris Bangle fought the good fight, rejecting consensus and complacency and adopting an attitude that commanded respect in an automobile world that tends to be conservative and cautious. He arrived at BMW in 1992, at the age of thirty-six. From the start he wanted to shake up the Bavarian firm's style by exalting its cars' sporty personality, with a design vocabulary emphasizing expressiveness, emotion, and sensuality—all of which was disconcerting for observers after decades of sleek, conventional design.

    Some years before his arrival at BMW the company had launched an autonomous creative unit, BMW Technik GmbH. This loose structure was reponsible for developing projects on the fringes of the company's usual commerical production. BMW Technik was authorized to pave the way for more futuristic, unexpected products with innovative technology. Between 1985 and 1989 the head of the unit was Harm Laagay, who would later become head of design at Porsche. In 1989 the designer Klaus Kapitza took over; it was he who developed the Z13 project, which was unveiled at the Geneva motor show in March 1993 before appearing at the Bagatelle concours in September.

    With this neat little car BMW revealed its intention to expand its market share by making inroads into the compact car sector—a strategy that would later be consolidated by BMW's takeover of the Mini. The Z13 was notable not only for its size (less than 138 inches [3.5 meters] long) but also for its interior layout, with a single, centered front seat for the driver and two passenger seats in back. Finally, the hot-tempered little BMW was propelled by an engine borrowed from a motorcycle.

224

Lagonda
Vignale
1993

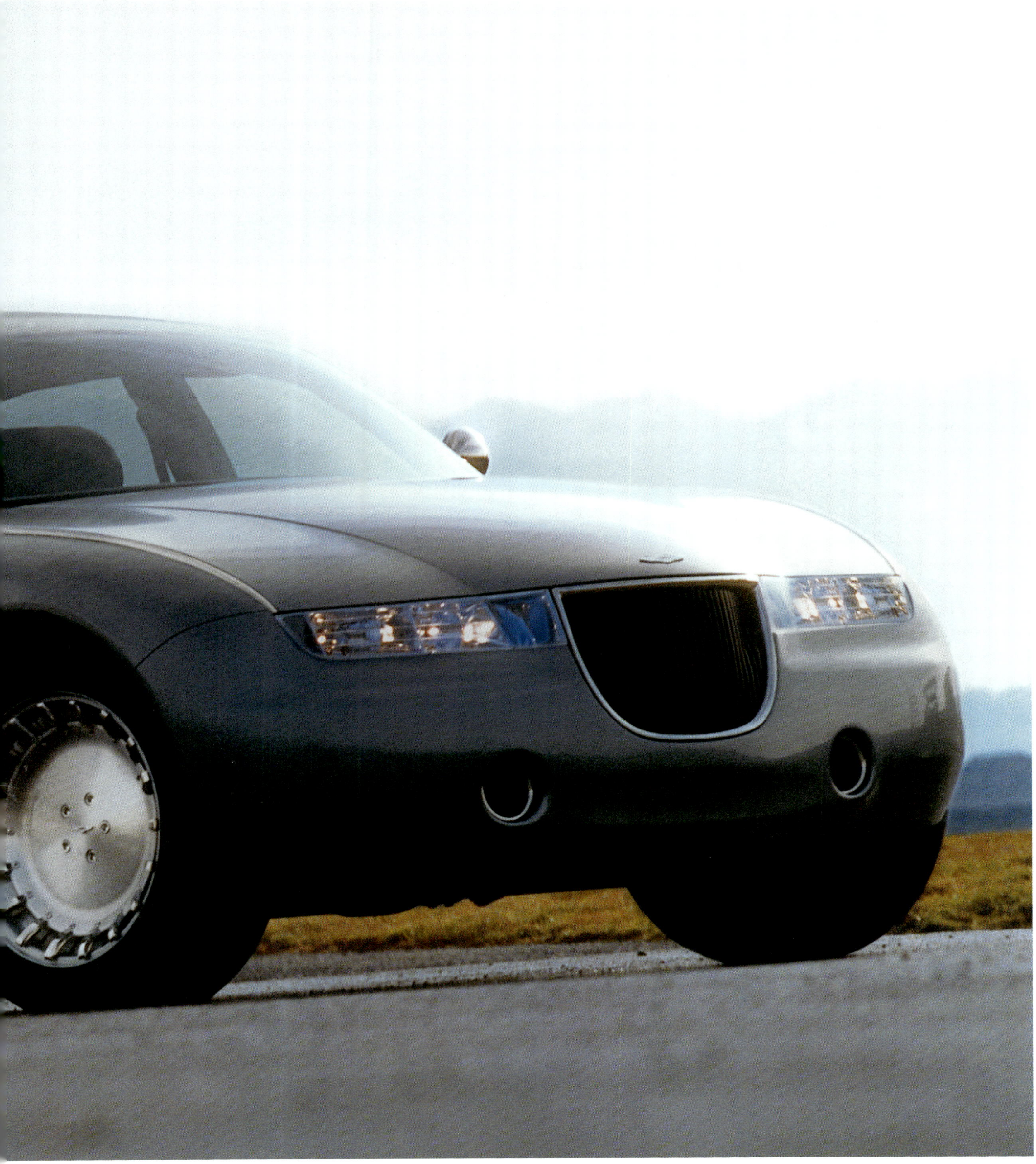

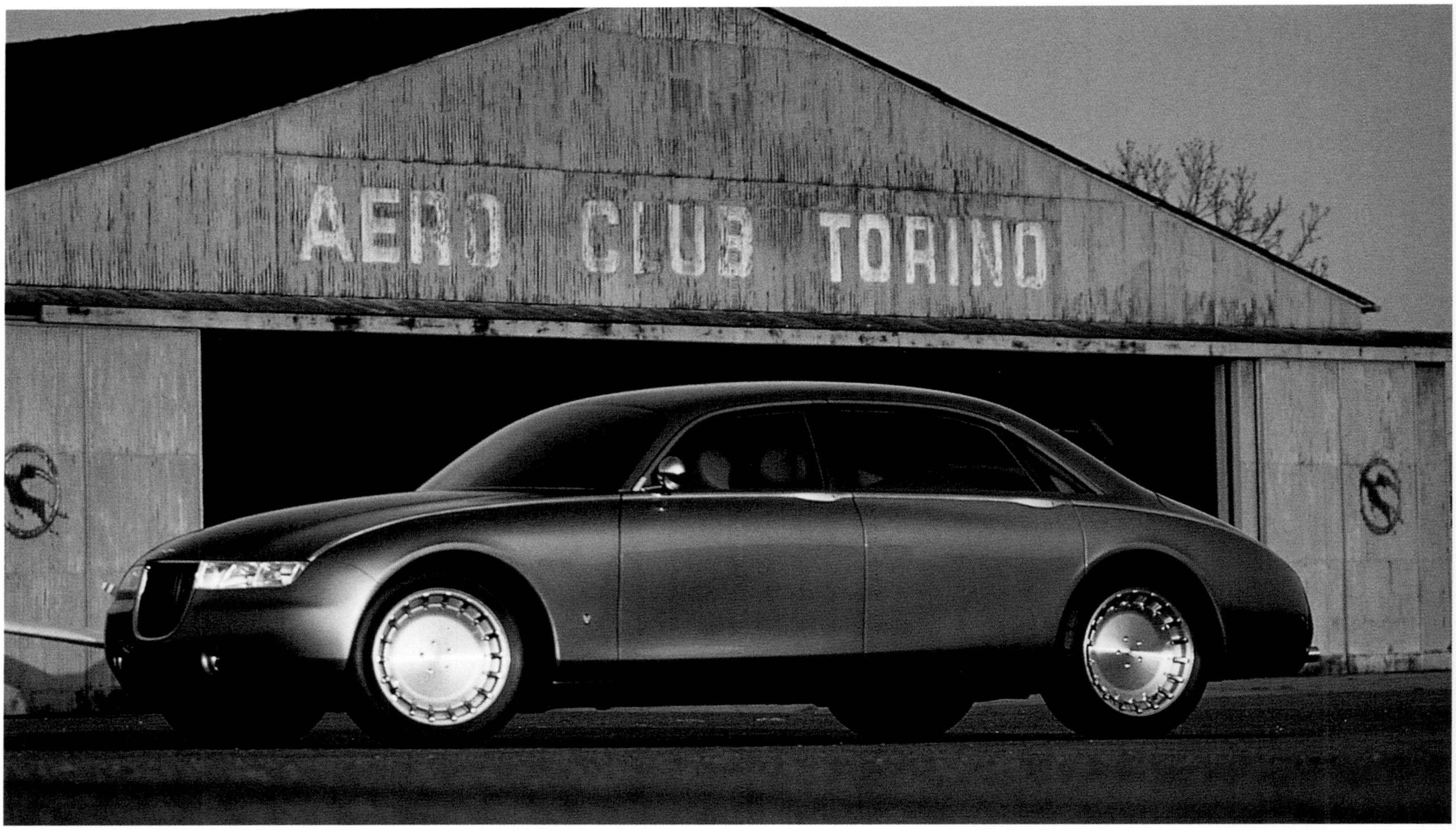
AERO CLUB TORINO

The venerable firm Lagonda joined Aston Martin just after the Second World War. Aston Martin specialized in sporty products, while Lagonda was dedicated to more conventional models. The brand was suspended for years, until the Vignale project came along. Aston Martin, intending to boost Lagonda's profile, furnished it with a V12, 400-horsepower engine.

Aston Martin had been through trials and tribulations in the decades before 1987, when the American Ford Motor Company acquired a majority stake—a welcome rescue of the British company after a number of liquidations and bankruptcies. Plans under the new ownership were to develop the Lagonda brand under the Aston Martin umbrella.

The two British names had been associated since 1947, when David Brown brought both companies to form Aston Martin Lagonda, but the two brands had always had clearly different goals. Aston Martin had been dedicated to the most sporting types of product, Gran Turismo cars and racing cars, while Lagonda had maintained the more conventional image associated with high-performance, luxurious touring sedans. Their affiliation continued until 1958, when the Lagonda make was abandoned. It was revived in 1961–64 as a very exclusive series. It returned again in 1978, and finally died out in the early 1990s.

Aston Martin would not give up on the possibility of another revival of Lagonda and sought a new life for the venerable brand. So Ford commissioned Ghia to look into a future Lagonda. Ghia was another of the prestigious names orbiting around planet Ford, a highly respected firm that had operated in Turin since the early twentieth century and had joined the Ford group in 1970. The new Lagonda project was called Vignale after another legendary brand in Italian bodywork. Vignale had failed and been absorbed by Ghia in 1969.

The Aston Martin Lagonda Vignale was unveiled at the Turin auto show in 1993, then shown at Bagatelle as a bulky sedan in an idiosyncratic neoclassical style. But its most precious asset was secreted away in the passenger compartment. The designers had dreamed up a nostalgic interior with Art Deco–inspired furnishings in a geometric composition of nickel and gray beechwood.

228 Cadillac Cien 2002

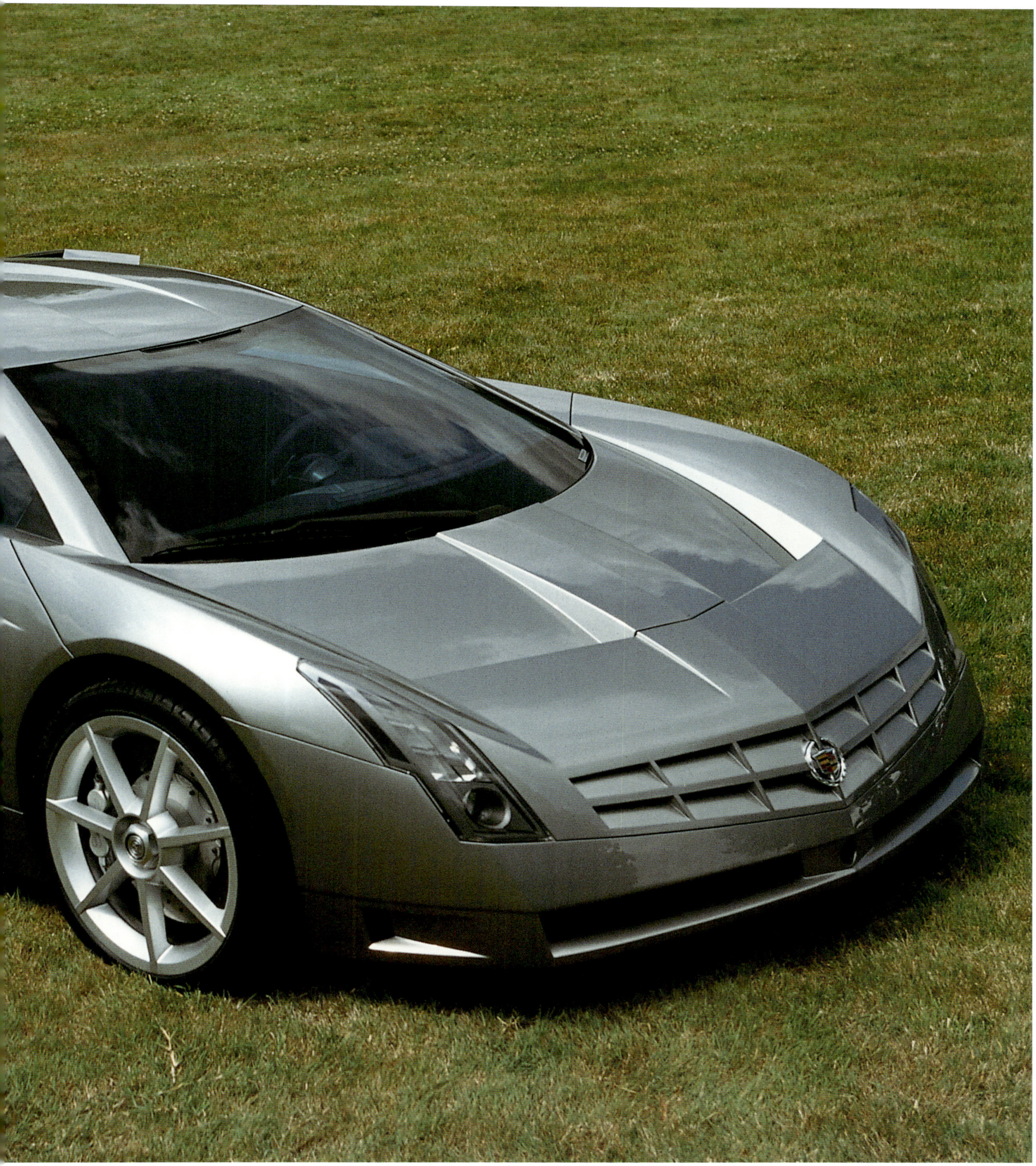

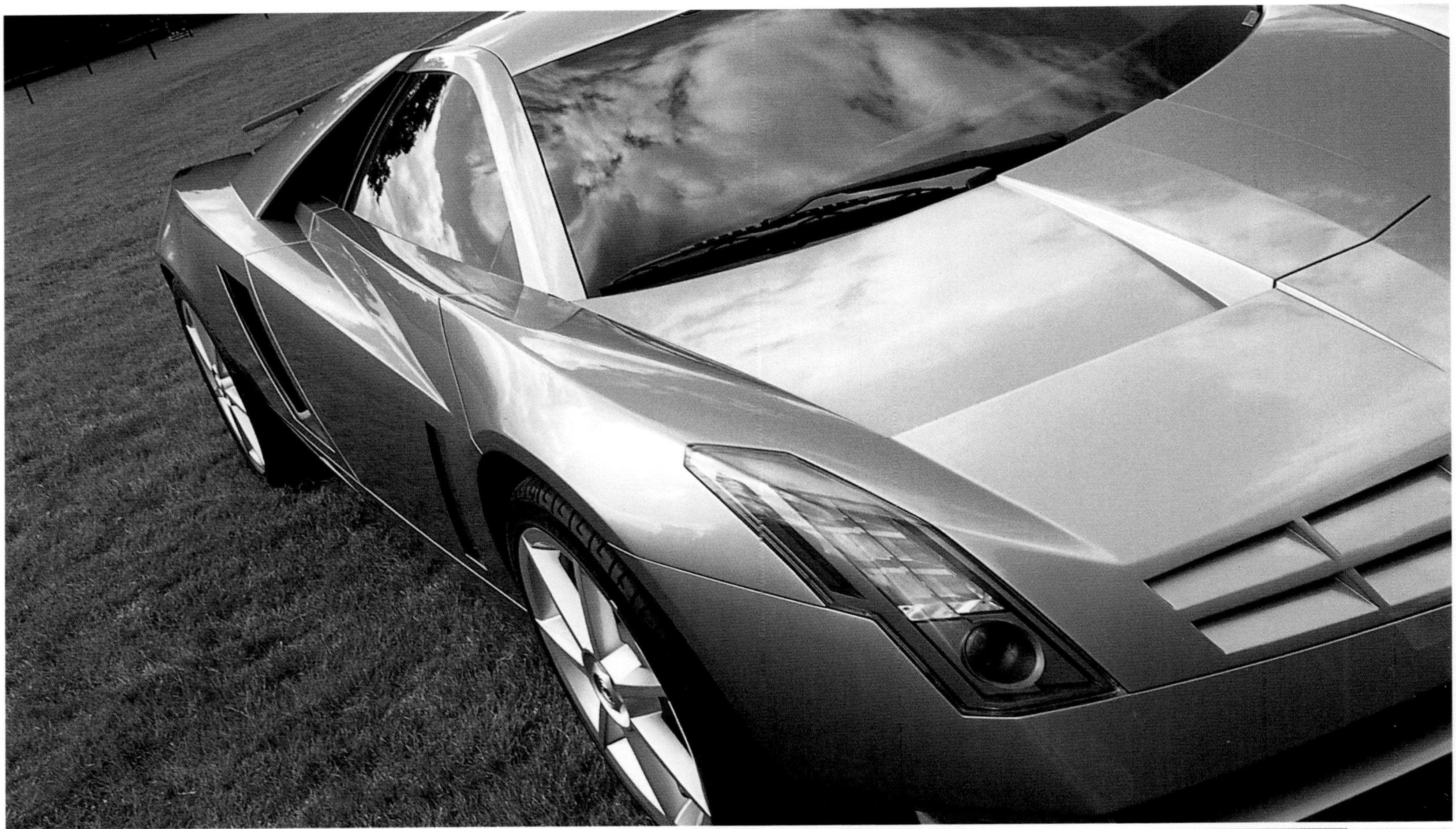
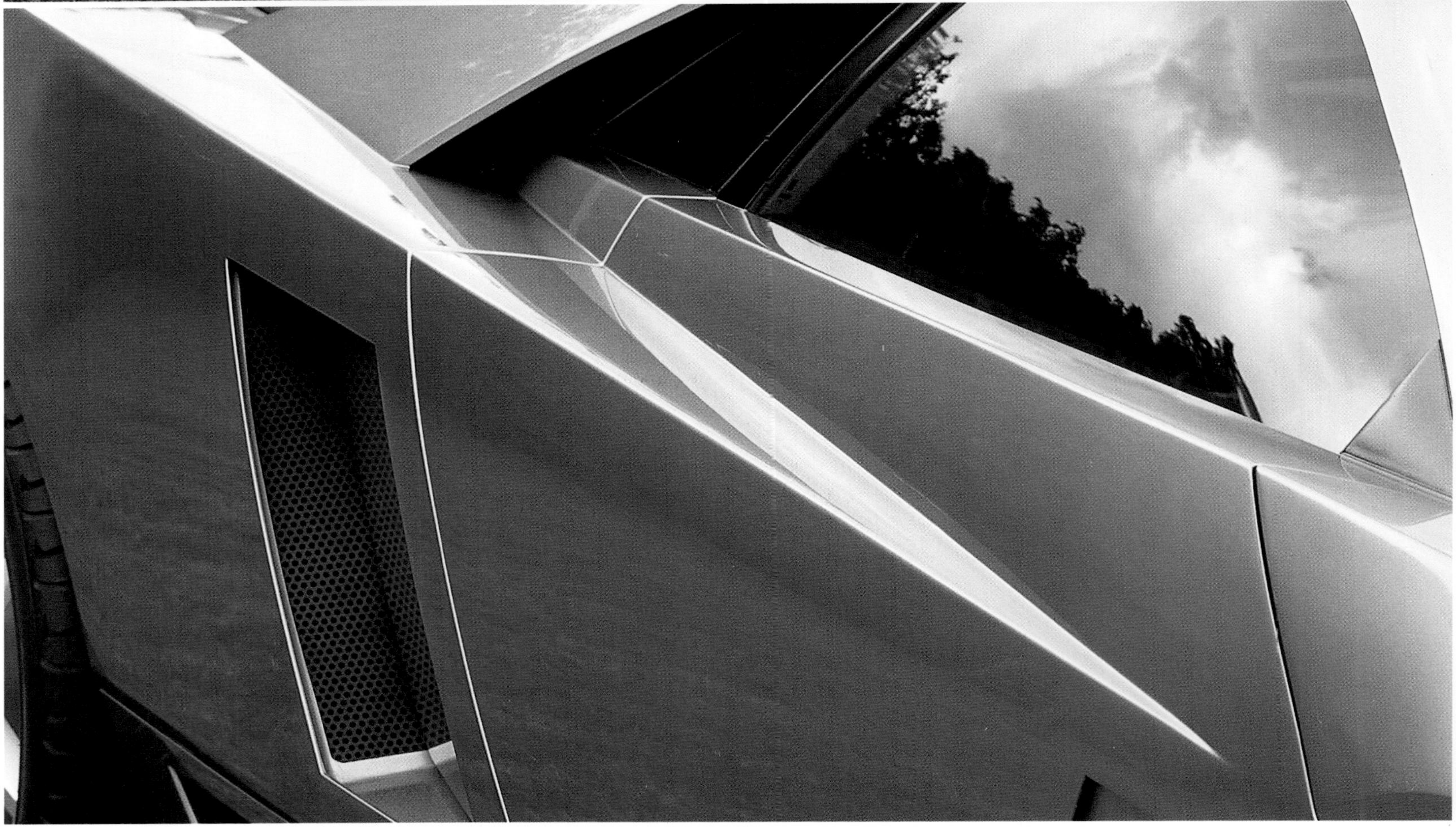

Cadillac's aesthetic identity has always relied on impressive proportions and aggressive lines. The Cien adhered to those characteristics while adding a more sporting dimension. To attract a younger clientele Cadillac had adopted a strategy based on competition, in particular the Le Mans Twenty-Four Hour Race. In conjunction with that plan Cadillac developed the Cien as a sharp, high-performance machine with a powerful engine—a supercar.

America has been an industry powerhouse since the dawn of the automobile, but Detroit has faced its share of difficulties over the years. Its might was taken down a peg or two by a succession of challenges, from the oil shortages of the 1970s to foreign competition. Confronted on their own turf by their European and Asian counterparts, American cars—even the emblematic Cadillac—found their chrome had lost its sparkle.

Throughout its history Cadillac had symbolized American opulence, with signature models such as the exquisitely refined Eldorado Brougham, a limousine outfitted with a set of silver tumblers, a makeup case, and a bottle of Arpège perfume. But it too had become vulnerable, in part because of the downsizing required by fuel economy standards.

Cadillac sought for some years to recover its strong design heritage, ultimately finding its way and even pushing forward with fresh inspiration. The Cadillac Cien is the symbol of this rediscovered pride. It is a coupe powered by an enormous twelve-cylinder engine, whose aggressive body styling is as sharp as a stealth bomber's. Developed for the 2002 Detroit auto show, the Cadillac Cien was one of the last concept cars created under the direction of Wayne Cherry, who had been head of design at General Motors since 1992.

The Cadillac Cien project was developed by the company's advanced design team, located in Great Britain and headed by Simon Fox.

232 Peugeot RC 2002

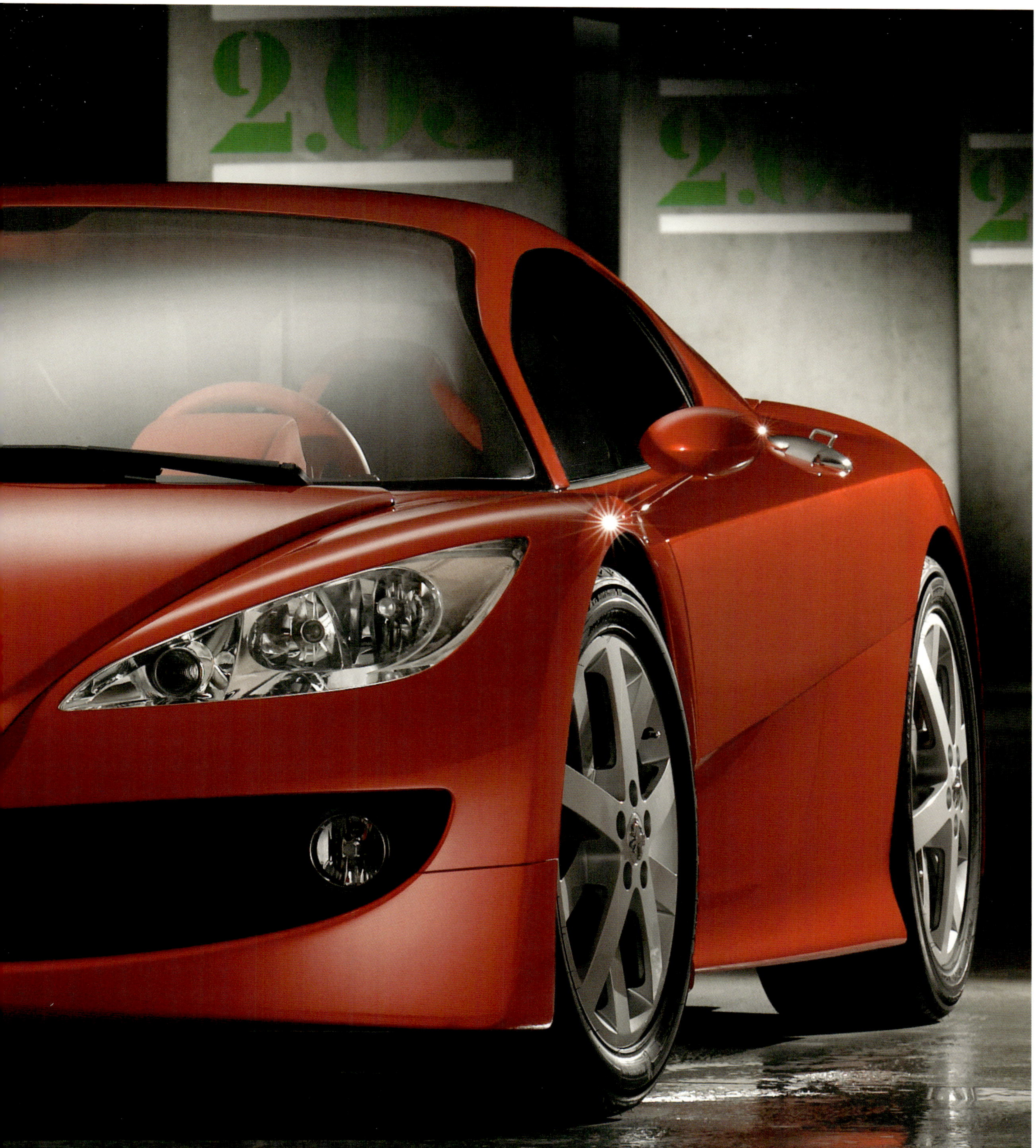

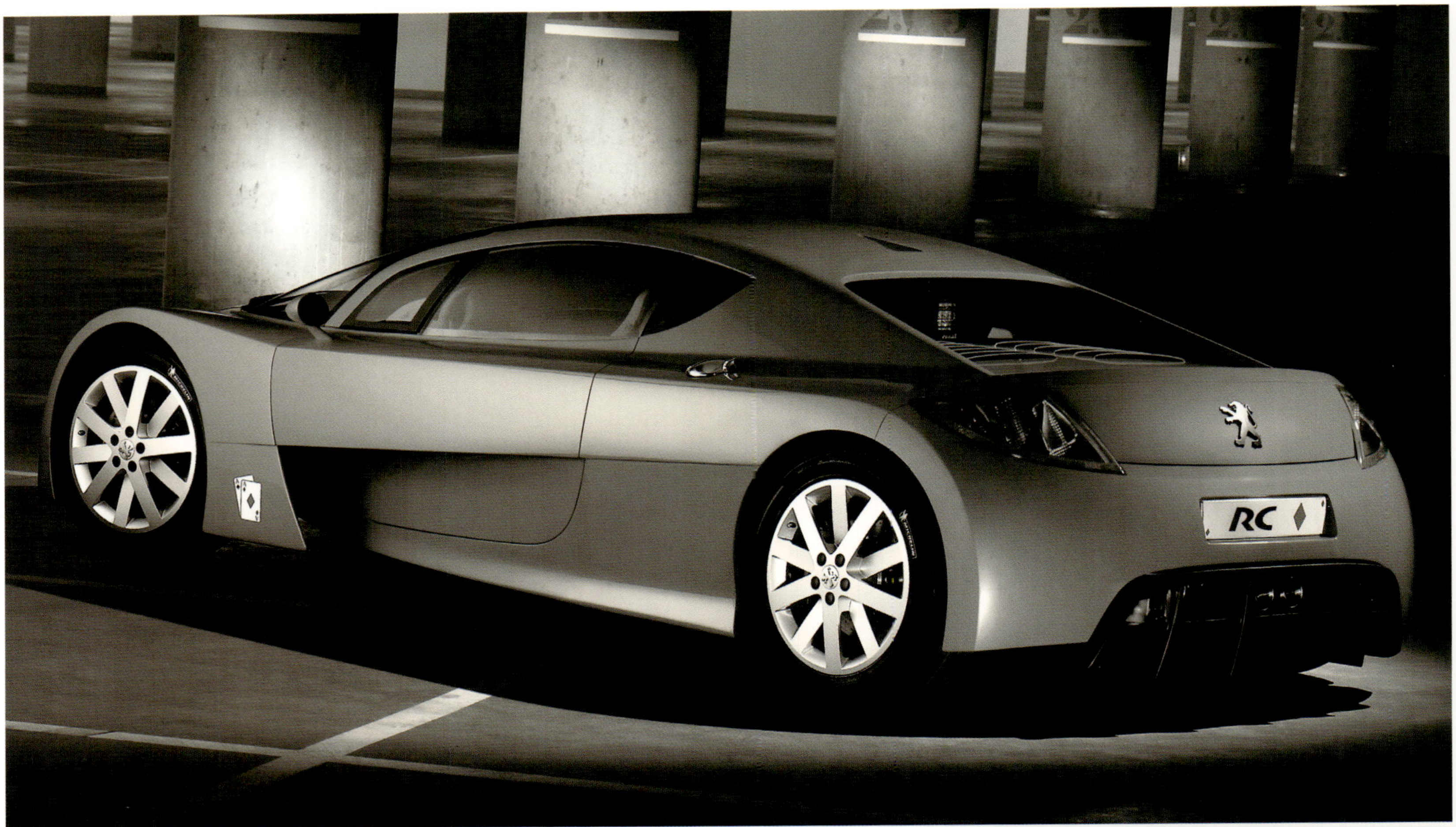
RC

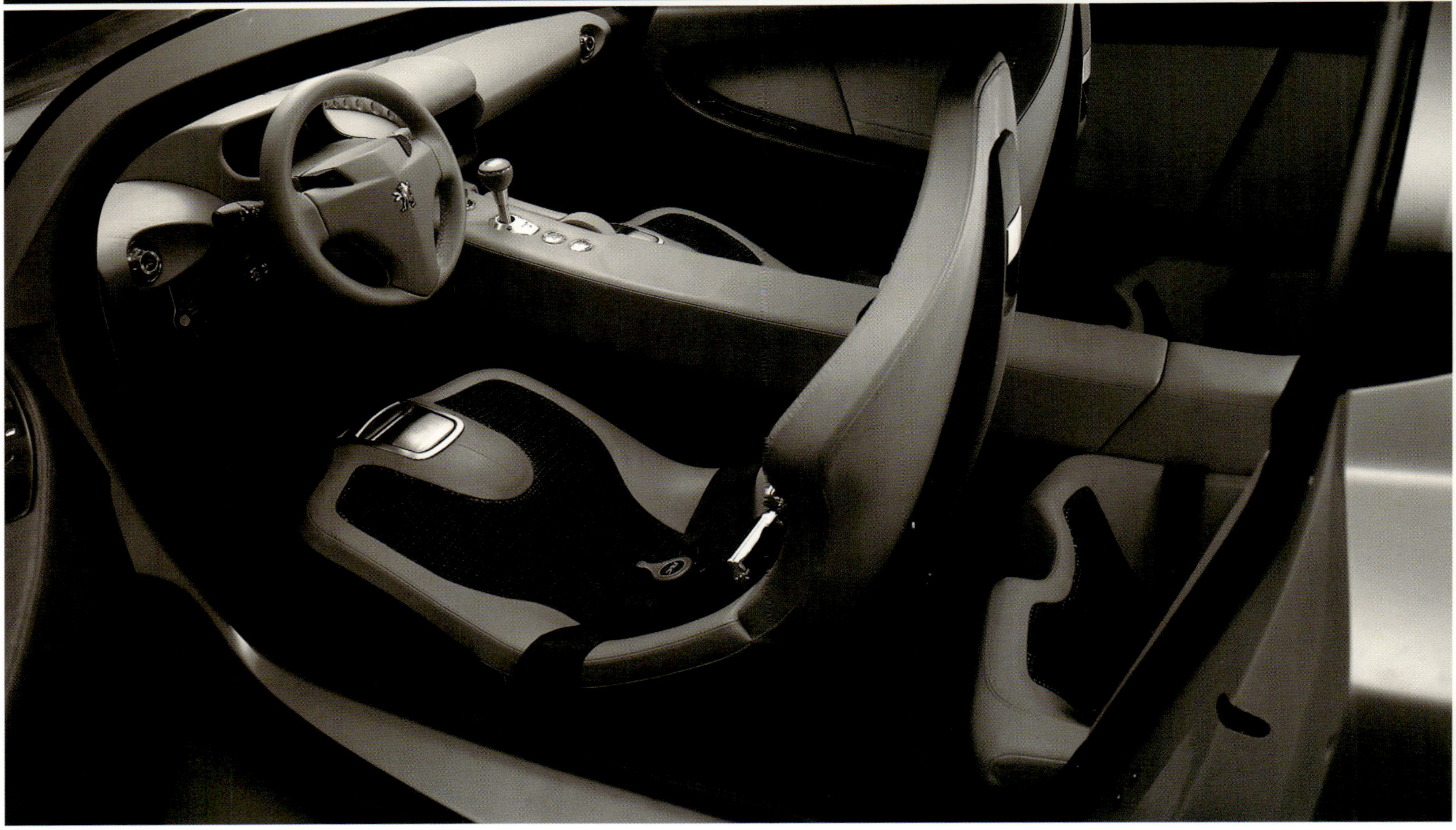

Unlike many concept cars, which are often ephemeral creations doomed to obsolescence, the Peugeot RC produced a concrete result: a monotype sports model to promote the biodiesel Diester. The research focused primarily on the engine, resulting in two prototypes: one with an engine that ran on gasoline (2-liter, 180 HP), the other with a diesel engine (2.2 liters, 175 HP). However, this focus on the engines did not prevent the Peugeot design team from giving the car an eminently sporty look.

Peugeot was keen to ensure that automobiles remained a passion. Its advertising campaign promised as much, and products such as the RC coupe delivered on that promise.

Gérard Welter, Peugeot's chief designer from 1980 to 2007, was a worthy and respectful successor to the company's longtime stylist, Paul Bouvot. A reserved, discreet man, he gave the members of his team complete freedom to express themselves on the exhilarating subject of concept cars. He invited the entire team to compete on every project.

The RC was no exception. Every designer in the company produced an enticing list of specifications for the design of a sports coupe; in the end the winner was Nicolas Brissonneau. The RC's mechanical architecture was determined by Jean-Christophe Bolle-Reddat, who works in the shadows on technical matters and was a loyal supporter of Gérard Welter. His chassis was characterized by a long wheelbase and the engine's central, transversal position. Previewed at the Geneva motor show in 2002, the RC created a sensation at the Bagatelle concours six months later—making good on the passionate claims of Peugeot's advertising slogans.

The Peugeot RC evokes memories of some classics in the history of the automobile. Peugeot presented two variants of its RC, one with a conventional gas-fueled engine, the other a diesel, underscoring its commitment to a technology widely promoted by the PSA Peugeot Citroën group.

236 Renault Fluence 2004

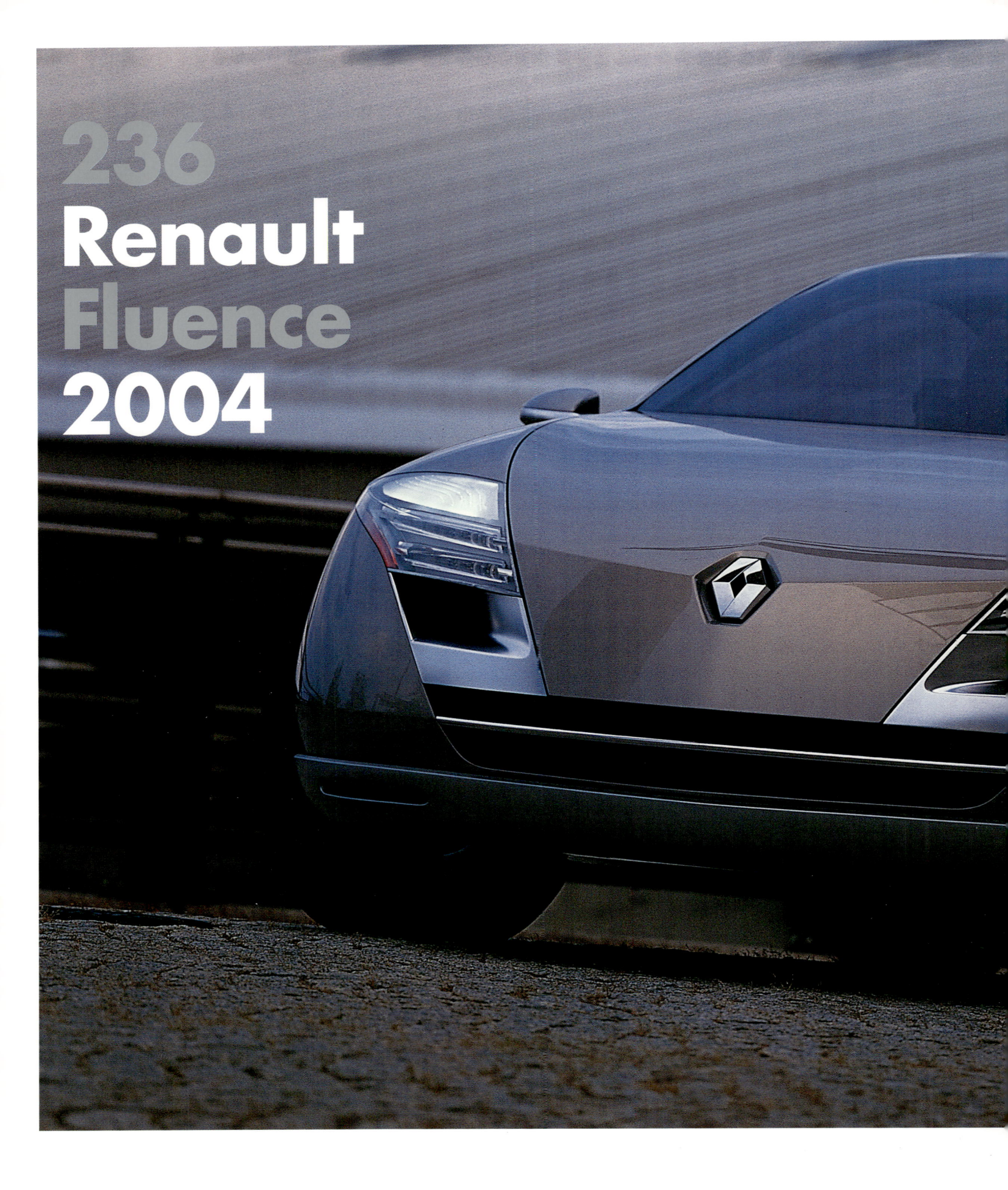

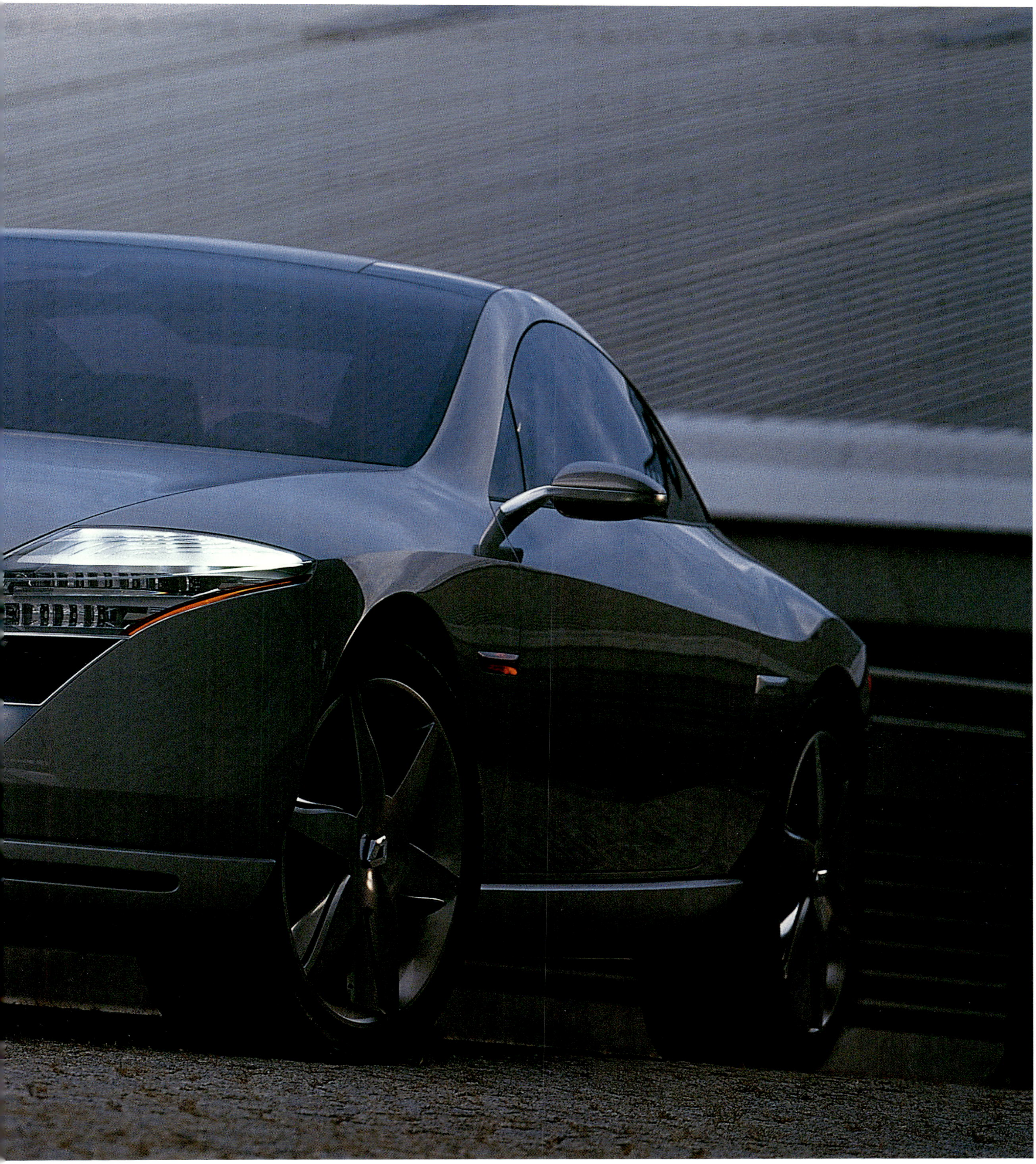

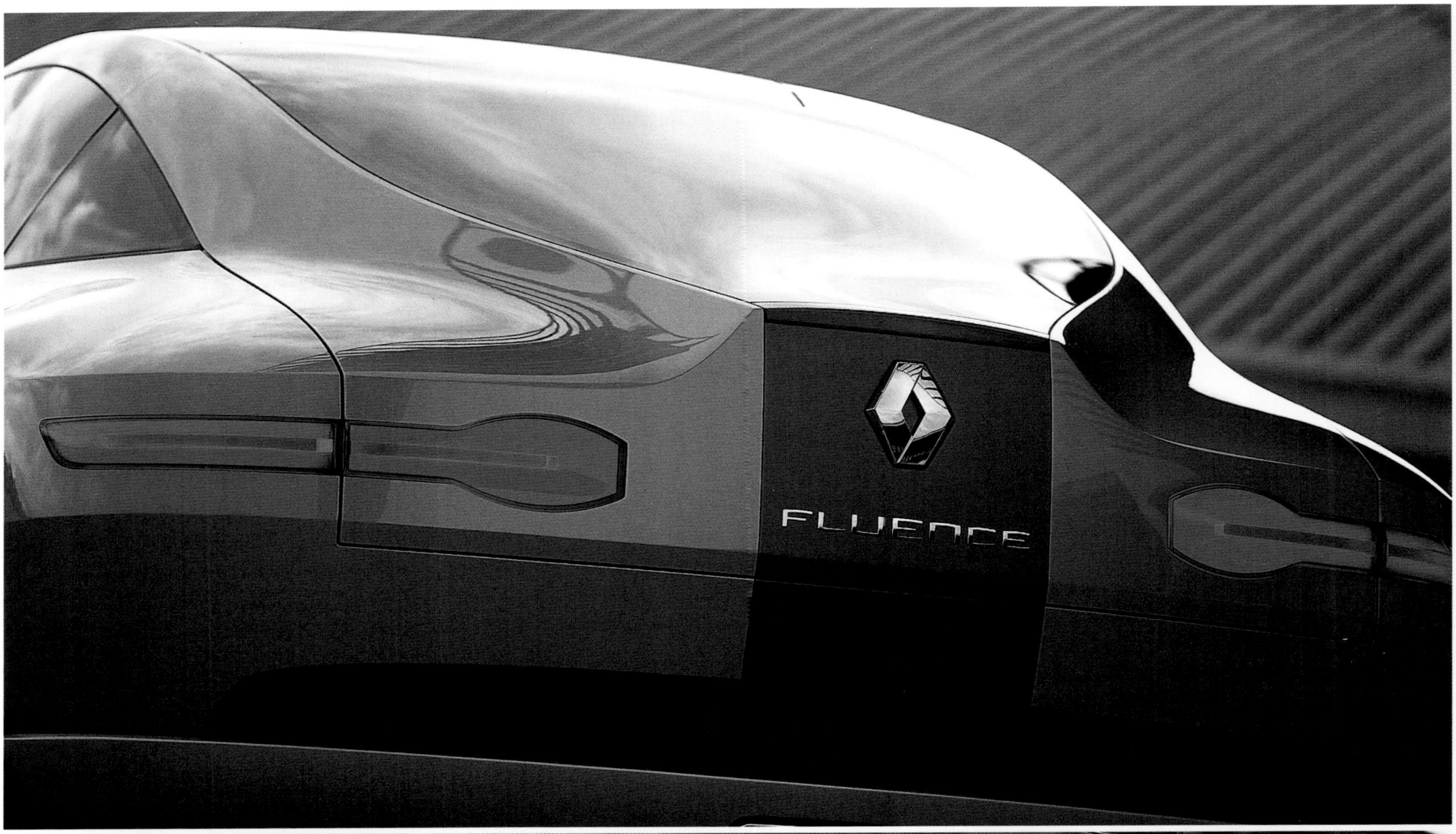
FLUENCE

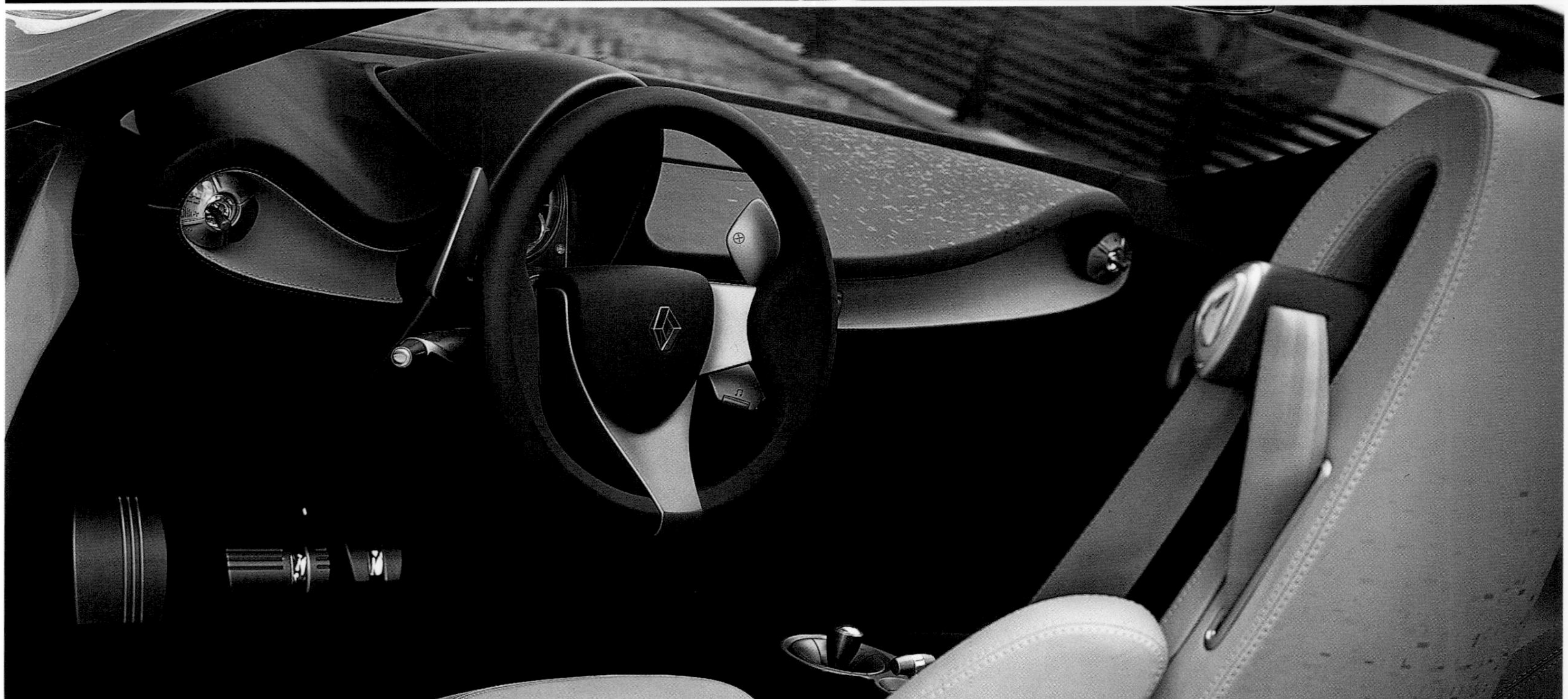

Launched at the Louis Vuitton Classic at Waddesdon Manor, the Fluence had the important task of indicating Renault's direction for the coming years. An elegant coupe, it also demonstrated the heritage of classic French bodywork: The exterior subtly combines strong, sharp lines and sensuous proportions, creating a sense of fluidity and harmony, while the interior illustrates Patrick le Quément's Touch Design concept.

The Fluence followed a long tradition of coupes in Renault's history but was infused with a new spirit, which was inspired by Patrick le Quément's Touch Design concept.

The specifications proposed to the designers of the Z16 could be summed up simply: to rediscover the foundations of the sports coupe. The designers were thus charged with creating a beautiful car at the top of the line, to dream up a high-performance touring machine that could be exhibited at a concours d'elegance. From the project's inception, the Louis Vuitton Classic was the prototype's designated destination.

But apart from making an impression at that fleeting event, the Fluence was intended to nourish a passion, to sustain the automobile's mythological status without resorting to a pumped-up sports motif, and to suggest the golden age of bodywork without edging into tired nostalgia.

The Renault Fluence was the work of two young designers, Nicolas Jardin for the exterior design and Paula Fabregat Andreu for the interior. They were overseen by Michel Jardin, who at that time was in charge of concept cars at Renault; he in turn reported to Patrick le Quément, who has presided over Renault Design since 1988. "Fluence is a continuation of a long tradition of outstanding French bodywork," he said upon the concept car's launch. The lines of the Fluence are fluid, supple, and shapely, defining the body's volumes in a skillful interplay. The clearly defined edges and flowing lines have the effect of sharp creases.

Inside, the dashboard undulates before the driver, as supple as a giant stingray, as light as a leaf, as suggestive as the curve of a lip. The burgundy leather, aptly named Margaux, imbues elegance and sensuality. It is all inspired by Patrick le Quément's philosophy of Touch Design, which seeks to enhance the relationship between car and driver with inviting ergonomics. The forms and textures arouse the desire to touch and make contact. The hand settles on the steering wheel, the fingers stroke the controls, the palm of the hand cradles the gear shift.

240 Pininfarina Birdcage 75th 2005

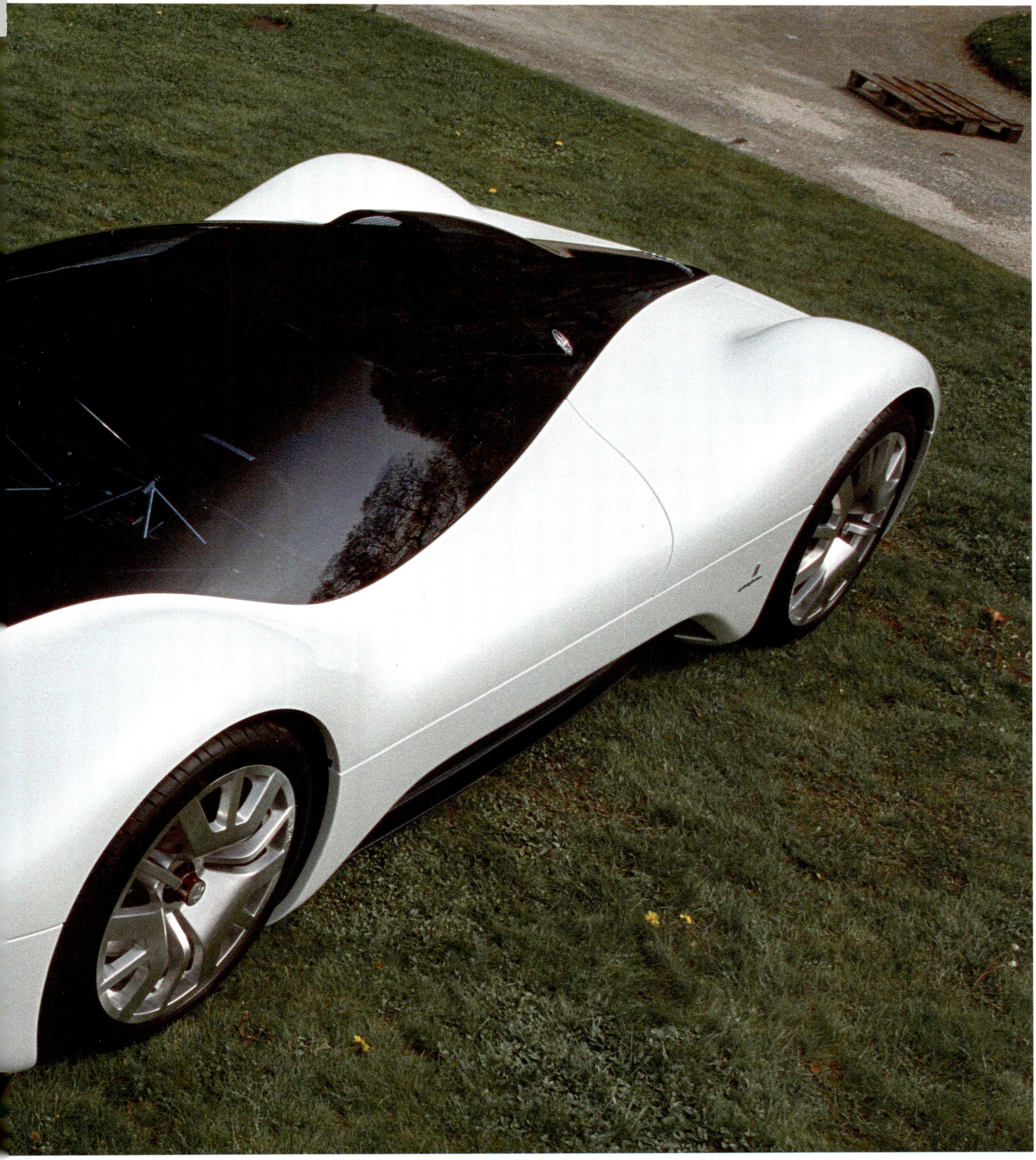

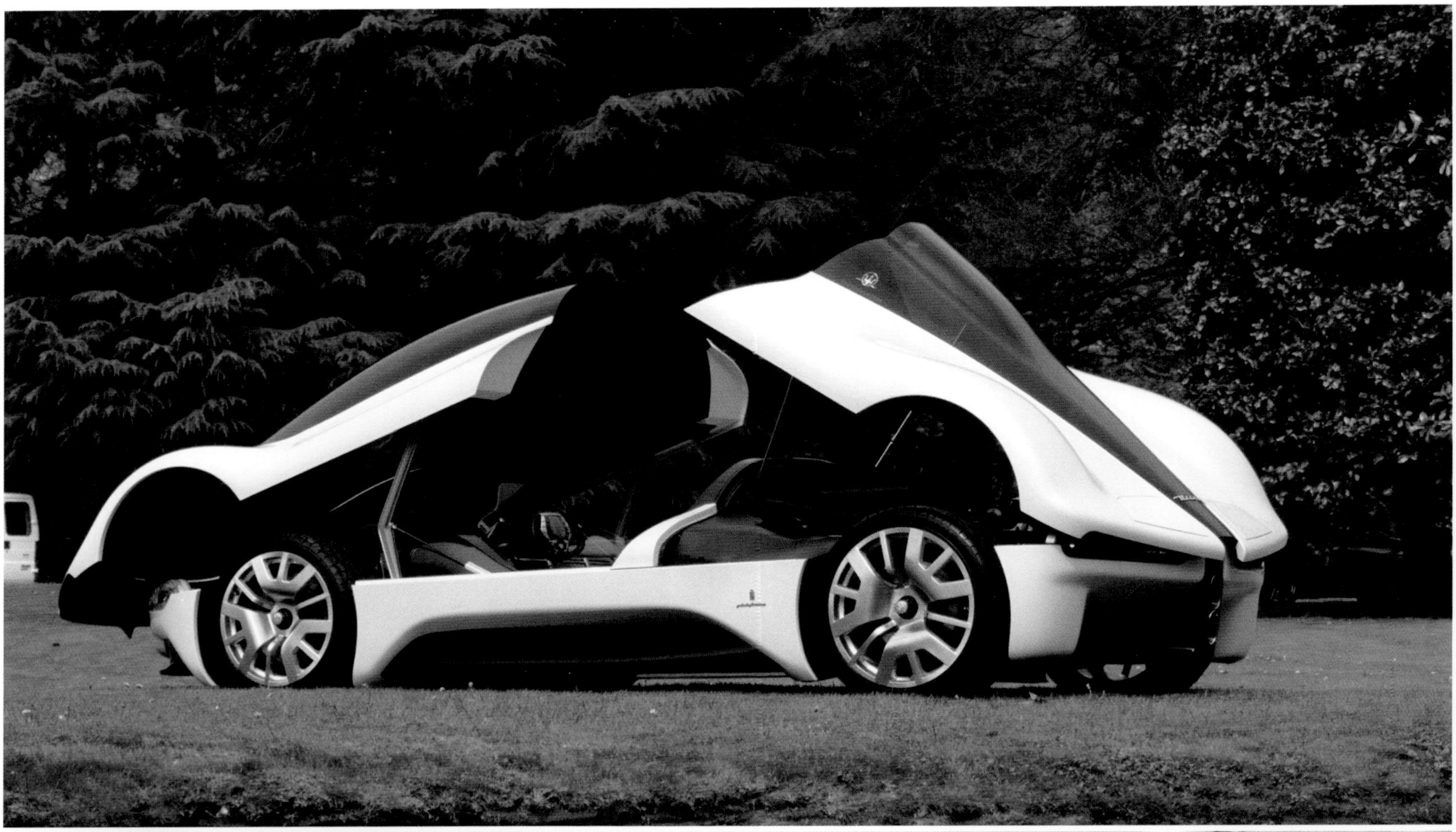

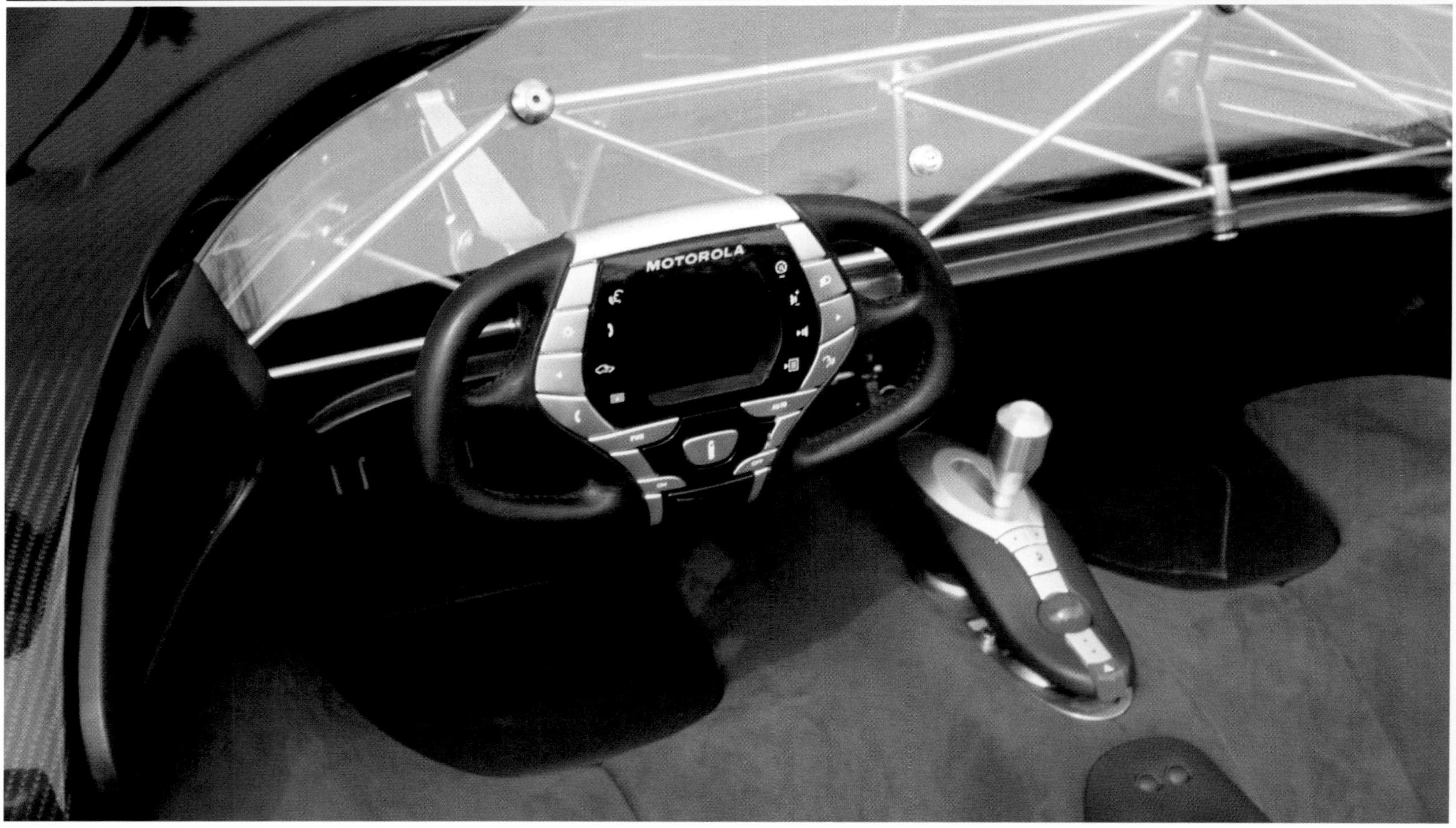
MOTOROLA

This spectacular Pininfarina creation was the winner of the first Louis Vuitton Design Award, which was presented in Paris in February 2006. The Birdcage 75th was selected by an expert jury headed by Christian Philippsen and including journalists, historians, designers, and collectors. In choosing this magnificent sculpture, the jury saluted an automobile that could win Best of Show in a concours d'elegance held in 2050.

To mark its seventy-fifth anniversary, Pininfarina paid tribute to Maserati with a futuristic concept car that reinterprets the MC 12 racing car.

Each year one auto-body maker takes pride of place at the concours d'elegance held at the Villa d'Este, in northern Italy's lake district; Pininfarina's turn came in 2005. The company was celebrating its seventy-fifth anniversary and marked the occasion by showing its Birdcage 75th, which had been unveiled in a sneak preview at the Geneva motor show a few weeks earlier and would win the first Louis Vuitton Design Award in 2006.

With the Birdcage 75th Pininfarina returned to the plane of dreams, excess, and extravagance. Lorenzo Ramaciotti, head of research and development, and Ken Okyuama, creative director, chose to build a superlative coupe on a Maserati MC 12. Within the family of exceptional automobiles is a rare and sublime species of thoroughbreds, a category that includes some road cars intimately descended from racing machines. With this one, Pininfarina again demonstrated the harmonious results that can arise from a preexisting foundation.

The Birdcage 75th's original design, seen in the first sketches by Jason Castriota, consisted of a flat form, a sort of upturned wing or undulating stingray, topped by an elongated bubble. These distinct forms were retained in the actual prototype, which plays on the opposition between the iridescent brightness of the paint and the deep darkness of the glass top.

The car's aerodynamics were researched with care and refined after testing in a wind tunnel, which led to the development of the retractable rear spoilers. The airflow modeled the surfaces: the half-open mouth at the front, the hollowed-out haunches between the wheels, and the skin that tightly hugs all the technical components. Just visible through the dark glass top are the engine and its carbon trumpets, the passenger compartment right in the center, the front suspension, the information screen, and the tubular frame. This little trellis of tubes is of course an allusion to the Birdcage of days gone by.

244
Citroën
C-Métisse
2006

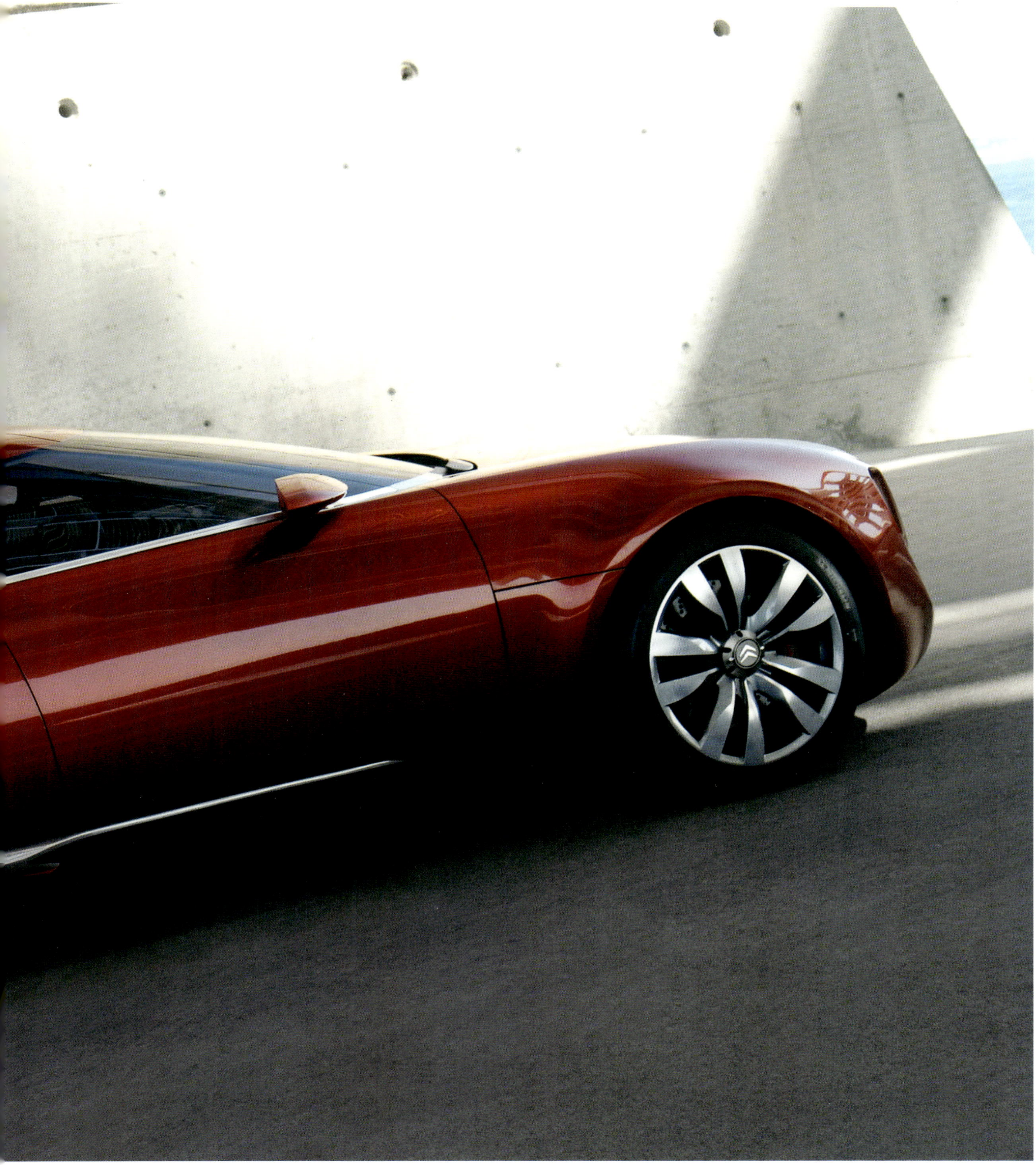

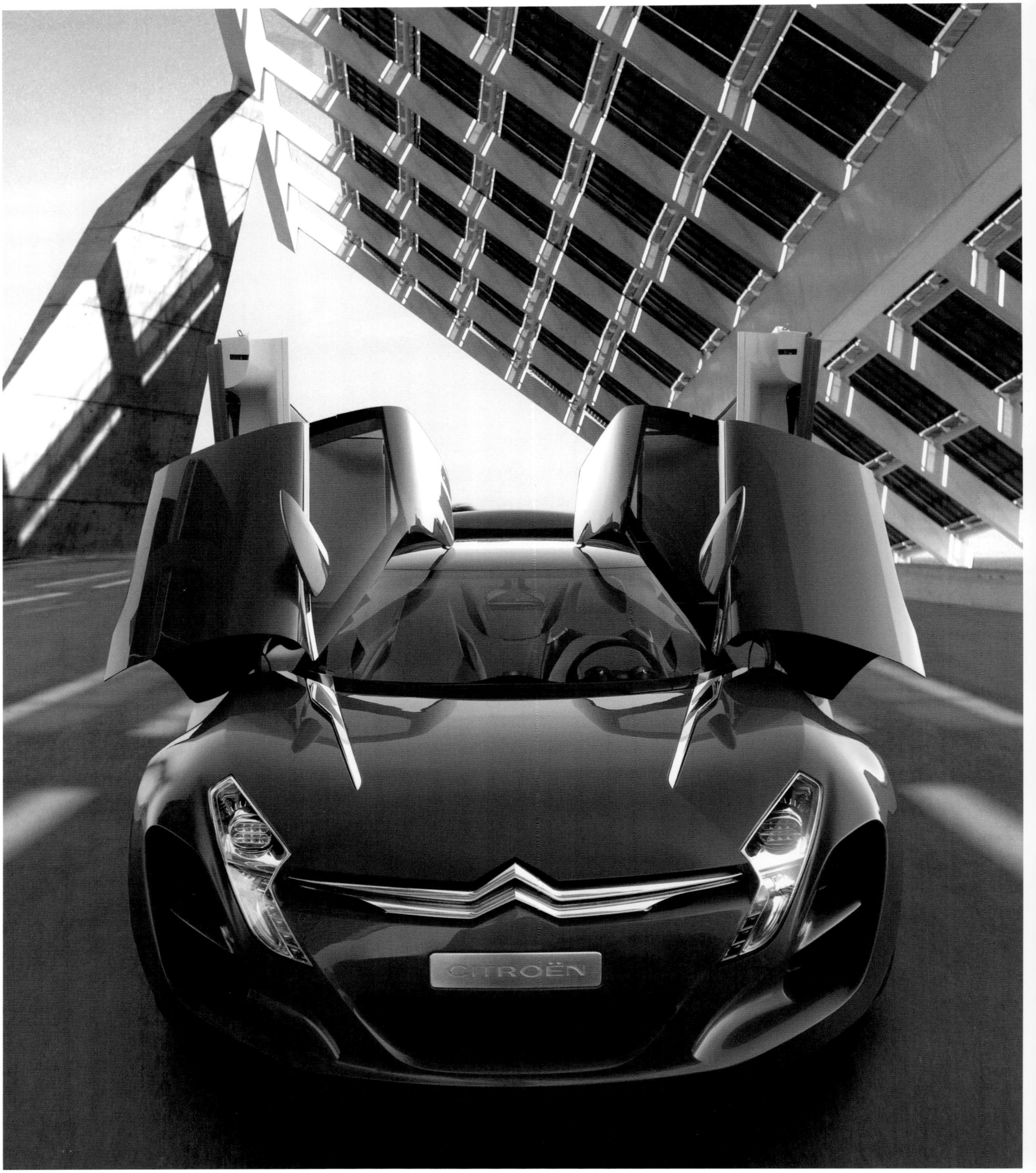
CITROËN

Winner of the second Louis Vuitton Design Award, presented in March 2007, the C-Métisse concept car symbolizes the revival of design at Citroën, brought about by the dynamic Jean-Pierre Ploué. This car demonstrates that it is possible to be passionate about beautiful cars and the pleasure of driving while remaining a responsible citizen; hidden beneath the frisky lines of the low bodywork is a well-thought-out engine that takes environmental issues into account. A hybrid, it combines a diesel engine (a 2.7-liter HDi V6 with 208 HP) and two electric engines for driving at low speeds.

With the C-Métisse project, Citroën combined a fiery, passionate design with rational technology. This superb mixture was recognized by the Louis Vuitton Design Award in 2007.

The notion of a four-door coupe is appealing to designers. The C-Métisse concept car prepared for the 2006 Mondial de l'Automobile (the auto show held in Paris every two years) represented a logical evolution toward a future high-performance touring car by exploiting this type of compromise.

The Citroën team worked on a touring machine that cultivated the ambiguity between a sedan and a coupe. The main players in the project were Gilles Vidal, who runs Citroën's concept car department, Emmanuel Lafaury, the technical expert, and Vincent Grit and Steven Platt, the exterior and interior designers. They were under the direction of Jean-Pierre Ploué, who became head of design at Citroën in December 1999 after rising meteorically from Renault to Volkswagen to Ford.

On the C-Métisse concept car, the body's masses play on the classic contrasts that inevitably yield attractive proportions: a long hood, a short, slanting back, and side panels curving toward a muscular rear. All the power is concentrated at the back of the car. The front is delightfully complex; the shapes clash, the lines cross or diverge, the surface planes break up. The aerodynamics succeed thanks to an excellent drag coefficient. Like the latest products from this make, the C-Métisse plays with curves, which are sometimes wide and sometimes tight.

On the technical side, the Métisse uses a hybrid engine system. The traction chain combines a diesel engine and two electric engines, which are set in the rear wheels to optimize motivity. The car's front doors open up like gull's wings, while the rear doors spin open in a spiraling trajectory.

The C-Métisse demonstrates that a passion for automobiles is capable of surmounting all the obstacles of long-established tradition and adapting to the change time brings.

A Discerning Eye

After hosting numerous concours and awards celebrating creativity, Louis Vuitton felt compelled to become involved in car design itself. On several occasions the prestigious label found its way behind the closed doors of the passenger compartment.

He has been spotted at many concours d'elegance, gauging a line or judging a form, observing a designer's brilliant invention or appreciating artisanal bodywork. Xavier Dixsaut casts a discerning eye over automobile design. It is not his profession but his passion, which allows his vision to be more free, fruitful, and ahead of its time. He has been in charge of innovation for Louis Vuitton for a quarter of a century. During the 1990s he persuaded management to embark on a flirtation with the car industry, thus returning Louis Vuitton to its roots: In the early twentieth century, the company worked closely with coachbuilders. Louis Vuitton's next logical step was to approach the management of Renault Design, which every year sent a concept car to the lawns of Bagatelle.

The creative teams at Renault Design and Louis Vuitton, run by Patrick le Quément and Xavier Dixsaut respectively, merged their visions for contemporary luxury by collaborating on the Renault Initiale in 1995.

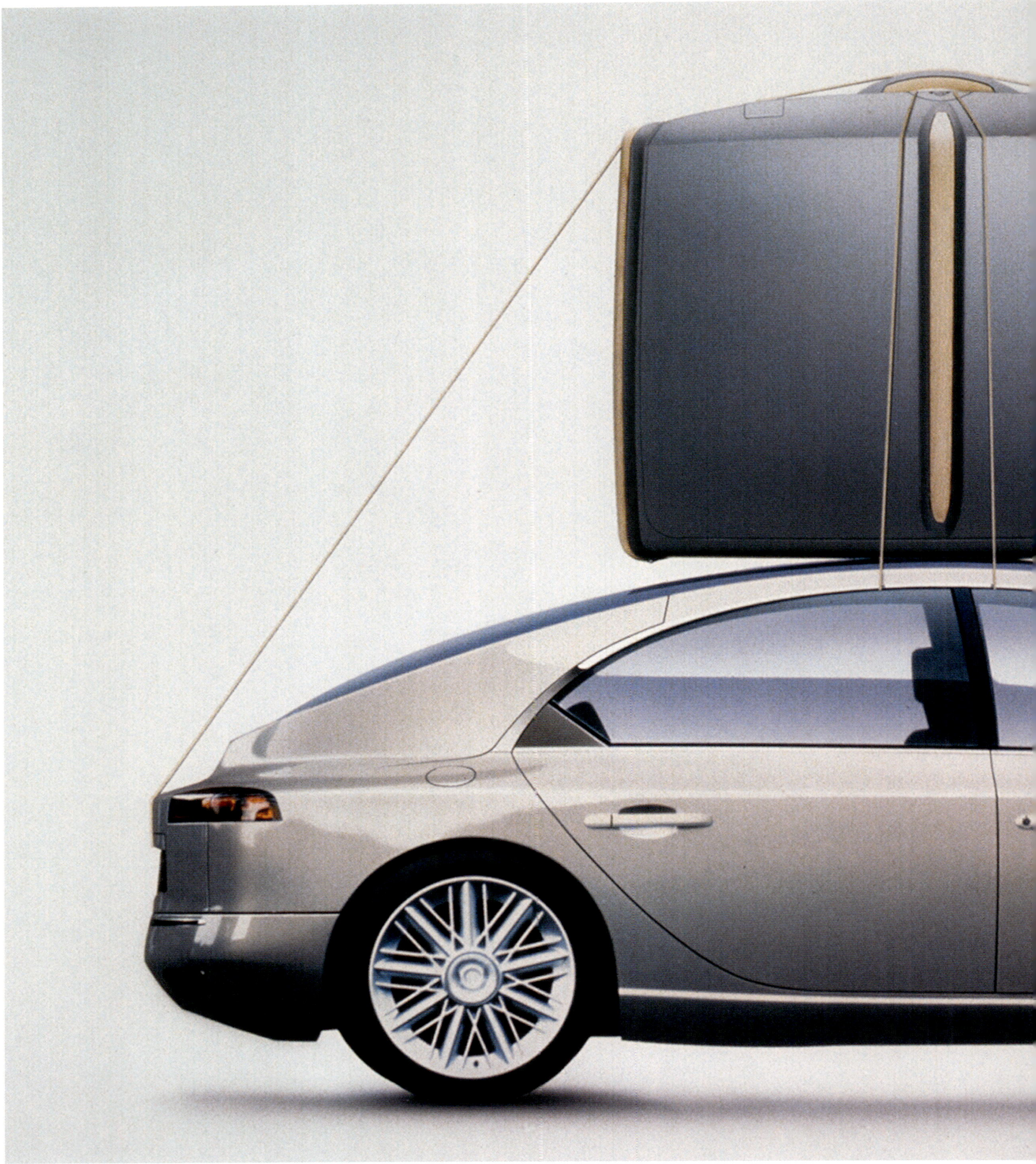

This advertisement was conceived by Rémi Peltzer.

The Launch of the Partnership

An ardent advocate of French design, Renault's Patrick le Quément wanted to provide a preview of one of his creations to the spectators at Bagatelle. Since taking the reins at Renault Design in 1988 he had transformed its structure to adapt to the profound changes shaping the car industry and had conceived a bona fide design philosophy. The second phase of the design department's evolution, which began in 1995, aimed to reinforce the brand's visual identity with a more individualized signature. As ever, the concept cars showed the way. One of these was the Initiale sedan, unveiled at the 1995 Automobiles Classiques and Louis Vuitton concours and intended to pave the way for Renault's rise. The front of the car, suggesting the legendary curved prow of Renault's 1920s "40 chevaux," made clear the company's renewed ambition.

Louis Vuitton had slipped into the trunk some luggage specially adapted to the car: two rigid suitcases and one vanity case, all in a combination of aluminum and beechwood that lent a contemporary feel. Without consulting one another, the teams of both Patrick le Quément and Xavier Dixsaut had been equally inspired by French elegance and arrived at the same conclusions. Together they restored travel to an art.

Renault's Fluence concept car, unveiled in 2004 at Waddesdon Manor, was also equipped with Louis Vuitton baggage, this time pieces in Damier Géant canvas.

Exploring Interior Design

Louis Vuitton was often courted by automakers who dreamed of benefiting from the company's expertise, but invariably the Parisian luggage maker refused to share its fine name and reputation with another manufacturer. Still, Andrea Pininfarina, the director of the eponymous firm, never gave up hope. He proposed that the two firms work on a common project that would debut at the Geneva International Motor Show in March 2003.

The project—named Enjoy, as if to tempt fate—would be a roadster entirely dedicated to the pleasure of driving, a tough, stripped-down car with no windshield or roof. This time Louis Vuitton's management agreed to collaborate—on the coy condition that its trademark initials would not appear anywhere on the car.

As soon as the Enjoy project hit Xavier Dixsaut's desk, ideas began to take shape. Xavier Dixsaut searched his memory and his archives, digging out a photo of a Chris-Craft from the 1950s. A theme soon emerged: The Enjoy's technical console would wrap around the passenger compartment, as on a motorboat. The trim would be in slightly faded red leather, as would the seats. The bodywork would be painted ivory. Xavier Dixsaut found himself thinking of a Jaguar, or perhaps a Hispano-Suiza, driving along Sunset Boulevard in Beverly Hills, in days gone by.

The instrumentation would be reduced to the basics: three dials, each in the style of a Louis Vuitton Tambour watch. Although the "LV" monogram did not appear, no one failed to pick up the references to the brand. The firm D3 created a model of the interior in its workshops near Paris. D3, which at that time was led by Bernard Pène and his deputy, Hermidas Atabeicki, has the finest reputation in France for producing manufacturers' prototypes and is an invaluable collaborator.

Of course, a car without a windshield requires that the driver wear a helmet. Louis Vuitton's Pont Neuf studio tackled the job, researching a helmet of leather, composite materials, and a built-in communication system by Bang & Olufsen that would match the interior. Louis Vuitton also designed shoes, while Dainese created a racing suit.

For an earlier experiment in the world of motor vehicles, in 2000, Louis Vuitton had produced three prototype scooters, with the help of Lecoq, the Parisian auto-body maker. These were customized versions of the BMW C1 named Nomad, Bagatelle, and Bond Street. Each had luggage and a decorative theme in keeping with its use: adventure, elegance, or modernity.

The quality and originality of Louis Vuitton's incursions into automobile design to date will surely lead to further explorations.

Xavier Dixsaut

Xavier Dixsaut joined Louis Vuitton in 1982 as its first in-house designer, contributing to a cultural revolution within the venerable company. He believed from the start that behind the firm's aura of tradition and respectability laid effervescence, open-mindedness, curiosity, and inventiveness. As a young designer Xavier Dixsaut had worked in town planning, but he realized that designers like Philippe Starck and architects like Gae Aulenti had not approached Louis Vuitton by chance. At Vuitton, Xavier Dixsaut became director of innovation, overseeing the firm's gradual shift from style to design and creating new design positions.

Louis Vuitton participated in the Pininfarina Enjoy project by designing the baggage, the driver's helmet, and the car's interior.

254

The Best of the Best

Best of Show Winners, 1989–2004

At the series of concours organized by Louis Vuitton, a succession of outstanding collectors' items was awarded the Best of Show title.

Automobiles Classiques and Louis Vuitton
Parc de Bagatelle, September 9–10, 1989
Delahaye 135 MS
Roadster bodywork designed by De Villars in 1938.
Shown by Roger Tainguy.

Louis Vuitton Concours d'Elegance
Stowe, July 28–29, 1990
Mercedes-Benz Type S
Convertible bodywork designed by Castagna in 1929.
Shown by Charles Howard.

Automobiles Classiques and Louis Vuitton
Parc de Bagatelle, September 8–9, 1990
Ferrari 330 P4 Spider
Made in 1967.
Shown by Albert Obrist.

Louis Vuitton Concours d'Elegance
Hurlingham Club, June 8, 1991
Aston Martin DB3 S
Made in 1956.
Shown by Dudley Mason-Styrron.

Automobiles Classiques and Louis Vuitton
Parc de Bagatelle, September 7–8, 1991
Talbot Lago Grand Sport
Coupe bodywork designed by Henri Chapron in 1948.
Shown by Nicholas Harley.

Louis Vuitton Concours d'Elegance
Hurlingham Club, June 13, 1992
Alfa Romeo 8C 2900
Spider bodywork designed by Pinin Farina in 1939.
Shown by Terry Cohn.

Automobiles Classiques and Louis Vuitton
Parc de Bagatelle, September 12–13, 1992
Talbot Lago Super Sport
Faux cabriolet bodywork designed by Figoni & Falaschi in 1938.
Shown by Jean-Pierre Schindelholz.

Louis Vuitton Concours d'Elegance
Hurlingham Club, June 5, 1993
Alfa Romeo 6C 1750 Super Sport
Spider bodywork designed by Zagato in 1929.
Shown by Keith Bowley for Sir Michael Kadoorie.

Automobiles Classiques and Louis Vuitton
Parc de Bagatelle, September 11–12, 1993
Bentley Speed Six
Convertible bodywork designed by H. J. Mulliner in 1930.
Shown by Terry Cohn.

Louis Vuitton Concours d'Elegance
Hurlingham Club, June 4, 1994
Rolls-Royce Phantom II Continental
Designed by Gurney Nutting in 1934.
Shown by Sir Anthony Bamford.

Automobiles Classiques and Louis Vuitton
Parc de Bagatelle, September 10–11, 1994
Cisitalia 202 MM
Coupe bodywork designed by Vignale in 1947.
Shown by Rudy Pas for Steve Tillack.

Louis Vuitton Concours d'Elegance
Hurlingham Club, June 3, 1995
Bentley Mark VI
Convertible bodywork designed by Franay in 1947.
Shown by Bob Gathercole for Gary Wales.

Automobiles Classiques and Louis Vuitton
Parc de Bagatelle, September 9–10, 1995
Mercedes-Benz 500 K Spezial-Roadster
Bodywork designed by Mercedes-Benz in 1936.
Shown by Naohiro Ishikawa.

Louis Vuitton Concours d'Elegance
Hurlingham Club, June 1, 1996
Isotta-Fraschini Tipo 8B
Sedan de ville bodywork designed by Dansk-Karrosseri Fabrik in 1931.
Shown by Robert Gathercole for William Haynes.

Automobiles Classiques and Louis Vuitton
Parc de Bagatelle, September 7–8, 1996
Alfa Romeo 8C 2900 B
Spider bodywork designed by Touring in 1937.
Shown by John Mozart.

Louis Vuitton Classic
Rockefeller Center, September 27–29, 1996
Bentley Speed Six
Streamlined sedan bodywork designed by Gurney Nutting in 1930.
Shown by Bruce McCaw.

Louis Vuitton Classic
Hurlingham Club, June 7, 1997

Rolls-Royce Phantom I
Sports tourer bodywork designed by Barker in 1929.
Shown by Charles Howard.

Automobiles Classiques and Louis Vuitton
Parc de Bagatelle, September 6–7, 1997

Ferrari 250 GT Competizione
Coupe bodywork designed by Bertone in 1962.
Shown by Lorenzo Zambrano.

Louis Vuitton Classic
Rockefeller Center, September 26–28, 1997

Alfa Romeo 6C 1750 Gran Sport
Spider bodywork designed by Zagato in 1931.
Shown by Edward A. Reich.

Louis Vuitton Classic
Hurlingham Club, June 6, 1998

Alfa Romeo Type B Grand Prix
Made in 1932.
Shown by Neil Twyman for David Uihlein.

Automobiles Classiques and Louis Vuitton
Parc de Bagatelle, September 5–6, 1998

Ferrari 375 MM Speciale
Coupe bodywork designed by Scaglietti in 1956.
Shown by Jon Shirley.

Louis Vuitton Classic
Rockefeller Center, October 2–4, 1998

Rolls-Royce 40-50 HP
Landaulet bodywork designed by Barker in 1907.
Shown by Terry Cohn.

Louis Vuitton Classic
Hurlingham Club, June 5, 1999

Bentley 8-liter
Fixed-head coupe bodywork designed by Gurney Nutting in 1931.
Shown by Charles Teall.

Automobiles Classiques and Louis Vuitton
Parc de Bagatelle, September 4–5, 1999

Delahaye 165
Spider bodywork designed by Figoni & Falaschi in 1938.
Shown by Peter Mullin.

Louis Vuitton Classic
Rockefeller Center, September 24–26, 1999

Bugatti Type 57 SC Atlantic
Made by Bugatti in 1938.
Shown by Paul Russell for Ralph Lauren.

Louis Vuitton Classic
Hurlingham Club, June 3, 2000

Ferrari 375 MM
Coupe bodywork designed by Pinin Farina in 1953.
Shown by Sir Anthony Bamford.

Louis Vuitton Classic
Parc de Bagatelle, September 9–10, 2000

Ferrari 250 Mille Miglia
Coupe bodywork designed by Pinin Farina in 1953.
Shown by Peter von Muralt.

Louis Vuitton Classic
Rockefeller Center, September 22–24, 2000

Alfa Romeo 8C 35
Made in 1935.
Shown by Peter Giddings.

Louis Vuitton Classic
Hurlingham Club, July 7–8, 2001

Isotta-Fraschini Tipo KM4
Made in 1911.
Shown by Ben Collins for Arturo Keller.

Louis Vuitton Classic
Parc de Bagatelle, September 8–9, 2001

Alfa Romeo 1900 Sprint a.k.a BAT 7
Designed by Bertone in 1954.
Shown by Paul Osborn.

Louis Vuitton Classic
Hurlingham Club, June 8, 2002

Aston Martin DB 4 GT
Coupe bodywork designed by Zagato in 1960.
Shown by Richard Williams for Peter Read.

Louis Vuitton Classic
Parc de Bagatelle, June 28–29, 2002

Alfa Romeo 6C 2500
Coupe bodywork designed by Touring in 1939.
Shown by Fabio Calligaris for Gérald Bugnon.

Louis Vuitton Classic
Domaine National de Saint-Cloud, September 6–7, 2003

Bentley Speed Six
Streamlined sedan bodywork designed by Gurney Nutting in 1930.
Shown by Peter Hageman for Bruce McCaw.

Louis Vuitton Classic
Waddesdon Manor, June 5, 2004

Rolls-Royce Phantom II Continental
Drophead coupé designed by Carlton in 1934.
Shown by Stephen Brauer.

Photograph Credits

Archives Louis Vuitton
6, 13, 14, 15, 16, 17, 19, 20, 21, 22–23, 25, 26, 29, 41, 43, 44–45, 47, 49, 50, 51, 52, 53, 54–55, 57, 58, 59t, 59bl, 60, 61, 62–63, 65, 77t, 81b, 85t, 86, 88–89, 90, 91, 94, 95, 97, 98, 99, 100–101, 108, 109t, 110–11, 119, 120, 121, 123, 124, 125, 126, 128, 131, 133, 135, and 136–37
David Chancellor: 113, 129b
Christophe Daguet: 87b
Élodie Gay: 127
Thomas Gogny: 252
Stéphane Muratet: 59br, 66, 67t, 68–69, 75, 76b, 109b, 115, and 143
Rémi Peltzer: 250–51
Mazen Saggar: 67b and 76t
Richard Young: 129t
DR: 35, 36, 37, 38–39, 48, 76t, 81t, 84, 87t, 93, 96t, 102b, 103, 104–5, 106, 107, 116–17, 122, 132, 134, 139, 141, and 253
Pascal Béjean, Labomatic
Endpages, 1, 2, 3, 258, 259, and 260
BMW AG
220–21 and 222
Citroën Communication
27, 140b, 244–45, and 246
Corbis
Philippe Heranian: 102t
Rune Hellestad: 114
Daimler Chrysler Communication
212–13
Ghia Communication
224–25 and 226
Xavier de Nombel
240–41 and 242
Peugeot
140t
Patrick Sautelet and Anthony Bernier
232–33 and 234
Cyril de Plater
228–29 and 230
Seat Communication/Rights reserved
96b
Peter Vann
208–9, 210, 216–17, 218, 236–37, 238, and 249
Michel Zumbrunn
148–49, 150, 152–53, 154, 155, 156, 158–59, 160, 161, 162, 164–65, 166, 168–69, 170, 171, 172, 174–75, 176, 177, 178, 180–81, 182, 183, 184, 186–87, 188, 189, 190, 192–93, 194, 195, 196, 198–99, 200, 201, and 202
Rights reserved
77b, 78–79, 80, 82–83, 85b, 92, and 214

Property rights
Works by Bernard Boutet de Monvel (29tr) and César (103b):
© Adagp, Paris, 2007
Work by Sonia Delaunay (103t):
© L&M Services B.V. Den Haag, 2007

Event posters
Works by Razzia (34, 40, 46, 56, 64, 74, 112, and 130):
© Archives Louis Vuitton/Razzia.

Acknowledgments

The author would like to thank the members of the Louis Vuitton team for their kind and efficient help; Marie-Laure Fourt and Florence Lesché for unearthing the rarest documents from their archives; Antoine Jarrier, himself the creator of numerous superb images, for searching through his memories; and Julien Guerrier for answering every question with tact and good humor throughout this book's production. At Éditions de La Martinière the author wishes to salute the unfailingly efficient and discerning partnership of Nathalie Bec and her assistant Cyrielle Martin, who briskly led this project to its completion.

Thanks also to Pascal Béjean and Frédéric Bortolotti at Labomatic, to Christine Bélanger, Yves Carcelle, Xavier Dixsaut, Isabelle Franchet, Juliette de Gonet, Brigitte Govignon, Christian Philippsen, and Nathalie Tollu, and to all those who contributed to the production of this work.

Translated from the French by Liz Nash

Project Manager, English-language edition: Magali Veillon
Editor, English-language edition: Nancy E. Cohen
Designer, English-language edition: Shawn Dahl
Production Manager, English-language edition: Tina Cameron

Library of Congress Cataloging-in-Publication Data
Bellu, Serge.
[Louis Vuitton et l'Elegance Automobile. English]
Louis Vuitton and the art of the automobile / By Serge Bellu.
p. cm.
ISBN 978-0-8109-9551-2 (hardcover)
1. Vuitton, Louis, 1821–1892 2. Automobiles—Miscellanea.
3. Industrial designers—France. I. Title.
TL154.B4313 2008
629.222—dc22
                2007029627

Copyright © 2007 Éditions de la Martinière, an imprint of
La Martinière Groupe, Paris
English-language translation copyright © 2008 Abrams, New York

Originally published in French under the title *Louis Vuitton et l'élégance automobile* by Éditions de la Martinière, Paris, 2007

Published in 2008 by Abrams, an imprint of Harry N. Abrams, Inc. All rights reserved. No portion of this book may be reproduced, stored in a retrieval system, or transmitted in any form or by any means, mechanical, electronic, photocopying, recording, or otherwise, without written permission from the publisher.

Printed and bound in France
10 9 8 7 6 5 4 3 2 1

HNA
harry n. abrams, inc.
a subsidiary of La Martinière Groupe
115 West 18th Street
New York, NY 10011
www.hnabooks.com

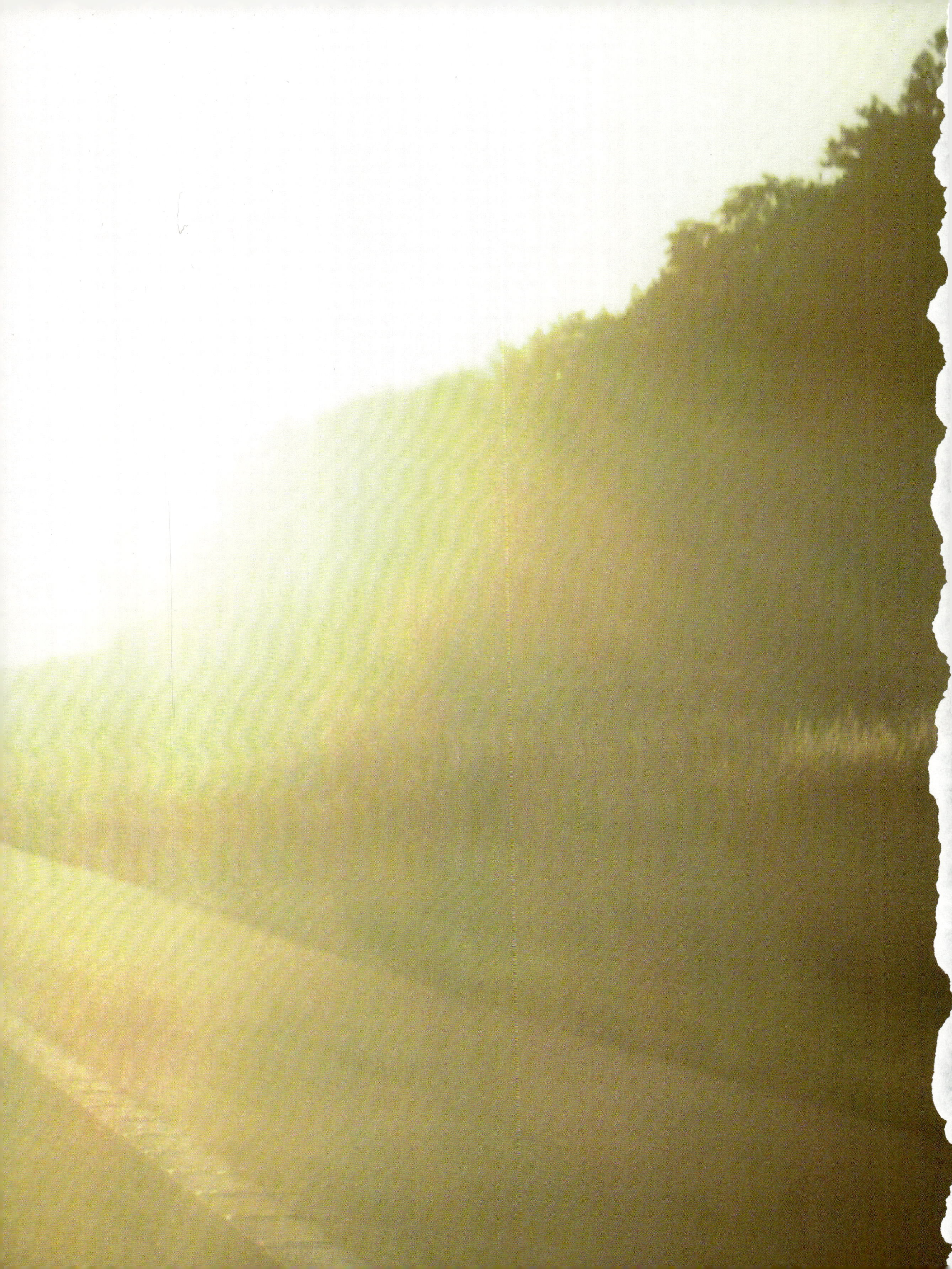